Praise from Admissions Officers
for *Great Applications for Business School* (second edition)

"A tour de force. Paul Bodine really understands the inside track and offers his readers a wealth of useful information. The book is thorough and wide-ranging, with lots of useful examples drawn from different business schools. I'm sure many candidates will find his advice invaluable. A practical and lively guide to applying to business school."

— CAROLINE DIARTE EDWARDS,
DIRECTOR OF ADMISSIONS,
INSEAD

"A very thorough and witty explanation of the admissions process on all levels, with excellent advice as to what not to do as well as what to do and how to do it skillfully."

— CHRISTIE ST-JOHN,
SENIOR ASSOCIATE DIRECTOR ADMISSIONS & RECRUITING,
DARTMOUTH TUCK SCHOOL OF BUSINESS

"Very insightful and a truly useful resource for candidates willing to travel the road of this wonderful 'leadership degree.' Paul Bodine's detail-oriented, fact-based approach is a powerful 'myth debunker' that will truly aid those willing to invest their time, and mainly themselves in this amazing, but truly challenging, process. The book's 'Put Yourself on the Couch' questions are a very helpful, insightful and a practical tool for self-assessment."

— JUAN FERNANDO JIMÉNEZ,
FORMER ASSISTANT DIRECTOR MBA ADMISSIONS,
HARVARD BUSINESS SCHOOL

"*Great Applications for Business School* has great advice for any student interested in earning their MBA from a top school! Real life examples, suggestions from Admissions Directors and tips for better applications can be found on nearly every page. Help for prospective students can be found inside this book!"

— RANDALL T. SAWYER,
ASSISTANT DEAN OF ADMISSIONS,
FIN̄⸻ ⸻ INCLUSION,
TH⸻ ⸻ UNIVERSITY

Praise from Admissions Officers
for *Great Applications for Business School* (first edition)

"Totally on target. *Great Application Essays for Business School* is a really terrific, practical, and insightful guide to the kind of writing that can make a difference in winning acceptance at a top MBA program. Many of the things recommended in the book are the kinds of things that I say when I speak with prospective applicants. I also love the level of detail. I really recommend it—a must-read for anyone with business school ambitions."

— Anne Coyle,
Former Director of Admissions,
Yale School of Management

"Paul Bodine's *Great Application Essays for Business School* is a great 'view from the trenches,' and a careful reading will offer many rewards to applicants. His overall messages—among them 'be yourself, answer the questions, showcase what you feel is important for schools to know'—seem simple but are hard to act on when you are sweating through deadlines. He gives you a practical guide to getting it done. Paul Bodine takes on the essay-writing process and breaks it down into actionable steps. He wants to help you tell your story. Paul knows there is no substitute for hard work and self-reflection, but his book should make an often daunting process much easier. *Great Application Essays for Business School* is a valuable how-to book with a generous spirit."

— Jon McLaughlin,
Former Assistant Director of MBA Admissions,
Massachusetts Institute of Technology,
Sloan School of Management

"Quite effective. If all MBA applicants take to heart Paul Bodine's counsel and advice, we would receive far stronger essays, and applicants would likely see even greater success in the MBA admissions process. *Great Application Essays for Business School* provides an easy-to-follow blueprint for preparing and writing effective essays."

— James Holmen,
Director of Admissions,
Indiana University,
Kelly School of Business

"Paul Bodine does a terrific job in *Great Application Essays for Business School* of capturing the essence of the MBA application process. This guide will be useful to every MBA applicant."

— Natalie Grinblatt,
Former Director of the Office for Admissions and Financial Aid,
Cornell University,
Johnson Graduate School of Management

Great Applications *for* BUSINESS SCHOOL

Great Applications *for* BUSINESS SCHOOL

Second Edition

Paul S. Bodine
paulsbodine.com

New York   Chicago   San Francisco   Lisbon   London
Madrid   Mexico City   Milan   New Delhi   San Juan
Seoul   Singapore   Sydney   Toronto

The *McGraw·Hill* Companies

1 2 3 4 5 6 7 8 9 10   DOC/DOC   1 9 8 7 6 5 4 3 2 1 0

ISBN: 978-0-07-174655-7
MHID: 0-07-174655-2

This publication is designed to provide accurate and authoritative information in regard to the subject matter covered. It is sold with the understanding that neither the author nor the publisher is engaged in rendering legal, accounting, securities trading, or other professional services. If legal advice or other expert assistance is required, the services of a competent professional person should be sought.
                    —*From a Declaration of Principles Jointly Adopted by a Committee of the*
                    American Bar Association and a Committee of Publishers and Associations

Library of Congress Cataloging-in-Publication Data

Bodine, Paul, 1959-
    Great applications for business school / Paul Bodine.
        p. ; cm.
    Rev. ed. of: Great application essays for business school. 2006.
    ISBN 0-07-174655-2 (alk. paper)
    1. Business schools—United States—Admission. 2. Exposition (Rhetoric) 3. College applications—United States. 4. Business writing. I. Title.
    HF1131.B543 2011
    808'.06665—dc22   2010037132

McGraw-Hill books are available at special quantity discounts to use as premiums and sales promotions or for use in corporate training programs. To contact a representative, please e-mail us at bulksales@mcgraw-hill.com.

This book is printed on acid-free paper.

For Tamami 永遠 の 愛 をこめて

For Linda Abraham, of Accepted.com, for her mentorship.

Contents

Acknowledgments

This book would have been impossible without my many clients over the years. It's been a pleasure learning about your lives, dreams, and successes. I thank the following successful applicants in particular for their help: Alex Assad, Avin Bansal, Allen Breed, Lidia Rekas Fluhme, Kate Harris, Elizabeth Holt, Joyce Huang, Soonbae Hwang, Abhey Lamba, Amanda Nelson, Anil Phull, and Brian Rothenberg. I owe a special debt of gratitude to Caroline Diarte Edwards (INSEAD), Rod Garcia (MIT Sloan), Alison Goggin (NYU Stern), Juan Fernando Jiménez, Randall Sawyer (Cornell), and Christie St. John (Tuck) for their generous time and attention. Thank you, Cindy Tokumitsu and Michelle Stockman for your help. Anya Kozorez of McGraw-Hill deserves special appreciation for her demonstrated ability to handle difficult authors.

Introduction

The stakes are huge. A newly minted Wharton MBA earned $145,000 in median cash compensation in 2008, according to *BusinessWeek*/PayScale. In 2008, Stanford MBAs earned an average of $225,000, according to *Forbes* magazine. And 10 and 20 years postdegree, the median pay-plus-bonus for Harvard MBAs was $182,000 and $232,000, respectively. Even given the breathtaking tuition costs at elite business schools, MBA graduates from schools like Tuck and HBS can expect to reach breakeven after only four years of post-MBA work.

Income is only one benefit of a top MBA, of course. The MBA remains preeminently a leadership degree, and for all the myriad MBAs making fortunes in nonmanagement finance or consulting roles, the job title CEO is still the benchmark for evaluating how far the MBA can take you. CEOs are not merely well remunerated; they are powerful—creating jobs, entire product categories, industries; deciding the professional fates of thousands; influencing the global economy, political system, and environment. For all the CEOs who have besmirched the MBA's good name (the Jeffrey Skillings and Dennis Kozlowskis), there are dozens of Fred Smiths (Fedex), Philip Knights (Nike), Indra Nooyis (PepsiCo), and Michael Bloombergs who have honored it. Indeed, a 2010 *Harvard Business Review* study of the two thousand most effective CEOs of publicly traded companies worldwide since 1997 found that the 32 percent who had an MBA significantly outperformed (judged by shareholder return) those who did not.

Even as the number of graduating MBAs grows, both MBAs and the people who hire them remain highly satisfied with the degree. According to a survey by the Graduate Management Admission Council in the recession year of 2010, 91 percent of MBAs who had received a job offer said that the MBA had "provided competitive advantage in the job market." Just as important, 77 percent of those who had yet to land a job agreed. On the recruiters' side,

99 percent of employers surveyed said they were satisfied with their MBA hires, 76 percent saying they were "very" or "extremely satisfied." Clearly, the MBA has sustained its reputation as a standard for "higher abilities in managing strategy and innovation, strategic and system skills, and knowledge of general business functions" (GMAC Corporate Recruiters Survey, 2010).

Though the MBA was once the feeder degree for a narrow segment of mostly white, mostly male, and mostly future Fortune 500 CEOs, it is a far more versatile degree today, opening doors to positions of great influence and impact far removed from conventional for-profit goals. A startling number of nonprofits are led by MBAs, from Habitat for Humanity International, Acumen Fund, and Alzheimer's Association to the Center for Applied Philanthropy, Children's Cancer Research Fund, and World Vision. Toss in the numerous MBAs who have made their mark in other ways (think former Treasury secretary Hank Paulson, ex-governor Jon Corzine, and even Dilbert's Scott Adams), and the message is as clear as ever: a top-tier MBA is a versatile, globally recognized qualification for those seeking to change careers—or the world.

A "top-tier MBA"—note the qualifying adjective. The number of business schools worldwide is well into the five figures (India alone has some 1,600), the number accredited by the Association to Advance Collegiate Schools of Business (AACSB), Association of MBAs, or EQUIS is 871, the number with truly international brands might be 50 (on a good day), and the number you probably bought this book to get into no more than 15 or 20. Gaining admission to these select handful is difficult not only because of the odds and fierce competition, but because the rules of entry are complex and subjective. The days are long past when impressive grades, ninety-ninth-percentile GMAT scores, and a fast-track career profile could assure you of a place in a top-drawer management program. With some 82,000 total applications flooding their admissions servers annually, the top 20 programs know they'll have their pick of applicants with stellar numbers and brilliant résumés. Today, they enjoy the luxury of cherry-picking a class fine-tuned for well-rounded variety not only in terms of industry and professional function but also cultural background, geographic origin, and even personal passions.

The raw data of your application can help schools weigh some of these admissions factors, it's true. But when admissions committees must choose between equally qualified superachievers, nothing helps them more than your own words. Enter the application essay. More than ever, the handful of essays that business schools typically require play the critical role in helping admissions officers see you as a unique person deserving of admission rather than a lifeless statistical "profile."

To write such mission-critical documents, you need more than one-size-fits-all "good writing" tips and a stack of sample essays you wish you'd written. As an admissions consultant since 1997 for Accepted.com and on my own (paulsbodine.com), I've written *Great Applications for Business School* to give applicants to the world's best business schools market-tested, MBA-specific methods and strategies for crafting essays and application packages that truly communicate the special qualities that make their personal stories too compelling for admissions officers to ignore. Whether you are a confident communicator or a writing novice, whether you're applying from an MBA feeder industry or are a card-carrying nontraditional applicant, the focused, practical advice in this book will show you the key "tricks of the trade" that have worked consistently for hundreds of admitted applicants at Harvard, Stanford, Wharton, Booth, Kellogg, London, Columbia, INSEAD, Tuck, MIT Sloan, Berkeley Haas—indeed, all the most selective management programs.

Great Applications for Business School is the only how-to MBA admissions guide to offer the following combination of features:

- Admissions and writing insights from one of the world's most experienced and effective admissions consultants. My advice has helped hundreds of applicants from every demographic and region of the world gain admission to the world's best professional schools year after year. (A sample of their testimony can be found on www.paulsbodine.com.)

- A flexible, practical system for finding your application's self-marketing handle, brainstorming your essays' raw material using personal data mining techniques, crafting an outline using theme and evidence sentences, and writing, revising, and editing effective essay drafts.

- Detailed strategies for answering the most common MBA admissions essay topics, from goals, accomplishments, and "self-revelation" essays to diversity, leadership and teamwork, failure, and creative or multimedia topics. *Great Applications for Business School* includes practical guidelines for understanding what schools actually ask, choosing your appropriate stories for each essay type, and structuring your essays so that they provide context, analysis, and the all-important takeaways.

- Forty-four actual, complete essays or admissions documents written by admitted applicants to the very best business schools (Harvard, Stanford, Wharton, Chicago, Tuck, Columbia, London, Kellogg, INSEAD, and MIT Sloan, among others). Each sample—an actual applicant's essay (with minor changes to protect privacy), not a "composite"—is annotated to highlight the tactics and decisions that made the essay click with admissions readers. Ten practical "what *not* to do" tips that recap the critical learnings in each chapter in light of the most common applicant errors.

■ New treatment of creative, PowerPoint, and multimedia essays. Special discussion of issues like handling social-impact career goals; discussing GMAT scores, grades, and other extenuating circumstances in optional essays; reapplying; and selecting and approaching recommenders.

■ Ten case studies showing how real applicants with specific challenges overcame their admissions obstacles to gain admission to top programs.

■ Five "Put Yourself on the Couch" question sets that will spark the kind of reflection and analysis from which truly self-aware essays can emerge.

■ Candid insights from 22 admissions officers representing 16 top schools.

■ Extended appendixes on admissions interviews (containing sample interview responses) and wait-list letters (featuring before-and-after versions of two successful letters). Supplementary content and bonus material on my web site, paulsbodine.com.

Chapter 1 of *Great Applications for Business School* guides you through the hardest part of the application process—actually writing the essays—by showing you how to create a self-marketing handle that informs your whole application, drill down to the themes and stories on which your essays will be built, use outlines effectively, and approach the first draft and revision/editing stages confidently. In Chapter 2, you learn what schools are really looking for in the goals essay while exploring practical strategies for writing the goals essays' key sections: career progress, goals statement, and the "why" questions. In Chapter 3, we consider what admissions officers expect in accomplishment, leadership, and teamwork essays and provide specific methods for structuring your essays, choosing your content, analyzing your examples, and developing the lessons the experiences you describe taught you. Chapter 4 provides detailed insights (and 15 individual essay examples) on self-revelation, diversity, failure, and challenge/growth essay topics. Special treatment is also given to "creative" and multimedia essay types.

Chapter 5 shows you how to take advantage of the opportunity that optional essays provide to do damage control on potential negatives or give schools new insights that strengthen your application. Finally, in Chapter 6, you'll learn the most effective strategies for selecting and approaching recommenders as well as practical tactics for tackling the most common recommendation questions. Two appendixes guide you through typical admissions interview questions and the wait-list process.

Great Applications for Business School is designed to offer motivated, self-reflective applicants to the world's best business schools a no-nonsense, thoroughly authoritative guide to admissions writing. I cannot promise, of course, that following the advice in these pages will ensure admission. "Magic bullets" or rigid systems cannot (thankfully) guarantee you success in a process that is so inherently complex and personal. There are many different ways to approach and write your essays, and I encourage you to use the advice here that helps you most and modify or ignore the rest. Indeed, I recommend that you take smart risks and define your own path.

The advice in this book is based on a simple but repeatedly forgotten truth: effective admissions writing isn't about trying to figure out what admissions officers "want to hear" or following the model of other successful applicants you know. Good writing and great applications must be about discovering and vividly communicating the special blend of skills, experiences, and values that only you possess. It demands self-understanding, honesty, analysis, and hard work. I have yet to meet a client who didn't have a unique story to tell. You have one too. Helping you find it is why so many of my clients have the MBAs they dreamed of.

A NOTE ON THE ESSAY SAMPLES

All the essays reproduced in this book are real essays—not composites or ideal models—written by actual applicants from a wide range of backgrounds who were admitted by the business school listed before each sample (and in many cases by other top schools as well). To protect these applicants' privacy, personal details like gender and cultural background, proper names, and other nonessential details have been disguised. Otherwise these are the same essays that the admissions officers read. It goes without saying that it is unethical to copy or adapt any of these samples for use in your own application. (Admissions officers, who have a nose for the inauthentic, will read this book, and you'll be toast.)

I would be happy to help you with your business school applications. Contact me directly at paulbodine@yahoo.com.

1

Getting Started

The most critical aspect of the application is the essay. We read them closely. They tell us a lot about you.

—RANDALL SAWYER, CORNELL (JOHNSON)

At first blush, it makes no sense. Why should essays—mere words—determine whether you're among the fortunate few who earn MBAs from the world's very best business schools? After all, CEOs aren't paid millions to turn colorful phrases; their job is to solve intractable problems, motivate organizations, and enhance shareholder value. Isn't your potential to do that better gauged by hard metrics like career progress, academic performance, and standardized test scores than by a batch of well-spun essays?

However counterintuitive it might seem, the preeminence of the application essay in the MBA admissions process is no longer open for debate. As the quality of applicants competing for top-tier schools spirals ever higher, the humble essay has become the decisive factor in helping B-schools choose the anointed few from the ranks of equally qualified also-rans.

And well it should. When applicants' work experience, recommendation letters, academic record, intellectual skills, and extracurriculars are all uniformly superlative (at the best schools they often are), business schools could make admissions decisions with a coin flip. How much fairer it is that adcoms take the time to let applicants' thoughts about their lives, dreams, values, and accomplishments guide their decisions. As subjective as words can be, business schools are actually doing you a favor by giving your essays so much weight. How so? Because of all the components of your application, the application essay is the one that gives you the greatest freedom and control and the one that most personally expresses the individual you behind the data. Your grades and work experience are by now all history; your recommenders may, or may not, say what you want them to; and even the success of your admissions interview depends on who your interviewer is, what you are asked, and whether the interviewer is having a bad-hair day. Your GMAT score can certainly open the admissions door for you, but only you can walk through it. Your essays can help you walk that walk like no other application component. From the themes you choose to capture your profile and the stories you pick to illustrate them to the lessons you draw and the tone you adopt, business schools give you the reins to shape their perception of your candidacy. Take them.

KNOW THY AUDIENCE

Why such generosity? Because, strange to say, admissions officers want to let you in. If you doubt that, consider the background of the typical admissions committee member. If you find any pattern, it may be that of the admissions careerist—that is, higher education–sector professionals with human-resource–oriented degrees who've worked their way up the admissions food chain, often at several schools. Rather than statisticians, demographic analysts, or business theorists, you'll find career development and educational administrators as well as eclectic multicareerists, from romance-language Ph.D.s, ex-opera singers, and attorneys to former ambassadorial assistants, marketing directors, and management consultants (some with MBAs). You'll find, in other words, "people persons" with polyglot interests who've made careers out of personal development and who value the same focus in applicants.

What the Schools Say

Please be authentic. If you enjoy writing your essays, we will enjoy reading them!

WHITNEY KESTNER, VIRGINIA (DARDEN)

Writing is really just a means of striking up a certain kind of personal relationship with the reader, and who you think that reader is will obviously affect what you say to him. Too many applicants doom their essays from the start by assuming that they're addressing the educational equivalent of a parole board—humorless, ranking-obsessed statisticians sternly sifting your past for hints that you've departed in thought or deed from the true MBA way. The essays of unsuccessful applicants often read like they were written for an audience of rubber-stamping, degree-issuing automatons or surly Dickensian gatekeepers waiting to pounce on signs of individuality. Though admissions officers must deny eight or nine of every ten applicants, you must assume that they approach each one with an open mind and the readiness to believe that your application is the one that will draw them a step closer to a rounded, diverse, interesting class. That's why the essays of successful applicants are usually open, relaxed, confident, and optimistic. That fact alone should tell you what kind of people your audience really consists of.

The Admissions Party

Imagine you're at a tony cocktail party where you find yourself competing with the best and brightest of your peers to make a lasting impression on your welcoming but overworked hosts. You're all splendidly accomplished, well-rounded types, but you know your influential hosts are only likely to remember a handful of you when the evening's done. When your moment comes, would you collar them and begin reciting your promotions and academic feats? Let's hope not.

You'd probably turn on the charm, complimenting them on their home, probing for areas of shared interest, telling a few of your choice stories, and generally captivating them with your engaging personality. On one level, your B-school essays represent this same interpersonal challenge: how to put your best foot forward when your personal distinctiveness, not your résumé, is what will separate you from the other super achievers vying for your B-school spot. If there are three applicant categories—the dings, the "doables," and the dazzling—it's in your essays that you can elevate yourself from the doable to the dazzling.

What the Schools Say

Effective business leaders are almost without exception also good communicators, and we make no bones about wanting to recruit good business leaders, rather than narrow analysts.

—ANDREW MCALISTER, FORMER WHARTON ADMISSIONS OFFICER

FINDING YOUR SELF-MARKETING HANDLE

The essay-writing process begins with introspection; there's no shortcut around it. Before you begin writing, even before you know the questions your target schools ask, begin developing a short personal "marketing" message or "handle" that integrates the key themes (strengths, values, experiences, interests) you want your application to communicate. Picture our admissions cocktail party again. Your hosts' time is limited. They must make the rounds with all their guests before the night's over. Since you can't give them your whole life story, everything you say must communicate a compact multidimensional message that's distinctive enough for your hosts to remember you by long after other partygoers have made their pitch. Take your time, cast your net widely, and ask friends and family for their input so the handle you devise reflects the key uniqueness factors from your professional, personal, community, and academic lives.

You Are Not a Brand

"Marketing yourself" to business schools simply means understanding that your application is an act of personal advocacy, not a workplace self-evaluation, class paper, or confessional. But don't get carried away with the marketing metaphors. Brands are often faddishly short-lived, skin-deep, and exhaustively focus-grouped. You should not be. All Apple iPads and Nike Air Jordans are essentially the same. No two humans are.

Thinking of yourself as a brand is the first self-falsifying step away from the self-reflection schools want and toward the pointless preoccupation with other applicants that they abhor. Before you know it you'll be wasting time trying to figure out what schools "want to hear" or which post-MBA goals are hot this year. Rather than projecting flashy, airbrushed images of yourself as the Maseroti or Budweiser of B-school applicants, conceive of yourself instead as a unique person who desperately needs to communicate something to the adcom. That something is not just your need for an MBA—it's deeper: what makes your life and experiences compelling to you. So, yes, market yourself, but your self, not some phony personal brand.

As a rule of thumb, construct your self-marketing handle out of four or five themes, each one rich enough to build an essay around. If you come up with, "I'm a natural leader with strong analytical skills and a social conscience," you're thinking way too broadly. (As an exercise in concision, try reducing your self-marketing handle to one tweet—140 characters). If your handle runs past a sentence or two, unless it's truly scintillating, business schools may garble it or lose it in the crowd. Your set of themes should emphasize your multidimensionality—who you are professionally, personally, and in the community. In other words, you're not only a testing team lead at Qualcomm; you're *also* a Norwegian-American raised in Ecuador who *also* loves taxidermy and tutoring immigrant kids for The Knowledge Trust Alliance.

Remember that your admissions "hosts" will be bringing a long memory of past conversations to your brief encounter. Simply telling them that you're a banker or a marketing manager will trigger all sorts of mostly valid assumptions about your skills and professional exposures. If you're applying from a traditional MBA feeder profession like consulting or investment banking, for example, your handle will come equipped with analytical and quantitative strengths. So round it out distinctively by including themes that B-schools don't automatically associate with your profession, such as creativity (e.g., your lifelong devotion to basket-weaving), social-impact causes (e.g., that stint training subsistence farmers in Malawi), or out-of-the-box professional experiences (e.g., your first career as a geography teacher). Or look for unusual childhood or family experiences, distinctive hobbies, or international experiences that offset the predictability of your professional profile, and incorporate these in your handle.

Conversely, if your profession is unusual (e.g., nonprofit or creative) B-schools will already be giving you points for distinctiveness, so balance your handle with themes that show them that you also have the quantitative, analytical, or business skills they automatically associate with consultants and finance types. Instead of "The award-winning African-American photographer who grew up in Portugal and organized her church's choir," pitch yourself as "The Lisbon-raised African-American photographer who runs her own five-person media studio and handles her church's finances." Like the consultant or finance professional, your goal is a handle that communicates multidimensional balance, but one that also reassures schools that you're MBA caliber (in addition to being unlike anyone they've encountered before).

What the Schools Say

After reading each application, I try to sum up in one sentence who each applicant is and what she or he will contribute to this class. The easier that is, the better your shot at getting in.

— KAREN SIEGFRIED, CAMBRIDGE (JUDGE)

Don't try to do this alone. Relying only on your own sense of your distinctive strengths may not be enough to separate you from your peers, especially if you're a member of a crowded applicant demographic. For example, a male technology applicant from India (a large applicant pool) could be forgiven for deciding that the strongest aspects of his profile are his degree from an ultra-selective Indian Institute of Technology, his leadership of his school's cricket team and cultural festival, and his fast-track career at Intel. Unfortunately, at the very top schools this stellar background will be only par for the course among Indian information technology candidates. To find a self-marketing handle that really sets him apart, our Indian friend will have to dig deeper—perhaps by focusing on unusual aspects of his upbringing (nonacademic obstacles overcome or cultural, geographic, or religious uniqueness factors) or hobbies or involvements that few of his peers will share. Experienced admissions consultants (moi, for example) can help you isolate the potential themes that can make your handle stand out.

Although a distinctive multidimensional handle is ideal, it must truly capture who you are. Don't try to force a theme—"internationalism," for example, or "creativity"—onto your profile if you don't have the experiences to back it up. Again, each of your handle's themes must be deep enough that you could write a full essay around it.

You don't have to figure out your self-marketing handle first. If it's easier for you, you can start the process with your best stories—the experiences from your professional, personal, and community lives that you're proudest of or that you identify most closely with. What do these stories say about you? What values or talents do they communicate? The answers to these questions can become the foundation of your self-marketing handle. The bottom line is that you be able to approach the essay-writing process with (1) an idea of the general themes that distinguish your application and (2) the specific stories that will illustrate them. Which you arrive at first is entirely up to you.

DATA MINING YOUR LIFE

Once you have your self-marketing handle, you have the multipart message that should inform all your essays for every school (albeit with some tweaking here and there to match particular schools' emphases). Now you need to find the best *specific* stories that illustrate that message. Unlike medical and law schools, which often give you carte blanche in formulating your subject matter, business schools help you by posing several highly specific "thesis-bearing" essay topics—topics, that is, whose theme (or themes) is contained in the wording of the question itself. Moreover, within each essay question, schools also usually pose several specific subquestions (What are your goals? Why do you need an MBA? Why now? Etc.). This may feel like cruel and unusual punishment when you're writing your essays, but by limiting the scope of the essays for you, schools at least spare you the agony of brainstorming your own essay topics.

✗ Stay on subject

Study the wording of each school's essay prompt carefully. You will hear a lot (in this book too) about "positioning" themes and thinking "strategically" about your essays, but none of that will make a whit of difference if you don't reflect in a sincere way on the question the essay poses. After all your savvy positioning, some of that sincerity must shine through, or your essays will read as blandly as a committee-written Hollywood script. Business schools put a great deal of thought (even ingenuity) into their questions because they're looking for the most effective and varied ways to get you to open up and let them peer inside at the unique you.

Since capturing your key uniqueness factors was exactly why I advised you to craft a self-marketing handle, schools' multiple essay topics should not intimidate you. Unfortunately, you won't usually be able to simply match each of your themes to your schools' individual essay questions. Some schools may force you to discuss several (or all) of your themes in a single essay. Other schools may pose questions that none of your self-marketing themes seem appropriate for. Many essay prompts ask you to address several things, so pay special attention both to the question's subject words (for example, *career progress, nonprofessional accomplishment,* or *leadership experience*) and the direction words (*describe, discuss, assess*). Columbia's "Please tell us about yourself and your personal interests. The goal of this essay is to get a sense of who you are, rather than what you have achieved professionally" might seem straightforward, but you can bet some applicants will discuss professional interests, assume "who you are" means "what you've done at work or school," or ignore the crucial "tell us about yourself" question and focus exclusively on their hobbies. And many programs pose much more maddeningly complex questions. So read carefully, break out all the subquestions, even shoot an e-mail to the school if you're unsure, but know what you're being asked.

Review your schools' essay questions to get a sense of the range of topics you'll face. As we discuss in Chapters 2 through 4, there are at least seven basic topic groups: goals (including, Why an MBA? and Why Our School?), accomplishments, leadership and teamwork, "self-revelation" topics, diversity, failure, and "creative" questions. Each school poses between two and seven essay questions. Assuming that you'll be applying to six to eight schools, you may well encounter all these categories in some form. Don't get too strategic here. Stay focused on the range of themes and stories within each school's essay set. Don't assume similar-seeming topics from two or more different schools can be answered with the same story. If you try to look for apparent topic "clusters" across a range of schools, you'll risk losing the focus that you need to find the right mix for each particular school.

Review the essay questions once a day for a week or so to get your mind working on them in background mode. Now you're ready to identify the individual stories you will build each essay around.

Mind-Plumbing Methods

The data mining or "life inventory" step is nonoptional. You should no more exclude it from the essay-writing process than you would omit gathering business requirements before developing a software application, rehearsing a piece of music before performing it publicly, or conducting research before writing a dissertation. It's that essential. Inventorying your own life is by definition a subjective process. Your memory can deceive you, stories you consider unexceptional may actually make outstanding essays, and stories that you're convinced are distinctive and impressive may actually be fairly commonplace. So at this early stage you want to suspend judgment and simply "brain-dump" as much as you can as quickly as you can. The goal here is to find different ways to bypass your inhibitions and trick your mind into disgorging details you overlooked, significant events you've taken for granted, passions you forgot you once had.

The following techniques may help you:

■ *Using your résumé as autobiographical timeline.* Your résumé can be a memory aid for generating essay material. Let your mind linger over each section of the résumé, recalling the challenges, breakthroughs, and changes each stage of your career offered you. Recall and write down the full details of the accomplishments listed in the résumé's bullets as well as the achievements you might have excluded from the résumé that could make good essay fodder. Since many of your essays will involve a chronologically ordered narrative (e.g., your career progress, your greatest accomplishment), this exercise can generate useful material and a timeframe for understanding your development.

■ *Recording thoughts or conversations.* If you are one of those people who find any kind of writing exercise inhibiting, a voice recorder may enable you to get your thoughts out painlessly. Either record yourself as you extemporize about your life or goals or record a conversation with a friend (over a beer if it helps) as he or she probes you with some of the basic questions listed in the Put Yourself on the Couch exercise elsewhere in this chapter. Transcribe this recording (minus the "um"s and "dude"s), and you may find that you have a rough but potentially useful data bank of essay content.

■ *Random listing.* Instead of shackling your thought to the rules of sentences and paragraphs, first warm up your writing skills by generating simple lists—favorite music; worst jobs; greatest accomplishments; best vacations; traits that define you, characteristics your friends admire in you; or most unusual things about your childhood, education, homeland, international travels, hobbies, and so on. Then take these lists a step further by looking for any connections between them. Perhaps your list of defining traits is illustrated by your list of achievements. Maybe certain experiences keep appearing in different lists—an indication they are important or defining for you.

■ *Journaling.* Nothing will get you into the discipline of writing better than a daily regimen. The operative word here is *daily;* anything less frequent will prevent you from writing naturally and un-self-consciously. The goal here is to get comfortable with the idea of expressing yourself in words (it's not an unnatural act). Pick a time of day when you can write uninterruptedly for 15 to 30 minutes. Record your experiences, victories, complaints from the past day—whatever you want—but do it without fail and without distractions. Avoid the trap of simply recording your comings and goings, however. Make it a practice to close each paragraph by drawing some conclusion or stating its significance. Writing thoughtfully is a habit you can learn. If you'd like a little help, try a Web tool called 750words.com, a private online journaling tool that gets you in the habit of writing three pages (about 750 words) daily by, for example, awarding "points" for every day you reach your 750 words. A similar site, springnote.com allows you to share your journal entries with others or create entries from your iPhone.

■ *Social media.* If it will help you commit to the writing process to post your exercises where anyone and everyone can see them—on the Internet—by all means go for it (but maybe keep the really embarrassing stuff to yourself). Facebook friends may respond in helpful ways to an anecdote you post (or at least tell you that it sucks when it does). Likewise, tweeting your memory of a defining moment or an idea you have for an essay theme may earn you some interesting feedback. But even if Web posting just gets you in the groove of thinking about your essay's themes and stories, it will serve a useful purpose. Twitter and other social media may get you into the habit of writing (albeit 140 characters at a time) and earn you feedback on your writing all at the same time.

■ *Visual mapping or clustering.* Write the four or five themes that constitute your self-marketing handle on separate sheets of paper (or use a mind mapping application such as Mindo or CrowdMap for iPad; Google "mind mapping" for other visual mapping apps). Around each of your theme words, begin jotting down whatever events, skills, values, or interests these words suggest to you. Each new term you jot down will suggest other words. Follow them where they lead, and connect each new term with a line back to the related term that prompted it. If you go with the flow here, you may gain insights into what you value most and the inter-connections between your themes. All these may prove useful when you begin writing your essays.

■ *Stream-of-consciousness writing.* Perhaps the least structured of tech-niques, stream-of-consciousness or "free" writing simply involves scrib-bling down whatever comes into your head without stopping, even if it's nonsense. As odd as this may sound, you'll find that, for all the useless verbiage you generate, you may also unwittingly produce ideas, phrases, and insights that may actually wind up in your essays. Try to group these ideas, phrases, and insights into related categories. At a minimum, this technique can help you overcome the angst of the empty screen.

What do all these exercises have in common? They get you writing *before* you begin writing your essays, when anxiety and your "internal editor" can cut you off from the creativity and personality that will make your essays live. The mere act of translating your thoughts into words—in whatever form—forces those thoughts to the next level of concreteness and leads you in new direc-tions, while also giving you a "paper" trail to refer back to as raw material for your essays. Writing, in other words, is a way of thinking, a kind of introspec-tion. The sooner you get into the habit of thinking on paper (or laptop, iPad, iPhone—whatever works), the sooner you'll be ready to shape that thinking into the rigorous, ordered thought that is the essay. Crossing the great divide between your thoughts and their verbal expression in concrete language is what separates would-be writers from nonwriters. It's not easy, but these exercises can help you do it with a minimum of pain.

Everything Signifies

Your data-mining or "life inventory" process should involve more then merely fleshing out the stories that best capture your self-marketing themes. You also want to be continually evaluating their significance—their *value* to you. How valuable was that Singapore internship to me? What did it teach me? How did it change me? To manage your data-mining effort, create a spreadsheet or log divided into sections, say, Career, Academics, Extracurriculars, Community/Volunteer, and Personal/Family. Within each section create three columns: one for describing the event, one for noting its "external" significance or impact, and a third for logging its "internal" significance for you. External significance will include the experience's impact on your career progress (earned promo-tion, raise, etc.), on your organization (won new client contract), or on others (helped tutoring student raise math grade to B). Internal significance will include how the experience changed you, enhanced your skills, deepened your perspective, strengthened your sense of your potential, and so on.

By getting into the habit of identifying and noting down the underlying significance of your stories as they come to you, you'll sharpen your ability to evaluate your essay material in the same way that admissions officers will, reducing your burden in the essay-writing stage. Don't perform the critical data-mining stage all by yourself. Your perception of your own life is likely to be highly subjective, so ask friends, family, and mentors for any key traits, memories, accomplishments you may have missed.

FROM RAW MATERIAL TO ESSAY CONTENT

If you've done it right, your data-mining process should leave you with a mass of raw material that could fill multiple admissions essays. As much as you may want to throw it all into the pot, essay length limits will force you to jettison the bulk of it. So get used to thinking early on in terms of focused stories or experiences that capture in microcosm what's essential about you rather than "overview" essays that superficially skim dozens of key moments. These latter essays usually come off as glorified lists that lack the detail and context that enable readers to remember your stories and, hence, you.

Look for discrete stories that can "stand in for" or serve as metaphors for your life's themes. By understanding these stories, in other words, someone could know nearly as much about who you really are as by hearing your full autobiography. Given the limited space schools give you, the only way you can convey the breadth of your life experiences is by exploring a key handful in depth.

Because you approached the data-mining stage with your self-marketing handle already defined, you were able to group your raw stories or data points into buckets that corresponded to the handle's three, four, or five themes. Your data-mining process may have shown you that your handle was overemphasizing one aspect of your profile or ignoring one that you now think is stronger. Be flexible; make whatever adjustments you need to. Get used to evaluating your specific stories (the ones you'll use in your essays) against your self-marketing handle, and vice versa. This way you'll be sure you're keeping both the forest (self-marketing handle) and the trees (stories/essays illustrating themes) in sight—and in alignment.

Now begin to evaluate your raw stories critically. Look for the ones that are most distinctive and that combine the greatest external impact and personal transformation. If a story is scoring high in unusualness, objective results or impact, and personal significance, you've probably got a winner. How well does this story illustrate your theme? You may have three stories for your "internationalism" theme: a college internship in Thailand; an implementation where you worked side by side with Belgians, Russians, and

Brazilians; and last year's two-month ERP engagement in Cairo. Because the internship happened four years ago in college and you were based in the United States throughout the ERP implementation, you tentatively decide to use the Cairo experience as your core story for any essays that focus on globalism or cross-culturalism. (Of course, it may also work for any team-work or diversity essays, and some schools may give you the space to discuss all *three* of your international stories.) Subject all the raw stories generated by your data-mining process to this same weighing or ranking process until you've arrived at a core set of stories that covers all the topics for the application you plan to tackle first.

Now—at last—you're ready to start the essays themselves.

WRITING YOUR ESSAYS

You performed the content-gathering steps in the last section. Now that you are beginning your first essay, you should not only know which stories best address each question but also have done enough raw writing to avoid blank page syndrome and other writers' ailments. Still, writing tends to bring out the procrastinator in all of us, so set tight deadlines of a few days or less for completing each stage of your essay. As in the data-mining process, your focus when writing the first draft of your essay is to get something down on paper. Many applicants believe that they have to complete a polished, finished draft in one sitting. Don't be so hard on yourself. Good writing is a base-at-a-time game; it's not about home runs. So forget about style, grammar, and word count when you're writing your first draft.

To keep the pressure off, you might start with the first application that comes out in early summer or with a school that's not your number-one choice. After you finish it, move on to the next school, but *don't* submit the first application. Finish the second school's application (and perhaps others) and then go back to the first school and polish it off in light of the tweaks you've made while working on later applications. In this way you can capitalize on the improvements that inevitably occur as you refine your essays, without jeopardizing the advantage of a first-round submission.

The Outline Is Your Friend

The outline may summon unpleasant memories of seventh-grade English, but it's one more useful method for reducing the anxiety and time drain of the writing process. If outlines make you nervous or stifle your creative juices, you *can* develop your essays in unstructured fashion by simply expanding the raw content you generated in the data-mining process into larger chunks or paragraphs, and then juggling their order until you find one that fits. The (substantial) downside of this approach is its haphazardness and inefficiency. By failing to map out your essay's organization from the start, you risk chasing tangents down blind alleys and wasting valuable time.

By bringing structure to your essay before you start writing it, outlines maximize your efficiency and enable you to perform a crucial early test of your essay ideas before you've invested too much in them. Do you have enough material to support your assertions or illustrate your experiences? Does the lesson you're trying to draw from your material have enough substance? Does it really grow organically from the story itself, or does it seem imposed and unearned? Outlines can help you answer these questions.

Each outline you create will have the following basic organization:

1. *Introduction.* One paragraph introducing the essay's themes and setting its tone.

2. *Body paragraphs.* Multiple sentences that provide evidence to support the themes asserted in the introduction. Each paragraph in the body should consist of:

    a. *Theme sentence.* The first sentence of the paragraph often states the topic or theme that this paragraph will "prove." "Though my formal roles are technical, all my growth opportunities have involved leadership roles."

    b. *Evidence sentences.* These consist of specific examples, anecdotes, or details that support the paragraph's theme sentence. "In my very first project, for example, I became the de facto team focal point when my implementation proposal was accepted as our project solution."

3. *Conclusion.* This paragraph pulls together the underlying lessons or themes of the preceding paragraphs. It generally includes lessons learned or insights (from the third column of your data-mining spreadsheet).

Good outlines are the safety rope that keeps you focused on finding that next secure foothold toward your essay's summit rather than staring dizzily into the abyss of the next empty paragraph. Don't cling to your outline cravenly, however. It may need to be revised as your thinking about the topic evolves. For examples of effective outlining refer to the two samples at the end of this chapter.

The First Draft

According to writing coach Elizabeth Danziger, you should devote no more than 15 percent of the total time you spend on an essay writing the first draft (with the remaining time divided between the brainstorming and revising steps). Whether that number's accurate or not, the moral is that writing your first draft should not paralyze you with anxiety or perfectionism. You've already done a major portion of your work (finding, selecting, and structuring your material), and the bulk of your remaining work (revision and editing) comes later. So lighten up! Run with your outline, and don't analyze what you're writing too closely—just get it down.

Some writers start with the sections of the outline that look the easiest or that they know the most about. And for many writers, the introduction is often the last piece of the puzzle. In the next three sections, however, we look at the three main components of every essay—the introduction, body, and conclusion—in that order.

Introduction

In your introduction, you must tell the reader what you will be trying to accomplish in the essay. This does not mean that your first sentence should be a monotonous statement of your theme ("In this essay, I will be ..."). But somewhere in your first paragraph—the last sentence is often good—you must directly signal that you will be answering the school's question and what the thrust of your response will be.

More than stating your theme, however, your introduction must catch and hold the reader's interest, which is battered daily by dozens of same-sounding essays. It's critical that the admissions reader finish your introduction thinking something like, "I wonder how this turns out," or, "Hmmm, intriguing," rather than, "Geez, here we go again." (See Chapter 2 for examples of the variety of ways you can open a goals essay.) Finally, your introduction must also provide some of the essay's key context (answering where, when, who, and what questions) and establish, primarily through word choice, the essay's tone (for example, dramatic and serious or wry and subtle).

Body

The body of your essay is also its heart—the human story and the corroborating "evidence" that justifies the claims or promises you make in your introduction. Every paragraph in the body should be built loosely on a basic pattern of *general assertion → supporting example.*

Whether you're writing a narrative-driven chronological essay, an example-driven "argument" essay, or a vivid detail-driven descriptive essay, each paragraph in the body should advance your case or further unfold your story. Usually, the specific sequence of your paragraphs will be dictated by the chronology of the story you're telling (from the past forward toward the present), but sometimes each paragraph will function as a separate example in a larger argument. In either case, your paragraphs will live or die by the degree of personal, vivid detail and insight you provide. You want to achieve a balance between data—the personal facts and stories that substantiate your themes—and analysis—regularly stepping back from an example or anecdote to tell the reader what it means. Too much data will make for a dull, impersonal essay. Too much analysis will cause your essay to float off into a sea of generalities unsupported by anchoring facts.

Perhaps the greatest disadvantage you face as an applicant is that you cannot read what the vast majority of other applicants write. If you could, you would immediately see how many essays sound identical. The reason for this sameness is almost always a lack of specific detail and personal anecdotes (that and many applicants have the same clichéd ideas about what business schools "want to hear"). So throughout the body of your essay, always be as personal and specific as you can be.

You know your essay's body is structured well when the opening theme sentences connecting each new paragraph to the preceding (often called transition sentences) seem to write themselves. For example, the transition sentence, "The eFunds engagement was not the last time I took on leadership roles outside my job description," smoothly links the preceding paragraph (about the eFunds engagement) to another leadership example the writer is about to narrate in the new paragraph. Try to avoid graceless numerical transitions ("Third, success for me means never having to say you're sorry").

Conclusion

Your conclusion needs to do several key things—and briefly. It needs to draw a synthesized (but not vague or banal) lesson or theme out of the body paragraphs that have preceded it. And it must do this without simply repeating the theme statement in the introduction or merely restating the key point of each body paragraph. The conclusion, that is, must create a true sense of "summing up," of loose ends being bow-tied, but in a way that injects deeper or larger insight than you previously provided in the essay. Moreover, to give the reader that peculiar feeling of coherence or unity that good writing often has, your conclusion should refer indirectly back to the language or details of the introduction—but as an echo rather than a mirror. Finally, the conclusion's tone should be positive and forward-looking. If you can smoothly refer to your goals or MBA plans, do so. Avoid "In conclusion" or any of its stuffy siblings.

As you work on your first draft, keep your outline in front of you so you don't wander off into tedious digressions. If you start to feel lost or bogged down, pull back and ask yourself, "What am I really trying to say here?" "What do I want the reader to feel, believe, or conclude after reading this?" These kinds of reorienting exercises can keep you on track and plowing speedily toward your objective: a reasonably coherent document within which lurks a finalized essay.

Try to think of your essay not as an argument ("Why I should be admitted") or a proposal ("Consider admitting me for the following reasons"), but as a story about an interesting and sympathetic hero (you) in pursuit of a distant but most holy grail (the MBA). Humans are hardwired to respond to human-interest stories. Tales of sympathetic protagonists overcoming conflict or obstacles by modifying their world to remove those obstacles appeal to our basic hopes in a way that impersonal proposals do not. This is not to suggest that you submit a ripe piece of fiction or melodramatic screenplay. But if viewing your essay more as creative act than as cold exposition infuses it with personality and reader-friendliness then go for it. You might, for example, use some object (your Brooklyn Element skateboard) or activity (belly dancing) that reflects one of your passions as a metaphor for talking about your whole life, connecting specific aspects of that possession or activity to examples from your life that illustrate them. The possibilities for creativity are unlimited.

REVISING AND EDITING

Now that your first draft is done, you must schizophrenically repress the un-inhibited Mr. Hyde who created it and summon your editorial Dr. Jekyll to make it presentable. You must cease expressing yourself, that is, and begin reading yourself as the admissions officers will. Writing and revising are distinctly different, even opposing, acts. Intermingling them, like trying simultaneously to be a stage actor and theater critic, is to risk misadventure.

Once you've banished your writerly self, your first act as editor is to completely ignore your draft, at least for a day. When you come back to it, you will immediately see things your creative self missed. Before leaping to fix them, step back and consider only macro and organizational changes first, such as contradictory themes or assertions, needlessly repeated points, yawning gaps in context or logic, or weakly developed or poorly placed paragraphs. If you find these, you may need to switch around paragraphs, expunge digressions, or add to, delete, or bolster your examples. By attending to these big-ticket problems first, you'll avoid spit-polishing prose that you later decide to cut.

Depending on how thorough your outline is and how effectively you elaborated on it in your first draft, your essay may go through one, two, or more macrolevel revisions before it's ready for editing proper. It's no fun, but you must revise your essays as many times as they require. Continually ask yourself whether your main thesis and secondary points will be clear to the admissions officers, whether your evidence will persuade them, whether you are telling this story as efficiently and clearly as you can—oh, and do all of these without editing the life and energy out of your original draft. Always choose the simplest, shortest, and most direct expression over the more complex or "sophisticated." Read your essays aloud. Do they flow? Did you notice miscues you missed earlier? Is the tone conversational, and does it sound like you?

Don't try to go through the revision and editing process alone. Whether you ask friends and family; colleagues, MBAs, mentors; or experienced admissions consultants like me, seek some reasonably objective and knowledgeable outside opinion. But be careful how many chefs you invite into the kitchen. Too much positioning and "helpful" tweaking will drain all the personality from your work (and some folks will just use your request as an opportunity to show off). They're ultimately your essays; keep it that way.

Revising is really the writing you do after your first draft is done. Editing, on the other hand, is not really composition at all. It is cleaning up the essay's mechanics and grammar at the sentence and word level after the writing is complete. Though the changes you make in this stage will affect your essay less fundamentally, they will be much more numerous and, if uncorrected, enough in themselves to torpedo an otherwise tightly organized piece of writing. The potential glitches that editing catches can involve everything from pronoun and subject-verb agreement, dangling modifiers, run-on sentences, and parallelism to punctuation and capitalization errors, word choice and misspelling, and active- versus passive-voice issues. If you're uncertain about any of these potential problem areas, review the redoubtable (and brief) *Elements of Style* by E. B. White and William Strunk Jr. Finally, have a trained editor vet your essays.

Letting Go

Too many applicants decide that their essays are "finished" only because the school's deadline says they must be, not because the essays are truly polished. Applicants who give themselves enough time risk the opposite danger: obsessively tweaking their essays until they have the bland plasticity of a corporate press release. Your essay is truly finished when you can't imagine how to make it say what you mean more candidly, vividly, or directly. When you've achieved that level of honesty, color, and tautness, let go.

ADMISSIONS ESSAYS: WHAT *NOT* TO DO

1. *Fail to answer the question.* The answer to their particular question is what the schools want, not the answer to another school's question. Remember that schools purposely customize the wording of their essay questions to differentiate themselves (and test your ability to follow orders). They don't want cut-and-paste responses. Often their particular spin or twist is subtle and can be addressed by modifying some key words or sentences in your introduction or conclusion. Thus you rarely need to start from scratch. Just be sure you're being sensitive to the particular nuance contained in the question.

2. *Write essays that lack a point or underlying thesis.* This mistake is often a result of omitting the data-mining or outlining stages of the prewriting process. Applicants appear to address the individual parts of the essay question, but when you look beneath the surface detail, you can't be sure where the essay is going, why the applicant is relating this experience, or what she thinks about it.

3. *Sound negative, whining, complaining.* Successful leaders are positive, forward-looking types who even describe their failures in terms of the constructive lessons they teach. They inspire respect, not pity. The ideal tone is conversational and confident; energized, fair-minded, and optimistic; and self-aware but world-directed.

4. *Use clichés or hackneyed ideas.* These reflect superficial or tired thinking whether they're committed on the micro or sentence level ("I broadened my horizons and learned that hard work and persistence are invaluable") or on the macro or essay level.

5. *Write a résumé in prose.* This blunder usually stems from the misguided notion that it's better to cram as much strong material as you can into an essay than to focus on one (or two) experiences in extensive detail. Believing that admissions officers evaluate human experience on some gross-volume basis, the applicant breezes through a long chronicle of mini-achievements, none detailed with enough specificity to distinguish him from any other applicant.

6. *Write what you think admissions officers want to hear.* Aside from the fact that this approach is insincere and won't help you stand out (because so many others do it), it assumes that admissions officers know what they want to hear. In reality, admissions officers live to be pleasantly surprised by a story or profile that answers their question and that they couldn't have anticipated because they've never encountered it before. Make their day.

7. *Fail to catch grammatical and spelling errors.* Don't rely on your own eagle eye or computer's spell-checker alone. Show your essays to other people, ideally someone with training in the rules and conventions of good writing and the English language. Read Strunk and White's deeply helpful guide to incisive writing, *The Elements of Style.*

8. *Leave out the passion.* Choosing boring material or writing about interesting material in a boring way sends the wrong signal to admissions officers, who are looking high and low for engaged, enthusiastic people with multiple interests and a zest for life. All your essays are ultimately about you, a subject schools naturally expect you to be somewhat excited about.

9. *Fail to be strategic about your essays.* This means knowing how to strike a balance between standing out from other applicants and having the minimal skills and values to be accepted by future classmates. It also includes the error of forgetting to view each school's essay set in its totality to ensure that you've included all your key stories and that your essays are a multidimensional mix of personal, professional, and community material.

10. *Omit the lessons learned or takeaways.* A B-school admissions essay (regardless of topic) that lacks a closing lessons-learned section should be a contradiction in terms. Whether the school asks for takeaways or not, give the committee reflection, thoughtfulness, and your analysis of the significance of the essay's subject matter in a single paragraph.

Put Yourself on the Couch

The following questions can help you dig deep enough to uncover the kind of thoughtful, searching answers business schools seek in admissions essays:

1. What makes you happiest? (Or, In what moment of your life have you felt the most joy?)

2. What do you fear more than anything else? (Or, What experience has frightened you the most?)

3. Have you ever been surprised when someone thanked you? What had you done for that person?

4. What one person influenced you more than anyone else in your life? What one experience or event best captures that person's shaping role?

5. What would your friends be most surprised to learn about you?

6. Aside from salary, what motivates you to do your best at work?

7. If you could choose your epitaph, what would it say?

8. What single event changed your life or your values the most, positively or negatively?

9. What was your greatest nonprofessional failure and what did you learn from it?

10. If you could be any person living or dead aside from yourself, who would it be? Why?

SAMPLE OUTLINES

The following outlines are actual examples (with some disguising changes) of essay outlines I developed with successful applicants to Harvard Business School and Kellogg.

Sample Outline 1: Vicky B. (Admitted to Harvard Business School)

What is your career vision and why is this choice meaningful to you?

I. My Facebook mental health pages have shown me that my passion is blending social media with social entrepreneurship. *[The opening sentence of the actual final essay was more vivid, but this placeholder enabled Vicky to start her essay with a clear theme in mind]*

   A. Helped hundreds of people affected by depression, worked directly with psychiatrists and social agencies to find social media-based methods for reaching out to, treating depression victims.

      1. Much more I can do.

II. Long-term goal: establish online mental health community that employs social media like Facebook and Twitter and technologies like iPhone to help isolated, depressed individuals find answers, compassion, professional treatment through Internet.

   A. Opportunities abound. FastCompany survey: 17 of America's 100 fastest-growing tech companies focused on $2 trillion social media market.

   B. To understand how my startup can survive new-venture process, my short-term goal: associate in top social media VC firm such as Andreessen / Horowitz, Accel Partners, or Greylock Partners. *[Vicky clearly has already researched her goals; her final goals paragraph was not much more detailed than this]*

C. Evaluating, investing in, guiding social media-based startups will prepare me to become entrepreneur myself.

III. Why MBA

    A. Experiences in mental health community work and social media taught me how to create online communities, lead teams, and gave me expertise in social media's technologies, trends, practices.

        1. But not gained tools to break into VC industry and launch own venture.

    B. MBA from rigorous, relevant business school will teach entrepreneurial fundamentals in accelerated fashion, give me VC-critical skills: evaluating business proposals, analyzing prospective investments, diligencing new deals, analyzing sectors, preparing sensitivity models.

IV. Why HBS

    A. Social Media *[Vicky has helped herself by having already done her Why HBS research before approaching her essays]*

        1. Case Studies like "Molson Canada: Social Media Marketing" and "Social Media: The New Hybrid Element of the Promotion Mix"

        2. Courses like "Digital Marketing Strategy"

        3. Professors like Mikolaj Jan Piskorski, "Understanding Users of Online Social Networks"

    B. Entrepreneurship

        1. "Entrepreneurial Manager" Required 1st year course

        2. 20 electives in entrepreneurship every year

        3. Business plan contest

    C. The HBS Difference

        1. Case method

            a. Class participation counts for 50% of grade

        2. General management orientation

        3. People:

            a. My visit to Cambridge and conversations with HBS students X and Y have convinced me that …

            b. Faculty: rich research tradition, truly thought leaders

            c. Alumni: conversations with alumni X and Y …

V. When reached out to first depression victim online worried only about helping out

    A. Never dreamed could one day think of building career out of battling mental illness

    B. With HBS MBA that dream can become reality

[Given HBS's length limits, Vicky's first draft will run long, but better too much content than too little (or, what's an editor for?)]

Sample Outline 2: Charlie K. (Admitted to Kellogg)

Each of our applicants is unique. Describe how your background, values, academics, activities and/or leadership skills will enhance the experience of other Kellogg students.

I. I still remember when I decided to find out where my father lived, to find out what kind of person he was.
    A. Parents divorced when I was 4.
        1. Only seen photos, heard stories
            a. Dad: Korean immigrant; mother: American
            b. When marriage failed, returned to Korea
            c. Mom didn't talk about him, were out of touch
        2. She married briefly couple of times
            a. Without father my whole life
    B. Not something I felt sorry for myself about
        1. Friends told me about playing catch or camping with their fathers
            a. Accepted family situation as reality, though wished I could know what they experienced
    C. Dad's absence not only challenge
        1. Mom is diabetic, depressive personality, didn't interact with me a lot.
            a. As child I spent time alone (no siblings)
        2. Mom is teacher: without second income, not a lot of luxuries
            a. Even new sneakers tough: "maybe for your birthday"
        3. Mid-teens: began to be curious about ethnic heritage, father
            a. With mom's help, eventually found where he was, contacted him
            b. Friendly call, "nice to hear from you," but clear had moved on, didn't seek relationship

[Charlie has lightened his essay-writing load considerably by already knowing his theme and many of his specific examples]

II. Despite these circumstances I always felt like "normal" kid
    A. Never felt sorry for myself
        1. Not sure why never got into serious trouble or struggled in school
        2. Only "rebellion" was decision at 13 not to be confirmed
            a. A shock for my very religious family
            b. Didn't feel right for me, stuck to my guns
        3. Lack of parental presence made me self-reliant
            a. Learned how to take care of things myself, make friends
            b. As soon as got license at 16, took car out on my own
    B. Self-reliance, inner drive key to how I dealt with childhood
        1. Early teens: remember thinking I would succeed

      2. No mentors, "uncles," teachers pushing me: came from within me

         a. Always good at school, math

         b. Threw myself into schoolwork, always top of class

      3. Turned into full scholarship at U. of Utah

III. Values of self-reliance and strength or drive began to blossom in college

   A. Expressing themselves as leadership

      1. Asian American Student Alliance

         a. What I did as president: created, organized A-A week

      2. In class

         a. Always leading discussion and groups

      3. In internship

         a. Though didn't have to, worked not only summers full-time, school year 30 hours a week in addition to school

         b. Because of my initiative, when acquisitions head at Idex offered me chance to move from accounting to investing side, I jumped at it

         c. Thrived: assigned to fly alone to Virginia to tour site, negotiate with seller on $X acquisition.

           i. Sellers took me at face value

           ii. Deal closed successfully

[Don't worry if your outline doesn't go to five levels like Charlie's—three levels is plenty]

         d. Experience so exciting quickly changed major to real estate/finance

IV. Growing up in Salt Lake City, can't ignore nature

   A. Always interested in outdoors, hiking, healthy living

   B. Four years ago: passion for hiking went in new direction

      1. Becoming "fourteener"

      2. Climbed ten of Rockies' 14,000-foot peaks

      3. Result: growing interest in environment

      4. Today: committed to integrating this concern into professional life too

      5. U.S. Green Building Council, helping lead Idex toward green emphasis

   C. Hiking also reflects my lifelong focus on health

      1. Believer in taking health supplements

      2. Last year decided to start business that would enable me to help people find the best supplements out of the myriad of good/not-so-good options available

      3. Hallyu Nutrition is result

V. Want to bring values of self-reliance/initiative, of leadership, of commit-
ment to environment/health to Kellogg classmates
   A. Venues or clubs at Kellogg where I can express these values?
      1. Environment or green clubs at Kellogg? Health-related activities?
      2. How will my leadership manifest itself specifically?
      3. How will my self-reliance/initiative help classmates?
   B. Concluding sentence

CHAPTER

Scoring the Goals Essay

Students with career goals and a logical, well-thought-out reason for an MBA ALWAYS do better in business school and the job search, good times and bad.

—Jennifer Brooks, University of North Carolina (Kenan-Flagler)

Make no mistake. Of all the essays you'll write for your business school application, the goals essay is the most important. It's the one essay in which schools most explicitly ask you to answer the central question that underlies your entire application—why exactly do you need an MBA? Not surprisingly, it's also the essay that schools give applicants the most space to answer (up to 1,000 words for some schools). Yet despite its importance, when admissions officials are asked "What's the most common mistake applicants make?" failure to describe MBA-justifying goals is frequently the answer. In fact, poor execution on the goals essay has been said to account for more than half of all dings.

The goals essay is key because—surprise—adcoms want to know what motivates you to go to all the trouble, expense, and opportunity cost of earning an MBA. No matter how staggering your qualifications, if you don't provide a clear reason for needing an MBA, your application stands an excellent chance of losing out to those that do. Business schools use the goals essay to do a reality check on your maturity and career savvy. Do you really have a career plan that extends beyond your next promotion? If you do, is the MBA really an essential tool for advancing toward that goal (maybe you just need more work experience or perhaps a master's in a specialized functional skill)? Schools know all too well that many applicants seek MBAs for the "wrong" reasons—as a desperate measure to escape a lousy job or looming pink slip or to gain a promotion or bigger salary—not because the MBA really prepares them to do something they could not do without it. A goals essay that implies you need the MBA for purely instrumental reasons or that has the aura of credential-collecting will be viewed dimly. Demanding well-defined goals is business schools' way of policing the focus and legitimacy of their applicants' aspirations.

But there are other, less obvious reasons for exerting extra effort on your goals essays. First, the goals essay is almost always the first essay question in each school's essay set, and first impressions do matter. Anything less than a compelling initial essay will put you in a hole that your subsequent essays, no matter how brilliantly executed, may never dig you out of. Start strong.

Second, admissions officers have a weakness for applicants who are, in the well-traveled term, "passionate"—burning with the right Promethean fire to pursue their dreams. It's only human to respond to enthusiasm. And projecting a well-defined reason for the MBA makes your enthusiasm much more credible and personal. "I need an MBA to advance my career and deepen my skills" won't generate much excitement, but a detailed, elaborated paragraph in place of this sentence could. If you can't define your goals well, you will also be unable to define why a particular school is the best fit for you. The crucial link between your goals and the school resources that support them will be missing.

Third, schools use goals essays to make an indirect read on the quality of your mind and thought processes. Do you think seriously about the problems in your company or industry? Are you a realistic person or a vague or flaky dreamer? Can you craft a compelling case in prose that links your past, your goals, and the school you're applying to? Finally, the goals essay gives you the least freedom of any business school essay for "creative" responses. This is because (1) you usually need to cover so much ground (career progress, short- and long-term goals, why an MBA, why our school) and (2) your goals themselves need to be grounded and savvy.

For all that, a secondary purpose of the goals essay is to learn about you as a person—that is, the distinctive experiences, values, and traits that make you unique. In other words, it's quite possible to submit a goals essay that is too factual, impersonal, or boring—that succeeds in answering all the school's goals questions but fails to introduce you as a person the reader would want to know better.

In this chapter, we discuss practical strategies for ensuring that your goals essay avoids all these pitfalls and touches all the bases, setting a compelling, concrete tone for your entire application. Let's start by examining the kinds of questions most goals essays ask.

WHAT SCHOOLS ASK

Though virtually all business schools pose the goals question in some form, the wording they use, the range of topics they include, and the length they require vary widely (a rare exception is MIT Sloan, which has no goals essay and has been known to discourage applicants from detailing their goals in Sloan's required cover letter). Some schools (e.g., Duke and London) even spread the goals topics over multiple essays, and programs like Virginia and Washington (Olin) care so much about goals that they don't ask about anything else.

Goals essays are always about more than your goals, of course. Almost every business school goals prompt also asks you to explain how an MBA from its program will help you achieve them. Similarly, many schools also ask you a backward-looking experience question, such as how your career (or other) experiences shaped these goals. Kellogg's essay 1 is a classic formulation, combining all three of these elements: "Briefly assess your career progress to date Elaborate on your future career plans and your motivation for pursuing a graduate degree at Kellogg." Because the range of topics you must cover in the goals essay is so broad (your past, present, and future), your biggest challenge may simply be answering everything the school asks in one coherent, readable essay. The remainder of this chapter focuses on how to do just that.

What the Schools Say

Essay 1 carries the most weight. You need to have a very clear sense of your goals and how Columbia can help you achieve those goals.

—Michael Robinson, Columbia Business School

WRITING THE GOALS ESSAY

The specific focus of your post-MBA goals colors almost every aspect of your application—from school selection (based on goals-relevant study tracks and courses, clubs and extracurricular events geared to your industry, number and quality of organizations recruiting for your industry, etc.) to the content of your nongoals essays to the guidelines you provide recommenders. For this reason, you should begin work on a basic goals essay very early in your application process, perhaps after you take the GMAT, but in any case, before you begin work on your application proper or on other essay topics.

Writing effectively about your goals starts with thinking about them. Many applicants begin the application process believing that sufficient reasons for seeking the MBA are:

- They have the "numbers" (GMAT, GPA) and work experience to get into a good business school.

- Their peers are in business school.

- Their organization expects them to earn an MBA.

- It's the next impressive credential for the fashionably superachieving applicant to acquire.

- Post-MBA salaries are high.

- They were just downsized or hit a career plateau and have nowhere else to go.

Though these are certainly common reasons for applying to business school, they all share the same drawback: they aren't goals. Your task is to move beyond these obvious or uninspiring motivations to goals that business schools will find interesting.

This book is not the resource for a crash course in personal career counseling. But if you really don't know why you need an MBA, abandon the application process until you do. Alternatively, consult your university's career services department; an accredited career coach; books like *What Color Is Your Parachute?* and *Do What You Are*; or sources such as CareerLeader (www.careerleader.com), The Birkman Method (www.birkman.com/), or Strengths Finder (www.strengthsfinder.com). If you do have a vague inkling about your career track, flesh it out by doing some due diligence. Do some serious informational interviewing with alumni or industry elders. Read industry magazines, attend meetings of professional associations in your area, or cruise the Web sites of organizations you'd like to join, noting the career paths of their top managers. Integrate your new knowledge into your post-MBA career story.

— Info Interviews

Put Yourself on the Couch

Use the following questions to explore the goals that now motivate you to earn an MBA. If they survive intact, congratulate yourself—you've done your homework:

1. Is your post-MBA career the same thing you would do if you were independently wealthy? Is it the same thing you currently do as a hobby?

2. Recall the evolution of your interest in your post-MBA industry. How did you learn about it? Imagine that the person or experience that made you aware of this career were somehow radically different—would that affect your interest in this goal?

3. Are the aspects of your current job that you enjoy more likely to be found in your post-MBA career? Are the aspects of your current job that you're best at more likely to be found in your post-MBA career? Think about the most unpleasant task in your current position. How likely is your post-MBA position to regularly present you with this or similar tasks?

4. To what extent will your post-MBA career make it easier or more difficult for you to enjoy the things you consider essential to your happiness outside of work?

5. To what extent are your post-MBA goals associated with a specific lifestyle or geographical location? If your post-MBA career were not associated with that lifestyle or location would you still be attracted to it?

6. Have you confirmed that your short-term goals are logical stepping-stones to your long-term goals? How many of the informational interviews or due diligence conversations you've had about your post-MBA career confirmed your plan for transitioning from your short- to your long-term goals?

7. How satisfied are you that you have sufficiently due-diligenced your post-MBA goal? If you drew up a list of the impressions and responsibilities of this field as described by your informational interviewers, would a consistent picture emerge?

8. If everyone you respected told you that your post-MBA goals were ludicrous or unworthy, would you still want to pursue them?

9. If anyone you trust has questioned your post-MBA goals, have you systematically addressed each of their concerns to their or your own satisfaction?

10. What is your Plan B if your post-MBA goals are not, for whatever reason, achievable? What is your Plan B for achieving your post-MBA goals if your primary path toward them becomes blocked or unavailable?

Let's assume that you do have a rough sense of your post-MBA path but you just need to refine it so that it passes the high muster of a B-school's application review. Stating that you want to be a partner at a strategy consulting firm is a start but is not nearly enough. For most schools, you'll need much, much more. Think of your post-MBA career not as a destination but as an evolving narrative, and take a hint from the short- and long-term language often included in business schools' goals questions to map out a career trajectory that evolves over time. Goals defined and schools selected, you can now begin to map your goals essay.

ORGANIZING THE GOALS ESSAY

As we discussed in Chapter 1, using an outline can minimize much of the potential grief of writing admissions essays. This is particularly true of goals essays, where you're often asked to discuss multiple topics, while also establishing the themes that unify your whole application. Fortunately, as we've noted, many schools' goals essays come with a built-in structure that can help you organize your material. UC Berkeley's "What are your post-MBA short-term and long-term career goals? How do your professional experiences relate to these goals? How will an MBA from Berkeley help you achieve these specific career goals?" gives you the same three-part structure we encountered with Kellogg's goals essay:

- Your professional experience or career progress: the broad trajectory (including any evidence of "fast-track" career pace), inflection points, and goal-shaping experiences of your career thus far (*not* a blow-by-blow walk-through of your résumé).

- Your career plans (short- and long-term goals).

- Your reasons for needing a Haas MBA (aka "Why Our School?").

Though Haas asks you about your goals first, it may make sense to structure your outline chronologically, from past (career progress) to future (goals + Why Haas): after all, your career experiences have shaped your goals, which have shaped your reason for needing an MBA from Haas. You still must decide how to start the goals essay and what aspects of your professional experience to include and what to leave out. But you now have a basic organization to guide you.

Don't assume that each of these three sections must be the same length or that schools care a great deal about the order in which you address these three topics. Just make sure that you address them. Structure your essay in the way that makes the most sense for you. If you've been certain of your career goal since high school, you might well discuss your goals first and your career experience second, since your goals have presumably been guiding your subsequent career decisions. Similarly, you could legitimately decide to open the essay with the reasons why a particular MBA program is best for you to highlight your enthusiasm for that school.

Whichever structure you choose, each section of your essay must be tightly integrated with the others. Your past, present, and future must be shown to logically support each other. Your career progress/professional experience section must leave readers feeling that the next inevitable step for you is an MBA and a career in your post-MBA field. Your goals section must describe objectives that seem to evolve naturally from (or are least adequately explained by) your past experiences, and your "why our school?" section must show the school as the perfect place for someone with your goals and educational needs. An effectively integrated outline can help you navigate through your past, present, and future without getting lost in minutiae or turning your essay into a glorified résumé. With your outline in hand you can begin to approach the individual sections of your essay.

What the Schools Say

For me, the question as to why an MBA is important is much more relevant than exactly where you're going, since goals change. The thought process that brought you to this place in your career is what interests me. I'm looking for a sense of direction and knowing what your needs are. If you have very refined goals, I would say that's great. But for the vast majority of people, if you really pressed them, goals were often created recently and typically just for the application. And, since the whole point of an MBA experience is to explore, expand, and develop a new understanding and awareness of one's abilities and passions, I don't get hung up on goals. I am, however, very interested in path, plan, and knowing one's self.

—Rosemarie Martinelli, University of Chicago

THE LEAD PARAGRAPH

There's no "right" way to start a goals (or any other) essay, but there are several wrong ones.

Many applicants are tempted to play it safe with a plain-vanilla lead:

- "My long-term goal is to become CEO of a major multinational corporation."

- "My career goals stem directly from my professional experiences."

- "I need an MBA so I can help benefit society."

While these gambits have the virtue of directness, they are catastrophically dull. Other self-destructive introductions include deeply clichéd quotations ("I took the road less traveled," "Be the change you wish to see in the world") and exhaustive or superficial autobiographies ("I was born in Sheboygan, the son of …" or "After finishing third out of 9 million test-takers in my state, I …").

Because goals essays focus on nitty-gritty matters like goals, skills, reasons for MBAs, and career choices, your opening paragraph is one of your few opportunities to inject a little pizzazz into this crucial essay. Creative leads can be divided into two broad types: content-focused introductions (where the emphasis is on what you say) and style-focused introductions (where the emphasis is on how you say it).

Content-Focused Leads

- *The direct statement of theme:* "The choices I have made in my career have been shaped by the constant interplay of two sometimes conflicting traits: my desire to gain broad international business experience and my need to positively impact my community."

- *The autobiographical or self-disclosure lead:* "I was raised by a family of inveterate dreamers," or, "I'm the inventor of something you sit on every day but probably can't name."

- *Statement of belief:* "I believe nuclear power plants can be designed that surpass solar and wind power sources for safety and sustainability."

- *School-specific leads:* "Sipping a latte in Huntsman Hall, Ward Dilever, WG'12, described a scene that sounded almost too good to be true."

- *The diverse list:* "An amateur organist, a rancher in Medicine Hat, a shortstop for the Beloit Bison—I've been all these things at one point or another."

- *The imagined future:* "It's March 2020, and the chairman of Afghan Mobile is admiring the scenic view from his thirtieth-floor Kabul boardroom."

- *Grand vision of goals:* "A truly global online 'postmortem' social network—a mall for analog caskets, cremation urns, and headstones but also digital remembrances and i-shrines—will give new life to the $21 billion death-care industry."

Style-Focused Leads

- *The vividly described image:* "In the clearing stood a huge, delicately carved statue of Hariti, the Indonesian fertility goddess, a quizzical smile etched into her red-lacquered face."

- *The "you-are-there" scene or anecdote:* "As the Lear jet's wheels touched down on idyllic Bekoe Island, Nordlink's CFO whispered two words that forever changed my career vision: …"

- *The question:* "Is there such a thing as a strategy consulting gene?"

- *The direct address of the reader:* "Picture yourself standing before an audience that includes Steve Jobs, Jeff Immelt, and Steve Ballmer, and you'll understand how I felt when …"

- *The (unclichéd) quotation:* "'If you don't know where you're going, you'll end up somewhere else.' —Yogi Berra"

- *The outlandish assertion:* "I am the president of an invisible company."

Which of these approaches—if any—should you choose? The key question is which one meshes best with your personality, stories, and themes. The goal is to engage the reader and project your individuality, so choose the lead that best helps you to do that. Whichever type of lead you choose, include a reference to your goals and, if possible, the MBA in your opening paragraph. This signals the admissions committee that your essay will, in fact, address the essay question directly, if not necessarily from the first sentence. Don't let adcoms think, "Where is all this going?"

What the Schools Say

We [have] found over the years … that the students who are able to do a real thorough self-assessment—an understanding of what their own skills and capabilities are, how those skills and capabilities match with what the companies need, and then are able to talk about them—those are the students who actually do quite successfully find the internships they want."

—Al Cotrone, University of Michigan (Ross)

THE PROFESSIONAL EXPERIENCES/CAREER PROGRESS SECTION

Common to longer goal essays of 750 to 1,000 words, the professional experiences or career progress section is really two sections in one: a highly selective narrative of your career's key decision or turning points or career-shaping highlights and an explanation of how your career goals have evolved to the point where you now seek an MBA. A goals essay that discusses your career path thus far without linking it to your goals will render your essay's goals section incomprehensible and your essay as a whole disjointed. No matter how superb your professional experiences, if you can't show how they relate to your post-MBA goals you won't come across as the focused applicant every school seeks.

Conversely, a goals essay that explains how you arrived at your career goals but fails to mention key career choices or pivotal moments will be a wasted opportunity to emphasize your strengths, inviting adcoms to give their own, perhaps less favorable explanations for the career choices you've left unexplained. Even when a goals essay question doesn't explicitly ask you to account for your career thus far, all business schools expect you to tell them not only what your goals are but why you have them, a question you usually must answer by referring to past experiences.

CASE STUDY: The Boring Becomes Exciting

Ankur was an Indian male with the usual profile: after graduating from a top-tier Indian engineering college, he'd earned his technical master's at a U.S. university and then joined a major technology firm, where because of the long gestation periods of his firm's products, he had risen no higher than R&D software engineer. Ankur's GMAT was high, his par-for-the-course extracurriculars showed no unusual leadership, and in conversation diffidence was the dominant note. To say that Ankur was a typical applicant, in other words, would be the understatement of all time: he was the living, breathing apotheosis of archetypal typicalness.

And yet. Digging further, I discovered that Ankur had suffered some personal stumbles, nothing egregious, but humanizing setbacks nevertheless, which had delayed his MBA plans and lent his profile depth. But the real discovery was that Ankur was not just any software engineer. As an R&D engineer working on advanced technologies at a global-brand firm, he didn't merely write code; he was an internal technology impresario who championed concepts and marketed their virtues to the company's global units, seeking their investment. Ankur was no mere software engineer. He was innovation personified—a globe-trotting evangelist of the cutting edge! Impressed by an applicant whose "career progress" was not the yawn it first seemed, Kellogg duly admitted him.

The biggest mistake applicants make in the career progress section is to assume that "career progress" means blandly marching through their professional history, project by project. In reality, schools want to know only about the inflection points or the key experiences that influenced or refined your goals. Ask yourself questions like:

- Why did you start your career with a business development job in interactive media and then jump to a growth equity fund?

- Why have you worked for three firms in five years (or the same firm for five years)?

- Why did you move from a strategic analyst role at Credit Suisse to a business planning role at Cirque du Soleil?

- How have your long-term goals changed over time? Why?

The professional experience section, in other words, gives you the chance to instruct the admissions committees on how to properly view the raw data of your résumé. Laying this interpretive, evaluative narrative over your career gives schools a context for understanding why you now need an MBA.

Your post-MBA goals may have taken shape during on-the-job exposure (even indirect) to the field: you interacted with Deloitte consultants during a reengineering project, you worked with the marketing department while developing technical requirements for a new product, you experienced leveraged buyouts as an analyst for a midmarket regional bank and became fascinated by the operations and investment side of deals, and so on. Your career-switch revelations can be the "takeaways" you learned from the "mini-accomplishments" you work into your career progress narrative. For maximum effect, you should also quantify the impact of these accomplishments in dollar or percentage terms. Always highlight what was atypical or "fast track" about your path relative to your peers.

What the Schools Say

Business school is a place to get it done, not to figure it out. Your résumé will be due as soon as you walk on campus. The first company presentations happen in October; interviews for internships happen in January. That does not give you much time if any for self reflection and introspection. If you're not really pretty clear in what you want to go do, take the time to figure that out and then apply to business school. You want to maximize the return on the investment and the best way to do that is to have a clear goal as to what you want to be doing when you get out before you even apply.

—ISSER GALLOGLY, NEW YORK UNIVERSITY (STERN)

If your work experience didn't expose you to your post-MBA field, explain what did. Perhaps a purely personal or extracurricular experience opened your eyes. Describe it. Maybe a friend's advice or a news article hinted that this particular career path might best match your personality, so you followed up with personal research and informational interviews with people in the field. Demonstrate that you did your due diligence in identifying the goals that motivate your application to business school.

Be strategic about the content of your professional experience section. What you highlight will obviously be influenced by the message you're trying to send across your entire application, by the negatives you're trying to compensate for, and by the topics of the school's other essays. If your GMAT quantitative score is lower than the school's average and you also want to emphasize your leadership skills to offset the fact that you have no direct reports, you could skew your career progress section to highlight accomplishments that show quantitative and leadership skills. Similarly, as we noted in Chapter 1, you need to view each school's essay set holistically. If a school has a separate essay on leadership, for example, you may not need to press the leadership theme quite as hard here in the goals essay.

THE GOALS SECTION

How you go about describing your goals in the goals essay will be dictated by the specific wording of each school's question. Many schools merely request that you describe your goals, period. A larger number insist that you at least divide your post-MBA plan into short- and long-term phases. A logical way to structure your goals section is chronologically, from short-term goals to long-term goals. Devote several sentences to describing what you plan to do professionally for the first three or four years after you graduate from business school. If your post-MBA plan includes an intermediate goal between your short-term career goal and your ultimate objective then briefly detail this middle period. Finally, close the goals section by describing your career's "end game." Since most schools don't expect you to know where you'll be more than 10 to 15 years after the MBA, you don't have to go into exquisite detail about what you'll be doing when you're 64.

If your short-term goal makes sense only as a stepping-stone toward your long-term goals, it's perfectly valid to describe your long-term goals *first*. You can then present your short-term goals as the bridge to your long-term goals. If the connection between your short- and long-term goals isn't immediately obvious (such as, short-term = consultant, long-term = partner), then make it so. It doesn't help you to have superbly detailed short- and long-term goals if the adcoms can't see how one leads to the other.

Regardless of the goals question's exact wording, you should strive to be as specific in your response as you can. From a purely practical perspective, understand that focused goals tell adcoms that you are more likely to thrive in their program. Instead of the leisurely four years you were given in college, business school gives you two years at most, sometimes only one, to master a comprehensive set of intellectual disciplines. The more focused your educational goals are, the more likely you'll be to make the right choices, minimize wheel-spinning, and rejoin the workforce as a productive alumnus capable of doing your alma mater proud.

Most applicants state vague objectives like, "To become a private equity partner" and leave the adcoms to fill in the rest. You must dig deeper. What kind of private equity fund will you join? A buyout fund? A venture capital fund? A mezzanine fund? If a mezzanine fund, which ones might you hope to join? Golub Capital? Peninsula Capital? Do you have preferences for geographical location? Which job responsibilities appeal to you—for example, running the day-to-day deal process or fund-raising? Maybe outline some of the challenges you'll encounter.

If space allows, you can also enhance the credibility of your goals by displaying deeper savvy about your future industry's fundamentals. Discussing trends or emerging challenges will further drive home the message that you know why you need an MBA. Briefly discussing why specific executives (by name) at the organizations you might join have been role models for you is another creative way to deepen your goal's believability. These discretionary elements can add value and resonance to your goals essay.

You won't be dinged if your description isn't a note-perfect rendition of the occupational realities of that industry. You could be if you sound like you've only done cursory homework on your goals.

CASE STUDY: Who Said Goals Are Created Equal?

Kay was an Asian American "associate" at a major financial advisory firm. Though she was only two years out college (with a respectable 3.3 GPA), her leadership and responsibility levels at work were negligible, her GMAT was a modest 640, and naturally—she was aiming high. Initially, I despaired. But struck by her never-say-die spirit and her affecting immigrant-builds-new-life story, I looked for angles. Her exchange year overseas enhanced her international profile, she had showed leadership in her sorority, and she evinced flexibility about her post-MBA goals. Seizing on this last opening, I explored her interest in a human resources career, a discipline all but abandoned by MBA applicants, in the finance industry (building on her career thus far). Intrigued, Kay proceeded to research this new goal with the fervor of a true convert. Aided by her atypical (and passionately presented) goals, Kay was admitted by Cornell, her first choice. The delightfully astonished voice message she left to share her good news made my hall of fame.

What the Schools Say

Admission to business school is like Willie Wonka's golden ticket. Once you are in, you can choose any path you like. We like to think that what you put on your application for career goal will not change, but it does for many people.

—RANDALL SAWYER, CORNELL (JOHNSON)

Finally, keep in mind that your goals statement doesn't necessarily have to be limited to your professional goals. Some schools deliberately welcome a wider-ranging discussion of how your professional goals meld with your values and life goals. If space permits, you may therefore want to include a brief discussion of your community/volunteer goals in your goals essay, especially if an MBA will help you achieve them.

Creative or Unusual Goals

The MBA has traditionally been a feeder degree for careers in investment banking, management consulting, venture capital/private equity, and executive management for Fortune 500 manufacturing and consumer goods firms. That business schools embrace nontraditional post-MBA career paths is amply illustrated by the prominence of nonprofit, public-sector, and just plain unique careers pursued by B-school graduates. A random walk through LinkedIn's directory for Kellogg's MBA alumni yields a bounty of distinctive careers:

- Executive director of a top-tier business school's part-time MBA program
- Film producer at an independent motion picture studio
- President and CEO of a major symphony orchestra
- President and CEO of the Chicago Botanic Garden
- Director of academic and operational evaluation at Chicago Public Schools
- Vice president of marketing at a leading test prep and admissions consulting firm
- Executive director of strategic marketing at *The New Republic* magazine
- Manager of slot operations and performance at Harrah's Entertainment
- Strategic planning associate for the U.S. Olympic Committee
- Nuclear surface warfare officer in the U.S. Navy

Did these nonconformists state these particular career objectives in their Kellogg goals essays? Probably not, but the point is that Kellogg's admissions committee is well aware of the staggering range of career tracks its MBAs follow. They are quite willing—even eager—to embrace such unusual career visions as long as you make them credible in your goals essay.

Business schools love candidates with unusual goals. But they also want to be sure they can place you. So feel free to state nontraditional goals (differentiation is the name of the game), but take the extra effort to prove to schools that your future career actually exists in the real world and that an MBA is an accepted or at least clearly helpful credential for achieving it. If the niche you want to fill is so specialized or new that the adcoms aren't familiar with it, you may have to educate them. If they are concerned about the marketability of your goals, they may ask a member of their career services office to evaluate your placeability. If you can, provide details of your own plan for using your established network to help place yourself. You can strengthen the credibility of your goals by addressing some the following questions in your goals essay:

- Does anyone in this career track have your kind of pre-MBA experience?

- Is an MBA a preferred or accepted credential for professionals in the position(s) you're targeting?

- Is your goal one that leverages specific strengths or resources of the business school you're applying to?

- Is this goal related in some direct and explainable way to your past professional or nonprofessional experiences?

If you can show the committee that the answer to these questions is yes (and provide evidence for your affirmation), then your goals will pass the adcom's credibility test.

Social Impact Goals

Once a nontraditional post-MBA career, social impact jobs are now all the rage. Aside from genuine concern over environmental issues and corporate corruption, this altruism is partly the result of the mainstreaming of corporate social responsibility in corporate boardrooms, the proven success of microfinancing organizations like Kiva, the maturation of green and clean technologies as industries, and even perhaps MBA applicants'/students acknowledgment that consulting and investment banking aren't always hiring. According to *BusinessWeek*, half the MBA students at Columbia Business School are involved in social enterprise through classes, student clubs, or the school's Social Enterprise Program. And nongovernmental organizations (NGOs) as diverse as the World Wildlife Fund, Saving the World, Outward Bound, Oxfam, The Bridgespan Group, the Bill & Melinda Gates Foundation, and the William J. Clinton Foundation India have MBAs in their leadership.

Indeed, social impact goals (encompassing social enterprise, microfinance, sustainability, and nonprofits) have become so accepted that some applicants embrace them as the kind of goal that business schools "want to hear." Suppose you are the heir apparent of a family-owned widget company in the Midwest. A passionate weekend sailor and devoted churchgoer (you now lead your church's fund-raising committee), your true goal is to rise to the top of your grandfather's firm and lead it well, sustaining your family's legacy. Because of your for-profit goals and poor track record of devotion to saving humanity, you've convinced yourself that unless you change your goals to microfinance in Bolivia, your application is doomed. You'd be wrong. Most schools would find your true goals appealing and would roll their eyes at your Muhammad Yunus imitation (the fourth they've seen that day).

Stating selfless career objectives to get a leg up on applicants who want to be consultants or investment bankers was a clever strategy 10 years ago. Today, however, when every mother's son declares a post-MBA social impact goal, you should do so only if it is in fact your true career goal. To ensure that your altruistic goals are taken seriously, you must be able to show through your work or extracurricular experience that public service has been a long-standing motivation for you. Make these past experiences the focus of the career progress/influences portion of your goals essay.

Reapplying

Given all the energy and effort a competitive application requires, why go to all the trouble of reapplying to a school that's scorned you? There are three reasonable answers to this question:

- You really love this business school. It is the answer to your educational dreams. If it dings you again, you'll just keep trying.

- The school has made encouraging noises, such as keeping you on its wait list, giving you actionable feedback the summer after your ding, or actually explicitly pushing you to reapply.

- You have significantly improved your profile since your first application, such as through promotions, new positions with higher responsibility levels, leadership roles outside of work, or 40+-point jumps in your GMAT score.

Ideally, your reapplication will be motivated by all these reasons together. Indeed, the first reason—infatuation with the school that dinged you—is simply not enough to justify a reapplication. And if the third reason fits you, it may not matter whether the school has encouraged you or provided feedback. Smart reapplications are never Hail Marys; they are the rational next step for the new and improved you.

Complicating matters, schools' attitudes toward reapplicants vary widely. Of 21 top schools providing reapplicant data in 2009, only 10 admitted reapplicants at a higher rate than all applicants, and of the top schools releasing data only Michigan and Columbia could be said to give a statistically significant advantage to reapplicants:

	Applicants admitted	Reapplicants admitted	Percentage of reapplicants compared to total applicants
Michigan	23%	31%	4
Columbia	15%	20%	11

Moreover, schools like Harvard and INSEAD have traditionally frowned outright on reapplication. In contrast, at some schools, reapplicants who follow the school's feedback can be admitted at twice the rate of first-time applicants, and most schools have heart-warming stories about serial reapplicants who got lucky on the fourth or fifth try. Reapplicants do bring certain advantages to the table:

- They have been through the application ordeal and now know the logistical pitfalls, the time-management challenges, and how much work the essays really take. Like the second-time GMAT taker, they are likely to improve on their performance.

- They have one additional year of work experience, meaning a greater likelihood of managerial opportunities and impact stories. (Note that the advantage of aging becomes a disadvantage for applicants older than, say, 29 who are targeting U.S. schools.)

- If they were wait-listed, they know that the school deemed them admittable, and they may also have received hard feedback (or "deny counseling" as USC gently puts it), giving them clear bulls-eyes to shoot for.

But the bottom line will always be improvement. In addition to the no-brainer application enhancements like promotions, subtler improvements can also make a difference: more concrete or realistic career goals, new recommendations, a better case for your "fit" at the school that sent you packing. Use your interapplication period to interview people in your post-MBA industry if you suspect your goals were poorly defined. If you think fit was the issue, spend the summer reaching out to students and alumni and maybe make another campus visit. But remember that fit is a deal-breaker: even if you're a test-taking genius (790 GMAT) and serial social entrepreneur, if you tend to steer clear of group community activities, Kellogg may not *ever* be the place for you.

What the Schools Say

Applicants should really think about the second application as a continuation or improvement. It's almost like a second draft. They get feedback from an English teacher on how to write their paper better and now they are resubmitting it. So you're not writing a completely different paper. You're just tweaking the things that were flagged as areas for improvement.

—Tina Mabley, University of Texas (McCombs)

Though many schools require only a single reapplication essay from those applying within two years of a ding, consider giving them more. You don't need to submit completely new essays, usually, but be sure your application gives the impression of having been thoroughly reworked (after all, it didn't do the job the first time). Some schools will review your first application as a matter of course; others only your application folder cover sheet. But don't change your application so much that they start wondering if you're the same person. Stating new goals is acceptable; as NYU Stern's admissions director Isser Gallogly acknowledges, "A lot can happen in a year of life." If your goal was vague last time and the recent experiences that refined it are impressive, then "changing" your goals in a reapplication essay is a positive move. But avoid goal changes that are too dramatic, and always provide concrete reasons for the change that are organic to your work or extracurricular experiences (rather than something you read or learned from a friend). Significant refinements to goals that are within the same industry or function as your first application are preferable to suddenly dropping supply chain management in favor of hedge funds.

THE WHYS

After polishing off the professional experience and goals sections, you may think you're home free. Not exactly. Many schools (those requesting longer goals essays) ask applicants to detail why they need an MBA and why now. And of course virtually every school insists that you explain why you are applying to its program.

Why an MBA?

Since schools give you only four hundred to one thousand words for the goals essay, asking you to explain why you need an MBA and then when you're done why you need their MBA might seem redundant. In reality, many schools separate the Why MBA and Why Us questions to get you to dig in and truly address the underlying needs or motivations that drive you to business school—any business school. In other words, it's entirely possible to provide 20 wonderfully specific reasons why Duke would be a great place to earn an MBA without ever really saying why you need one in the first place. Though "Why an MBA?" is an important question, too many applicants answer it with boilerplate, if at all.

The best way to approach the question is to write terrifically compelling career progress and goals sections. If you do those sections right, you will have created so inexorable and compelling a case for needing an MBA that the adcoms may feel they can answer "Why an MBA?" for you. "Of course she needs an MBA. She's proven she can lead culturally and functionally diverse teams. And since that L'Oreal project, she's obviously known that operations management is the best way to use her leadership and problem-solving skills." If you've managed to get adcoms rooting subconsciously for you like this, you needn't belabor the Why MBA section with vague references to "enhancing my skill set" and "honing my soft skills." (Quick test: if your Why MBA section reads like it could describe every person who's ever graced the campus of an accredited business school, then you need to dig deeper.)

There are, of course, several solid reasons for wanting an MBA: it is an accepted, even required, credential for advancement in many industries; it's a universally recognized degree that will enable you to jump from one industry to another or from one function, region, or country to another; it gives you the broad management skills to launch and then lead a start-up business, and so on. These are compelling reasons, but they are so general and commonly held that they almost go without saying. Worse, these reasons aren't too far from the "I need a shiny new credential" type of reasons that schools are loathe to dignify. Never forget that business schools view themselves as temples of personal metamorphosis, not diploma mills.

So if you do state a general reason for needing an MBA, fortify it with some concrete reasons specific to you, like the functional skills—for example, accounting, marketing, operations—that you lack. Starting with your goals section, (1) list the functional skills usually required in the career track you've specified and (2) inventory your own skills. Subtract (2) from (1). In your goals essay simply state which of the post-MBA career skills your education and work experience have given you and which goals you still need. This is the heart of your Why MBA section—what skills will the MBA give you that you don't already have? A few plain-spoken sentences will usually suffice.

Since it is unlikely that business school is the only route to gaining these skills, you should also note that the MBA is the most accelerated, rigorous, and integrative path to these skills, one that also provides benefits (network, soft skills) that work experience alone can't give you. It's perfectly fine to tell schools that you seek the pure intellectual challenge of learning more about market segmentation or financial derivatives; just don't let them think that such scholastic motivations are your main purpose—there are other, research-oriented or specialized degree programs for that.

If length limits are an issue, consider combining your Why MBA and Why Our School sections. That is, state the functional deficiencies you have that an MBA can fill and then follow this directly by describing the two to three specific resources at your target school that address your needs. You will be fine as long as you show schools that you know that needing an MBA and choosing a school at which to earn it are two separate things.

Why Now?

Some schools explicitly ask you to explain why you are applying now:

- "Why pursue an MBA at this point in your life?" (NYU Stern)

- "Why is an MBA the best choice at this point in your career?" (Michigan)

- "Why is this the right time for you to pursue an MBA?" (London)

Why do they ask this? In one sense, it's another way of getting a fix on how certain you are that an MBA is right for you. That is, the Why Now question is a back-door maturity and focus question and, as such, a complementary variation on the goals and Why an MBA questions. You may have detailed, rock-solid career goals and an airtight case for how the MBA gets you to them, but if you can't say why you need to begin the MBA process *now*—rather than two years from now—adcoms may conclude that you're applying now for the "wrong" reasons.

So, whether your school asks the Why Now question overtly or not, you need to provide an explicit or implicit answer. The implicit answer will be the subliminal message that should be flashing throughout your career progress section: that the trajectory of your skills, leadership roles, and functional breadth has been rising inexorably, so only the lack of an MBA keeps you from bursting in glory into the management ranks. Your explicit answer will support this subliminal answer along the following lines:

- *Career plateau:* Your learning curve has flattened, and no new challenges are foreseeable in the next two years. If you stay any longer in your current career path, you will risk being pigeonholed as a (insert your job here), and breaking out will only become harder.

- *Goals epiphany:* You have only just recently realized what your career's purpose (post-MBA goal) is, and now that you know it, there's simply no reason to delay.

- *Post-MBA goals have time element:* Your post-MBA plans are linked to trends that will begin to gel by the time you earn your MBA. You can't afford to wait to gain the skills to capitalize on these trends.

- *Maturity:* You finally have the professional and personal savvy, balance, and perspective to make the wise decision to invest in your long-term future. (This is the acceptable way of saying "My age matches the median age of your admits.")

- *Natural break in career:* You're approaching the end of a clearly demarcated career phase, such as a bank or consultancy's two- or three-year analyst program, a corporation's two-year management training program, or an expat posting overseas.

The Why Now issue is even more important for applicants who are younger (two years of work experience or less) and older (say, 30 years old or older for U.S. programs) than the norm. Younger applicants will have to go out of their way to convince schools that they can't wait another year or two more. The best way to do this is to show that you are exceptional for your age. You have the skills, career progress, or leadership responsibilities of an older applicant. If you aren't exceptional professionally, you can compensate by outlining well-defined goals. Schools may admire your career focus and overlook your relative lack of experience. Alternatively, you may argue that, while your work experience isn't the equivalent of older applicants, you can compensate by bringing other positives to your class—perhaps unusually deep international experience, a personal story that shows maturity and fortitude, or distinctive extracurriculars.

Older applicants will be expected to have more sharply defined career goals. This is partly because they are expected to be more mature professionally and partly because the school's career services office may have more trouble placing them and will expect them to play a bigger role. For this latter reason, older applicants have to be careful about stating goals that represent radical career switches, particularly into fields like management consulting and investment banking. Entry-level positions in these time-intensive professions are typically filled by younger types with the energy and unencumbered personal lives to work the appalling hours. In their goals essays, older applicants will have to convince the adcoms that they already have the professional network and job opportunities to "place themselves" after the MBA.

What the Schools Say

It is never about age. It is always about realistic goals and how they plan to achieve them.

—Linda Meehan, Columbia Business School

Why Our School?

Today, otherwise superb applicants with superhuman numbers and glowing résumés are regularly dinged simply because they don't show that they've given any thought to their potential match with the schools they apply to. Admissions officials do not believe it is their obligation to figure out whether you would fit in well in their program; they expect you to make that case.

Perhaps the best way to view the Why Our School section is as an elaborate courting ritual involving a somewhat conceited future spouse. She (or he) will not surrender to your overtures merely because you are handsome, rich, and charming. You must also flatter her that it's *personal*, that despite all those *other* schools you've known, you are sincerely, passionately, and uniquely interested in her tastes and self-image and will defend her reputation and honor as a generous future alumnus. This wooing metaphor is not entirely facetious. The application process is undeniably a human, subjective process, not a scoring system of numbers and indexes. A convincing—that is, a highly specific—answer to the Why Our School question persuades adcoms that despite the marriage proposals you've casually tossed out to six other rivals, you will actually pick their school if they say yes. For adcoms, as for potential marriage mates, the yield factor is critical.

For this reason, you should avoid giving any reason for attending a school that can also be said to any other school. "I'm attracted to School X because its flexible curriculum, collaborative learning environment, strong alumni network, and outstanding faculty are unique." Unique? Virtually every school accredited by the Association to Advance Collegiate Schools of Business could claim that this sentence described it. You must refer by name to aspects of the school's program that will individualize your areas of interest. For example, almost all business schools have some program for getting students involved in the community, but only INSEAD's Social Innovation Centre will enable you to study the Middle East's health-care value chain and delivery systems through INSEAD's Abu Dhabi Centre. Simply by citing this opportunity by name, you lift your Why Our School section one level above the typical applicant's.

What the Schools Say—

Don't even think about starting the essays until you have researched the school and MBA thoroughly.

—David Simpson, London Business School

It's hard for us, especially when so much of the applicant pool is admissible. It comes down to who fits the life, spirit, and culture of an institution.

—ROSEMARIE MARTINELLI, UNIVERSITY OF CHICAGO

Any effective Why Our School section must involve serious personal research on the school, not just a quick skim of the school's Web site and *BusinessWeek*'s B-School forums. As Michigan (Ross) tartly notes, "Providing generic reasons for Ross, or quoting information from our materials and Web site, is not helpful." A visit to the school is essential (whatever the schools may tell you) unless it's financially burdensome or you live an ocean or two away. Schools like NYU Stern, Berkeley Haas, and Duke, which ask you to write separate essays detailing how you learned about their programs, make it even harder to rationalize away the effort of making a campus visit. However, even attending information sessions in your city can give you a better sense of the school than impersonal research. Contact your target schools for names of current students open to answering applicant questions, or use your own network to find alumni and students willing to speak with you. Business schools' student newspapers can also give you a relatively spin-free, student-level version of campus realities that will help you grasp the school's all-important "culture":

- Harvard Business School: *The Harbus* (www.harbus.org)

- University of Chicago: *Chicago Business* (www.chibus.com)

- Columbia Business School: *The Bottom Line* (www3.gsb.columbia.edu/botline/)

- University of Michigan: *The Monroe Street Journal* (www.themsj.com/)

There are no rules regarding the length of your Why Our School section or the order in which you should present your reasons. If your belief in the school's match with your needs is deep and you have many examples that demonstrate it, your school section may be comparatively long, say, three paragraphs in a two-page goals essay. If the school's curricular resources perfectly complement your intended specialization, then you could devote more space to these academic factors and perhaps launch your school section with this information. Similarly, if your campus visit is what really sold you on the school, consider talking about it first (or even opening the essay with it) and giving it the most space.

The only guideline is to take the space you need to show that your interest is genuine and specific to that school.

Content

You do, of course, want to show that your interest in a program is multidimensional—not only academic resources but extracurricular and cultural factors too. The following four categories of school-specific information may help guide you:

1. *Academics:* This includes everything from academic tracks or specialties, specific courses, and nontraditional learning environments to faculty members (including research interests), teacher-to-student ratio, teaching methods, and joint-degree opportunities. *Hint:* Research books, articles, or case studies by professors whose interests match yours. Consider mentioning one or two of these publications in your essay to show the school you've done your homework.

2. *Extracurricular features:* This is where you show them that you are a joiner who enjoys people and means to contribute. You can refer to everything from student clubs, athletics, and social groups to the alumni network, overseas or exchange opportunities, internships, business plan contests, and community involvement initiatives. *Hint:* If the school has no organization in one of your interest areas, consider stating that you will start one (if you would). Adcoms may be impressed by your initiative.

3. *General and cultural features (aka "fit"):* This is where you show that you understand the school's specific culture, its self-image—the message it sends about what it believes makes it unique. This is where you might discuss Chicago Booth's idea-driven culture of intellectual questing, MIT's tradition of creative innovation, or Michigan's pragmatic action-based learning. *Hint:* Refer back to the notes you took during your school selection process. Many of the reasons you originally used to winnow your list can actually be mentioned in this section, as long as you also link them to specific school resources by name: for example, urban versus rural campus, large or small school, proximity to cultural or business opportunities, and so on.

4. *Campus visit and personal interaction:* Making a campus visit is the best way to show interest. Capitalize on your visit by noting which classes you sat in on, which adcoms and students you spoke with (by name), and what you learned about the school that you didn't know before. You can use all this information in your goals essay to personalize your Why Our School message. But such personalization can also extend beyond a campus visit. If you know alumni, mention them by name, how you know them, and what you have learned from them about the school. *Hint:* Consider contacting one or two faculty members whose research interests genuinely match yours and respectfully arranging to discuss your interests with them. You could then refer to these conversations in your essay.

Be School-Specific

This process of customizing your application to the specific offerings and culture of each school is an essential part of the goals essay. If you expect your application to be taken seriously by a top-twenty business school, don't write a generic goals essay that you submit unchanged to every school. Customization is all.

Though business schools don't have "preferred" career goals, they are aware of how well your goals match their resources, whether they stem logically and reasonably from your work experience, and whether they seem typical or distinctive. Schools also have distinct strengths, and they are not always the obvious ones, like Kellogg = marketing. While you will earn no points informing Chicago that its finance resources are top drawer, you may impress its admissions committee if you describe how Booth's strength in marketing (ranked sixth by *U.S. News*) will help you launch a career as a market research director. Similarly, Wharton is not just a great finance school; it is also an outstanding general management and entrepreneurship program (ranked fourth and fifth, respectively, by *U.S. News*).

You may have mixed goals that allow you to modulate your goals description to emphasize your fit with particular schools. For example, if your post-MBA goal is health-care–related social entrepreneurship and you are applying to Duke and Michigan, for Duke you could emphasize the health-care goal and Duke's rich health-care management resources, and for Michigan you could emphasize the social entrepreneurship goal and Ross's deep social responsibility offerings.

The Why Our School section is not the only place in the goals essay where you should be sending your customized school-specific message. The whole essay should be communicating school fit on some level. Revisit your entire goals essay to see if its themes and key words need tweaking to match the school's particular culture.

THE CONCLUSION

Because the goals essay is your application's first and most formal essay, you need to be extra careful not to commit any of the blunders applicants typically make in conclusions. One is to simply let the essay end abruptly: "Fourth, Stern's International Passport Day will enable me to share my Estonian heritage (from red beet potato salad to runo-songs) with my diverse classmates." Even if you have room to insert only one sentence, add a summarizing closing thought, lest the adcoms think you hastily submitted a rough draft.

The most common error in closing a goals essay is to rely on stale boiler-plate prose: "I am confident I can succeed at Booth and look forward to making an invaluable contribution to my talented and diverse class." This kind of language adds no value because (1) it could have been written by anybody, (2) it could apply to any school, (3) it doesn't reinforce any of your specific themes, (4) it doesn't (one hopes) echo your opening paragraph, and (5) schools see millions of conclusions like this so it doesn't help you stand out.

As we discussed in Chapter 1, the safest way to avoid these deficiencies while also creating a nice sense of closure is to echo or refer back to your opening sentence or opening paragraph. Think of this as repeating your lead but with a twist—restating what you began with but with some forward-looking variation on it. Locate the key word, phrase, or idea in your opening sentence and find some way (it can be indirect) to connect it to a positive, flattering, declarative statement about this specific school:

Lead: "When I asked my friends what they thought of my decision to leave Lance & Boyle, they replied in unison, 'You're out of your mind.'"

Close: "Earning my MBA at Haas makes the best personal, professional, and educational sense. In fact, I'd be out of my mind not to."

Lead: "In 2010 I was the key client contact for the largest strategy consulting engagement in Chinese business history."

Close: "With an Anderson MBA the next historic engagement I witness will be the one I lead."

Lead: "My father once told me: 'Put your trust in friends, your faith in hard work.'"

Close: "Put my trust in friends, my faith in hard work? Of course, but I'll also put them in the transformational power of a Stern MBA."

Echoing your introduction like this is a convenient way to avoid the generic ending. If your introduction is, as it should be, personal and engaging, then your conclusion in echoing it will borrow some of that flair. Finally, the short-is-sweet rule of thumb applies to goals essays too. A brief, punchy final sentence can give your essay a nice closing jolt like an exclamation point:

- "More than ever, I'm ready to seize that chance."

- "I can't wait to begin."

- "My next step is clear: a Columbia MBA."

Now, that you've finished your goals essay, go out and treat yourself—you deserve it. You've cleared a major hurdle on the way to a successful application.

GOALS ESSAYS: WHAT *NOT* TO DO

1. *Start your essay with a bland lead paragraph:* "My career goal is to …". The range of topics business schools ask you to address in the goals essay prevents you from getting too creative, but this doesn't mean you should start the essay like an auditor's opinion letter. An anecdote, a vivid moment, a pivotal scene from your career—each of these can give your goals essay a bit of color while projecting your themes.

2. *State the obvious or the impolitic:* Increased salary, promotions, or the prestige a top-ten degree confers on your résumé are not the reasons for earning an MBA that schools want to hear.

3. *Be vague:* You must be specific about your career progress thus far, your goals, and your reasons for applying to this business school. If you're avoiding concrete details (1) because you think the schools aren't interested, think again; (2) because you don't think you have enough space, then find an editor to help you make it all fit; (3) because you don't want to think that hard, then you're not taking the application process seriously enough. Specify!

4. *State goals that are too creative or off the wall:* Yes, you want your application to be distinctive and stand out from the pack. But off-the-beaten track goals must be thoroughly nailed down and domesticated so the adcoms don't have to worry about your placeability. Anchor your goals in reality by doing thorough research into actual career paths for MBAs in your desired field.

5. *Make the mistake of writing your essay without an outline:* A good outline can help you ensure that your goals essay's three sections—your relevant career experiences, your goals, your reasons for an MBA—all interconnect and comment on each other.

6. *Fail to connect your goals to the past experiences that shaped them:* It is imperative that you explain what experiences or influences prompted your decision to earn an MBA and select the post-MBA path you hope to pursue. If your goal is strategy consulting, perhaps you worked with strategy consultants on a key company project, learned about it through a friend in the field, or saw an *Economist* article that prompted you to read *The McKinsey Engagement*. Whatever the reason, explain it.

7. *Neglect to create a Why Our School section that discusses resources unique to that school:* The garden-variety goals essay will chatter on unctuously about the school's "student-driven learning environment and sense of community," "powerful alumni network," and "balanced teaching methods

and flexible curriculum." But since these things can be said about 90 percent of all business schools, you must go several steps further and connect these "selling points" to specific resources (by name) at the target school.

8. *Write a résumé in prose: Career progress* does not mean a blow-by-blow account of your work experience since college. It means explaining why you've made the career choices you did (think inflection points) and using brief descriptions of a few of your key accomplishments to account for the origins of your post-MBA goals.

9. *Forget to explicitly address the Why Now question:* You don't need to devote an entire paragraph to explaining why this is the right time to earn the MBA, but adding at least one declarative sentence about the timing of your business school decision will show the adcoms that you're answering the question.

10. *Fail to inject some of your values, personality, or nonwork uniqueness factors into your essay:* Even if the school does not explicitly ask you to, try to communicate the scope of your contribution: "In turn, I will offer my classmates my intensive experience in the bioinformatics industry, multicultural depth as a Japanese-Canadian who has lived and worked in Europe, and creativity as reflected in my award-winning poetry and saxophone compositions."

SAMPLE GOALS ESSAYS

The following six sample essays—written by actual applicants admitted to Harvard, Wharton, Stanford, Kellogg, and Columbia (though somewhat disguised for confidentiality)—show the room for creativity and variety even the staid goals essay topic allows you.

Sample Essay 1: Joyce H. (Admitted to Harvard Business School)

What is your career vision and why is this choice meaningful to you?

9:43 a.m. August 29, 2017. Delhi, India. The meeting regarding Project Swabhiman, an effort that helps domestic violence victims through job training and ethically-sourced garment businesses, has been a success. Project Swabhiman—meaning "self-respect" in Hindi—is a program co-supported by Gap and will continue receiving sponsorship from local partners. Smiling, I shake hands with the Director of Delhi's Social Welfare Department and local NGO executives. The meeting adjourns, and I jump in a cab full-speed to the airport. [←*Effective use of 'imagined future' introduction nicely showcases Joyce's social impact goals.*]

Four hours later, I'm in Sri Lanka leading 60 Gap employees who have volunteered to join the Gap Foundation—Gap's charitable arm—Community Corps. We've partnered with Habitat for Humanity to build houses in underserved communities; this time the project has taken me to Batticaloa, Sri Lanka. My team and I race against the setting sun to drive the last nail into the wall and I'm beaming the whole time, wiping sweat caked with dust from my brow. *[←Adept use of vivid language and physical details to hold reader's interest]* I'm Chief Foundation Officer of the Gap Foundation—and I love this job.

Looking forward ten years from now, my career vision is to combine my two distinct career interests—retail and nonprofit work—and become executive director of an international retailer's charitable arm and focus on corporate responsibility. *[←Direct declaration of the goals that the first two paragraphs illustrated.]* Community service has always been my passion, from nonprofit consulting with Inspire, to my work on L.E.K.'s pro-bono initiative, to personal volunteering at hospitals and homeless shelters. However, I've also had a lifelong love affair with retail; I pore over fashion magazines, am helping to build L.E.K.'s Retail Practice Group, and collaborate on the monthly Retail Sector Report highlighting industry news and trends. *[←In two meaty sentences, Joyce both explains why her goals are "meaningful" to her and cites examples that make them more credible.]*

Although I have a strong foundation in business strategy, retail, and nonprofit work, an HBS education will provide me with the platform to achieve my career aspirations and combine my interests. Firstly, I'll need the rigorous general management training HBS provides to give me greater business sophistication and in-depth understanding of day-to-day operations. Secondly, by participating in the Retail and Apparel Club and Social Enterprise Club, I'll develop long-lasting relationships with a network of individuals who share my passions. Lastly, Harvard's Social Enterprise Initiative will enable me to explore issues in corporate social responsibility and equip me with the skills to run a successful nonprofit organization with ties to a for-profit retailer. While I'll take full advantage of Harvard's exceptional resources, I also believe my unique background of for-profit, nonprofit, retail, and international work experiences will make me a valuable member of the HBS community. *[←Solid paragraph establishing HBS's social entrepreneurship credentials is weakened somewhat by a generic-sounding conclusion.]*

Sample Essay 2: Rohit B. (Admitted to Wharton)

Describe your career progress to date and your future short-term and long-term career goals. How do you expect an MBA from Wharton to help you achieve these goals, and why is now the best time for you to join our program?

"Sachin's Master Blaster" was a computer game that pitted cricket's best batsmen against each other in gruelingly realistic matches. My friends enjoyed it, and I got a real kick out of teaching myself the programming skills to design a functioning computer game all on my own. But while some might see this early demonstration of technical wizardry as proof that I had a great software career before me, I've always seen it as the first act of a budding entrepreneur. My programming skill was just a tool; it was creating something tangible that others enjoyed that really mattered. [←*Uses a childhood anecdote to not only personalize himself to the admissions committee, but to establish the "why" behind his goals.*]

In one sense, my entire life since then has been about finding a way to get back to that act of creation. [←*Deftly pivots into his "career progress" section.*] Following my technical talents, I earned degrees in electrical engineering at IIT Kharagpur and computer science at University of Arkansas. But with the dot-com jobs disappearing in the bursting bubble, I had to get creative and soon discovered a role managing club card promotions for Wal-Mart's Sam's Club headquarters. I was quickly promoted to a pricing analyst role with increased scope in which I managed regular retail prices. In my spare time I built a system that integrated with our mainframe and automated my department. This not only hugely increased efficiency and reduced cost but also caught the attention of Wal-Mart's director of pricing strategy, Susan Benitos (WG '00). She promoted me to analyst on her strategy team to create business solutions for pricing. I completed a major overhaul of our pricing systems, producing a cost savings of $2 million a year, yet after two years at Wal-Mart my role still remained highly technical. [←*Integrates accomplishment into his career narrative.*] To own more of the business and drive key business decisions, I accepted an offer to join J. Crew Group's inventory management team.

J. Crew gave me the freedom to take both technical and business lead roles in a redesign of its systems for end-of-life inventory management. Promoted to manager for my efforts, I then led a three-person team plus one off-shore contractor in building an inventory management application that fundamentally changed J. Crew's inventory distribution process and saved over $27M annually. [←*Works in another accomplishment without interrupting the flow.*]

After two years on J. Crew's inventory management team, my learning curve started to flatten so I began to look for new "stretch" opportunities. My old mentor, Susan Benitos, offered me a job on Saks Fifth Avenue's Strategy team in New York and convinced me that a role on her team would expose me to a broader part of a company with a strong brand. Today, as manager of corporate strategy at Saks, I shape the strategic direction of the organization by driving analytics on and insight into our brand proposition and future growth potential. Working with MBAs from top schools (including two Wharton grads), I provide recommendations directly to Saks' executive leadership team, including C.E.O. Steve Sadove, on such diverse topics as real estate growth, pricing architecture, and store cannibalization. [←*Unusual career role helps him stand out; repeated references to Wharton colleagues don't hurt either.*]

I'm thrilled that I've managed to exploit my technical skills to create a fast-track career in strategy at the very top of a retail leader. However, over the last two years I've become heavily involved in a quite different enterprise that has reignited my teenage dreams of entrepreneurship: my family's franchise, Tandoori Bites. In building a site evaluation model to select a location to purchase, a sales forecasting tool to make more profitable labor and inventory decisions, and a price elasticity analysis to determine our promotion strategy, I've leveraged my experience and abilities to drive real profitability to the store's bottom line—and had a blast doing it! Our small Tandoori Bites's franchise has reminded me that I really want to lead and grow a business. [←*Somewhat surprising secondary career connects essay back to opening entrepreneurship goal and sets up direct statement of post-MBA plan.*→]

Therefore, my short-term post-MBA goal is to enter a general management rotational program at a strong retail brand such as H&M or Gucci and gain management experience across functional areas. For example, Gucci's Europe-based management development program offers rotations in finance, sales, HR, brand marketing, and supply chain. After gaining this broad holistic experience, my long-term plan is to lead, as CEO, a small growing retail brand in the apparel or accessories niche—whether my own company or a start-up that enables me to set its strategic direction and brand proposition, and drive its growth.

To gain the broad management perspective to make sense of my deep operational knowledge I'm convinced an MBA is essential and that now is the right time. With seven years' work experience in three different retail industries, intensive exposure to three diverse operational areas, and a technical/engineering foundation, I bring a breadth of experience that will enable me to both benefit enormously from and contribute enormously to business school. [←*Rohit's Why Now argument is that he's done enough to know what he wants and is ready to contribute to his classmates. Why wait?*] And I'm convinced that Wharton is the best place to complement my experience and goals. I first learned that Wharton is a great fit for me from one of my good friends in New York, Atul Shekhar (WG '07). In discussing how amazing his experience was, he really drove home for me how much Wharton's students shape it, citing the 110 student-run clubs and his own experience as president of the Marketing Luxury Club. On my subsequent campus visit and tour, I thoroughly enjoyed Prof. Jonah Berger's Consumer Behavior class and in speaking with him I learned more about the strengths of Wharton's Entrepreneurship program, from the Business Plan Competition to the Venture Initiative Program. [←*References to class visits and student/alumni interaction are always a good idea.*]

But Wharton's retail and marketing programs are just as strong! Classes such as "Retailing" and "Marketing Management: Strategy" and clubs such as the

Fashion and Luxury Goods Club speak directly to my educational objectives. *[←Rohit does a nice job of showing that Wharton has the resources to match his goal.]* Wharton also offers broad strength in its finance, real estate, and strategy programs, as well as in its multitude of clubs, collaborative students, and strong alumni base. The relevance of Wharton's strengths to my goals truly cannot be overstated.

Sample Essay 3: Markus L. (Admitted to Stanford GSB)

What are your career aspirations? How will your education at Stanford help you achieve them?

My long-term career goal is to build an art auction company as a social enterprise that discovers talented artists in isolated regions, especially South America; develops the Latin American art market globally; and reinvests the profit into public exhibitions and art education for Latin American communities. *[←Because Stanford's essay length limits are tight, Markus cuts right to the chase with a direct assertion of his goals.]*

My aspiration formed in 2007, when I traveled with my brother, a glass-blower, for five months in South America holding art exhibitions with local artists in Bolivia and Guyana. Seeing villagers shed tears because they were touched by beauty they had never seen before abolished my prejudice that art is a mere luxury in areas where subsistence is a daily struggle. *[←Effectively explains the "why" behind his unusual goals.]*

At Boston Consulting Group I have learned how to apply economic mechanisms to the nonprofit sector through KIASMA Museum of Contemporary Art and Sibelius Academy projects in Finland. Desiring to directly implement initiatives, I became involved with The Foundation for Contemporary Art Guyana in 2010. However, in Guyana, I discovered that funds from World Bank and elsewhere often never reach the artists or art organizations. Lack of grant monitoring enabled the foundation directors to purchase $500 chairs and hire personal cooks, neglecting the mission. Meanwhile, for five years the Castellani House, Guyana's national art gallery, could not afford new exhibitions. I developed an intense commitment to bringing business acumen to arts promotion in South America. *[←Establishes that his goals will solve a problem, fill a gap.]*

My short-term career goal is, therefore, to work in an established art auction house such as Christie's or Sotheby's that have developed emerging art markets in Russia and Poland. As a buyer, I will learn how to identify and market new artists effectively, how to finance and value artworks, and how to build relationships with collectors, ideally based in New York or Moscow. I am already enrolled in Bonhams and Butterfield's program in London to start my preparation.

[←Evidence that Markus has already initiated his career transition before business school gives his goals much greater credibility (it helps that they're also unusual).]

I believe Stanford GSB is the best bridge to develop the global management and social entrepreneurship skills my goals require. Stanford GSB appeals to me because it will enable me to take tailored courses even during my first year and offers me opportunities to deepen my interest such as the Global Management Immersion Experience and Service Learning Trips in the public management program. By giving me unprecedented access to renowned faculty like Jonathan B. Lovelace, who has researched the economics of Sotheby's on-line auction, and the Center for Social Innovation's Dale T. Miller, James A. Phills, and Jesper B. Sørensen will help me learn more by applying management theory to real-world business problems. *[←Identifies Stanford resources that are directly relevant to his goals.]*

Through interactions with alumni like Veijo Lano (MBA '08) I have learned how Stanford GSB's alumni connection and Career Services office epitomize Stanford GSB's collaborative culture. That culture will help me build a strong network of future business partners, friends, and mentors such as Ernesto Casona (MBA '80), who established Casa Museo Nuñez del Prado, one of the first not-for-profit, independent art centers to be developed in Bolivia. *[←Mentioning the names of Stanford people he's spoken to shows that Markus personalized his Why Our School due diligence.]*

Sample Essay 4: Diane W. (Admitted to Kellogg)

Briefly assess your career progress to date. Elaborate on your future career plans and your motivation for pursuing a graduate degree at the Kellogg School.

For me, there is nothing as amazing as a photo of an evening cityscape: the lights, the traffic's constant motion, and most of all the buildings' dazzling steel and glass. To some, these soaring structures are nothing more than offices, condos, or hotel rooms, but to me they are concrete masterpieces. In them, I see beauty, yes, but also opportunity. I'm a future real estate investor. *[←Vivid, straight-from-the-heart intro explains the "why" behind Diane's goals and adds a little color to an essay about a subject, real estate, that could sound dry.]*

I've been fascinated by real estate since I first laid eyes on a photo of Manhattan as a young girl. Focusing my college studies on general business and real estate with an emphasis on finance, in my junior year I began interning with K. Bellow Sons, a private shopping center syndicate, to learn more about real estate investment. For the next two years I interned in virtually every part of the business, from finance and accounting to acquisitions. Gladly accepting a full-time position at Bellow after graduation, I worked for the next fourteen months on the acquisitions and dispositions team, sourcing and underwriting more than 100 prospective acquisitions. While the exposure this position gave me to the industry truly crystallized my passion for real estate investment, I also learned that by becoming an analyst at a large firm I could develop core competency in institutional transactions, sharpen my analytical ability, and gain a strong due diligence background—all essential to one day running my own broad-based real estate investment fund. *[←Foregrounds goal to let reader know where essay is going, but delays full goal statement until end of "career progress" section.]* I began the search that led me to AMB Property Corp., the world's leading provider of logistics real estate.

Moving to AMB in October 2007, I joined the North American due diligence team, which handles financial analysis and due diligence for AMB's $1 billion in annual transactions. Doing financial modeling of potential acquisitions and single-building acquisitions in major industrial markets, I began to understand the due diligence process and how institutions perceive the risk/return relationship of assets across the country. Not incidentally, earning the responsibility for tracking all the investments approved by our Investment Committee and Board of Trustees also gave me my first exposure to "green" development, from solar panels on a building in Spain to energy efficient buildings in Japan. The focus of AMB's senior management on environmental impact gelled with my own growing conviction that green development is the future of commercial real estate. *[←Introduction of "green" angle gives Diane's goal depth and helps position her "for-profit" goal as socially impactful.]*

Gradually working on larger and larger transactions, after a little more than a year I was selected to lead our five-person team through the due diligence and secured financing of an $800 million portfolio that would seed our latest North American Joint Venture Fund. Since then, I have led more than $400 million in additional secured financings, work typically reserved for Associates. When I'm promoted to Associate in the next year (more than a year ahead of the typical pace), I will become AMB's youngest Due Diligence Associate ever. *[←These two "fast-track" sentences send very strong signals about Diane's impact and potential.]* While I'm excited by the challenges and successes of my current role, even as an Associate I will not gain the exposure I need to achieve my long-term goal: becoming a principal or partner with a private equity real estate company such as Blackstone Real Estate or Colony Capital who manages an opportunity fund that seeks out real estate worldwide. Ultimately, I envision building and developing a fund that invests in "green" buildings, whether office, retail, or industrial space, built by developers who understand how important environmentally sensitive buildings are to their clients, employees, and communities. Toyota Motor Sales USA's office campus, for example, was constructed with such energy-saving improvements as a solar rooftop and low-flow water taps—all at a cost comparable to traditional construction and yielding Toyota a 10% ROI. [←*Fine to devote only two sentences to goal statement since preceding paragraphs have established that Diane knows her industry.*]

To realize this ambitious goal, I need an accelerated, rigorous way to more fully develop my financial skills, knowledge of marketing and management (vital elements in development and investment funds), and understanding of real estate beyond the analysis. Kellogg's full-time MBA program precisely answers my needs. First, Kellogg has outstanding ties to key figures in the real estate community, such as John Montaquila, Principal, Macquarie Capital Partners, and Jeffrey Johnson, Chief Investment Officer, Equity Office Properties, both of whom spoke to Kellogg students in recent years. The Real Estate program's independent study projects will also enable me to pursue a broader understanding of the kinds of capital that seek institutional real estate and their reasons for doing so. Similarly, "The Human Element in Private Equity Investing" (ENTR–926–0) will expand my knowledge of the specialized private equity world and its key players. Outside the classroom, the Real Estate Club, Private Equity and Entrepreneurship @ Kellogg (PEEK), and Energy Management Club will help me strengthen my real estate network and align myself with other professionals with similar career interests. [←*Diane effectively convinces the reader that Kellogg is an appropriate program for someone with her goals.*]

Conversations with Chad Bevington (Class of '10) have convinced me that I will excel in Kellogg's aggressive curriculum and thrive as a team member and leader in the collaborative environment that Kellogg is highly regarded for. With a Kellogg MDA, in other words, I can not merely admire cityscapes; I can help build them. [←*Refers deftly back to introduction and forward to Kellogg.*]

Sample Essay 5: Stuart F. (Admitted to Harvard Business School)

What are your career aspirations and how can an MBA help you to reach them? Why now?

I plan to devote my career to building successful businesses in health-care, an industry expected to grow from 15% GDP to 19% in the next 10 years. I am attracted to the financial and social benefits of this industry, which has ample room and high demand for improved quality of care. Recent Medicare and other reforms, combined with an aging population and increased utilization of health benefits, create favorable reimbursement and demographic trends. I will leverage my private equity experience and network (entrepreneurs, consultants, lawyers) to build service businesses that improve my customers' quality of life. [←*Opening paragraph directly states goals but also explains the "why" behind them.*]

I hope to change the way that health-care services are delivered, starting with outpatient surgery, a highly fragmented and mismanaged market with no company holding more than a 5% market share and many stand-alone centers operated unprofitably. My focus will be on the patient experience: creating a comfortable environment like a hotel, where surgeries are performed in a soothing setting. Additionally, by improving billing standards, I will create a business model that withstands regulatory changes and cracks down on unethical billing practices while improving the economics for physician owners. Starting with the acquisition of an unprofitable surgery center, I will turn it around, building a network of profitable centers, which will then expand across regions. Eventually, I will create a base to branch into other health-care arenas including home health and hospice care. [←*Meaty paragraph lends credibility to Stuart's highly specific goals.*]

Now is the time to pursue an MBA. With 3 years of private equity experience, I have built health-care industry expertise. [←*Stuart briefly answers Why Now?: he has sufficient private equity and health-care industry expertise.*] I now need to examine the industry from the viewpoint of corporate decision-making: coordinating business units, reacting to competitive threats, hiring competent managers, and efficiently allocating financial resources. I am a competent advisor and investor, but I need exposure to issues that CEOs face daily. An MBA will provide this through case studies, coordinated projects with companies, and discussions with other students of different professional backgrounds. [←*Directly tackles Why an MBA question.*]

Post-MBA, I will return to private equity as a health-care-focused VP, spending substantial time on corporate boards, collaborating with management teams, and applying my MBA lessons to portfolio companies and deal opportunities. The MBA and a return to private equity is my bridge to my entrepreneurial goals and the health-care industry leader I envision becoming in the future. [←*Makes judgment call to omit Why HBS section so he can devote more space to fleshing out his goals. Chose wisely—HBS admitted him.*]

Sample Essay 6 (Reapplication Essay): Jang D. (Admitted to Columbia Business School)

How have you enhanced your candidacy since your previous application? Please detail your progress since you last applied and reiterate your short-term and long-term goals. Explain how the tools of the Columbia MBA will help you to meet your goals and how you plan to participate in the Columbia community.

As I sliced through the ribbon in front of GridSys's new Mexico City office this past February, a crowd of executives, clients, and city officials broke out in applause. *[←Opening anecdote is visual and immediate but also shows that Jang has filled VIP roles.]* Since my transfer to GridSys's Los Angeles office in summer 2006, I've been working with our Mexico distributors to expand GridSys's territory into Latin America through a joint venture called GridSys Ltd. Mexico. As the CEO of this 12-person satellite office, I have led my team in leveraging promotional marketing to achieve 20% revenue growth and established partnerships with distributors in Guatemala and Honduras. *[←Immediately begins using impact examples to show he's continued to grow since his first application.]*

This is only one way I have strengthened my candidacy since my first Columbia application in June 2008. Because of my familiarity with Spanish culture and language (I spent two summers there during college), GridSys assigned me its Spanish account in summer 2008. Knowing Spaniards prize personal business relationships, I flew to Barcelona that August and, building trust, convinced them to choose our products over price-competitive Chinese batteries. Consequently, last December we convinced Spain's biggest wholesale supermarket, Spemax, to supply our batteries to its 50 customers—a $500,000 contract. *[←Another impact example that also shows Jang's impressive international credentials.]*

Because of these accomplishments, this past January I was promoted to Director of GridSys's new $6 million Flexible Lithium Polymer batteries division. *[←Director of a $6 million division? Impressive stuff.]* In March, I exploited the tracking capability that paper-thin FLP batteries make possible (when combined with radio frequency identification [RFID] tags) to implement FLP-powered tracking into GridSys's inventory system. After I led a five-person team in launching the tag-scanning system and embedding the product codes into the tags, our inventory loss rate fell by 15% and the shorter time-to-warehouse improved turnover tremendously.

Finally, beginning in May, I led GridSys's sales/marketing team in convincing smart-card manufacturers such as Omaxx ID and security software companies like STB to choose our FLP batteries for integration into next-generation bank smartcards (capable of online banking authentication). After marketing efforts that included major trade shows such as CARTES in Paris, in August I convinced the card suppliers of Citibank of America and PayPal to sign $12 million agreements to use our FLP batteries over China BAK's batteries beginning in January 2010. To increase the production capacity to drive these sales, in September I also approved $2.5 million in production line investments, which will lower our unit costs. *[←Relentless exposition of impressive examples creates momentum toward inevitable conclusion: This time you should let me in.]*

All these successes have only deepened my commitment to pursuing the goals I stated in last year's application. In the short-term, I will return to GridSys to lead the growth of our FLP battery unit, whose products will be embedded in smart cards and for RFID applications such as supply chain management. Longer term, I will develop the FLP division so it can be spun off from GridSys and ultimately achieve an IPO on the NASDAQ. My ultimate career vision is to return to GridSys to continue my family's sixty-year-old business legacy, not only by growing the company in its core businesses—dry-cell and lithium polymer batteries—but by transforming it into a "green" innovation leader producing solar and hydrogen fuel cells. [←*Ambitious goals with a nice green twist to show Jang's social conscience.*]

A Columbia MBA is the most efficient and intensive way to strengthen the managerial and functional skills I'll need to realize these goals. Since applying to Columbia, I've reached out to more students and alumni and revisited the campus to better understand my fit. Bill Asté (MBA 2010) inspired me by describing the wide range of leadership opportunities Columbia offers, such as serving as a representative for the Hermes Society. Doug Kapproff (MBA 2010) stressed the January program's advantages and suggested valuable entrepreneurship classes such as Professor Low's "Introduction to Venturing." Amanda Carlson's Los Angeles information session in September confirmed my decision to reapply. [←*Amply demonstrates that he has continued to personally explore Columbia since his ding.*]

My appreciation for Columbia's entrepreneurial resources—the Eugene Lang Entrepreneurship Center, courses like "High Technology Entrepreneurship" and "Entrepreneurship in Large Enterprises," the Entrepreneurial Sounding Board—has only grown since my first application. The family business panel events hosted by the Family Business Network and Professor Michael Preston's courses (such as "Family Business Management") also speak directly to my plans for GridSys. [←*Makes a good case that Columbia's resources are relevant to his goals.*]

My initiatives for GridSys in Mexico, Spain, and the U.S. have taught me that "localizing" one's understanding of each culture's business environment is the key to global business success. Completing the advanced-level Spanish courses at Institute for Spanish Language Studies in Los Angeles, for example, is helping me to maintain strong partnerships with our exclusive distributors in Spain. The Chazen Institute's language program and Columbia's exchange program at IESE will enable me to continue studying Spain's language and business culture. I also look forward to organizing a study tour for my classmates to GridSys's solar cell plants in South Korea.

Finally, after speaking with the presidents of Columbia's Energy and Green Business club, Kathleen Gabarro and Herminia Reardon, respectively, I'm excited about sharing what I know about GridSys's renewable energy initiatives by sponsoring events such as Clean Tech Month and participating in the Green Business Club's campus greening projects. *[←Jang clearly knows Columbia's program.]*

In taking on extraordinary new responsibilities—managerial, international, and operational—at GridSys, I've substantially improved my candidacy over the past year. More than ever, Columbia's January accelerated MBA program is the best place to continue my education in leadership.

Getting to Know You: Impact, Leadership, Teamwork

In addition to leadership, we're looking for applicants who have a track record of engagement, initiative, and impact. None of these things requires that someone be a leader in an organization.

—Soojin Kwon Koh, Michigan (Ross)

Leadership is leadership. It is a demonstration of a skill, no matter what the setting. Be sure to give good examples.

—Kellee Scott, USC (Marshall)

There, it's done. You've hammered out your goals, short and long, crafted a gripping account of your career thus far, and persuasively detailed the reasons why Elite Business School is your life's destiny. Surely it's all smooth sailing from here. Alas, your goals essay, though critical, is just one of several legs on which your candidacy must stand, or fall. In addition to it, almost all schools pose two or three other essay questions (some as many as six or more) whose intent is basically the same: to get to know the person behind the goals. What specifically and uniquely do you—as a person—bring to their program? The essay topics discussed in this and the following chapter all play variations on this single insistent theme.

If you cannot demonstrate a consistent ability to affect the world, lead others, and energize teams, you will have a tough time convincing business schools to admit you. In this chapter we discuss essays—whether focused on work or extracurriculars—that show you have advanced interpersonal skills and know how to deploy them to get things done. Though accomplishments, leadership moments, and teamwork stories can often be the same experience seen from different angles, simple "cutting and pasting" usually won't fly. You will have to rethink your stories to highlight the impact (Why is this your most significant accomplishment?), emphasize the leadership (What did you learn about leadership?), or underscore the teamwork (What exactly did you do to empower your teammates?).

ONE GOOD DEED: THE ACCOMPLISHMENT ESSAY

On one level, accomplishment essays enable admissions committees to gauge whether you have the "right stuff" for business school. Do the accomplishments you describe indicate you are capable of having the kind of world-shaking impact proclaimed in your goals essay? Have you been successful in translating your skills into concrete results that demonstrably benefit your organization or community? Do your accomplishments suggest that your career is unfolding at a faster pace than your peers? What do the kinds of things you accomplish say about what you value or how you operate with others?

Business schools value accomplishments that show significant impact and interpersonal skills. The applicant who writes that her achievement led directly to a multi-million-dollar revenue gain has an advantage over the applicant whose greatest achievement affected a minor module of an obscure product that's still in development. Similarly, the applicant whose accomplishment involved motivating six older client team members to help wind down a department and ultimately their own jobs demonstrates far superior interpersonal skills to the applicant who developed—on her own—a world-beating software application. Scale and context matter.

Qualities That Accomplishments Can Reveal

Dedication or focus

Persistence

Ambition

Vision

Expertise or special talents

Concern for something larger than oneself

Initiative

Modesty (or lack of it)

High personal standards

Leadership

Team skills

Energy

Self-discipline

Organizational ability

Similarly, *how* you describe your accomplishment also tells the admissions committee a great deal. If you give the impression that you rammed an achievement through with no regard for teammates, schools may question your team skills. The same interpersonal doubts may be triggered if your accomplishment essay focuses on the procedural or technical aspects of your achievement rather than the interpersonal dynamics. Finally, the committee will learn much from the reasons you give for valuing this accomplishment. If you say only that you're proud of this achievement because it led to an early promotion, they'll wonder why it didn't teach you deeper lessons.

The accomplishment essay, then, is considerably more than a résumé bullet point writ large. Before discussing strategies for ensuring that your accomplishment essay gives adcoms the personal insights they seek, let's look at how schools ask the accomplishment question.

What Schools Ask

Many schools word the accomplishment question broadly to give you maximum leeway:

- ■ "Tell us about your most significant accomplishment." (Berkeley Haas)

- ■ "What achievement are you most proud of and why?" (Yale)

Because these questions give you so much freedom, you need to evaluate the accomplishment stories you choose with extra caution. Consider carefully before saying that your accomplishment was "getting into IIT" or scoring the winning touchdown in your high school championship game. Unless you execute these well-worn topics extremely well (and even when you do), you may give the impression that you have a narrowly competitive or superficial definition of achievement or that you're living in the past, with no significant accomplishments since the onset of adulthood.

Many schools deliberately narrow the potential scope of the accomplishment essay to force your answer in the direction they prefer:

- "Describe your accomplishments and include an example of how you had an impact on a group or organization." (MIT Sloan)

- "Tell us about a time when you made a lasting impact on your organization." (Stanford)

- "Discuss a time when you navigated a challenging experience in either a personal or professional relationship." (Wharton)

- "Please describe a time when you took responsibility for achieving an objective." (MIT Sloan)

- "Describe your greatest professional achievement and how you added value to your organization." (Cornell)

These topics not only compel you to confine your definition of accomplishment to specific areas of your life; they also signal what the school values: MIT values evidence of atypical impact, Stanford values legacy-caliber change, Wharton values 'relationship management' skills, Cornell values other-directed achievement.

Accomplishment questions also vary by the quantity of achievements they expect you to discuss. Harvard's "What are your three most substantial accomplishments?" is the classic formulation of the multiple-accomplishment essay. Here, the conundrum, "Should I use a professional or personal achievement?" solves itself. To avoid sounding like a work-obsessed drone or an unaccomplished underachiever, you can answer such multiple-accomplishment essays with one professional, one community, and one noncommunity personal accomplishment. Ideally, you also want each of the three accomplishments to show you making an impact in varied ways. Your professional achievement could show you having an impact through analytical skill and team leadership, for example; your community achievement through teamwork and consensus-building; and your personal through creativity and risk-taking. For many applicants two professional accomplishments will make sense, but the nature of the accomplishments should differ: don't describe the largest and second-largest leveraged buyout you worked on if your role in each was similar.

Finally, all schools want you to not only describe the accomplishment but to tell them what you think of it, why you value it, what it means to you.

What the Schools Say

We aren't looking for "number of leadership experiences" and we don't have categories of leadership that we're looking for. I'd focus on the impact you had, how that experience developed you as a leader, what you learned from that experience that will enable you to be a stronger leader in the future, etc. When we look at leadership, we're not just looking at actual experiences, we're looking for "indicators" and "signals" for future leadership potential as well—qualities in applicants that indicate to us that he/she has the makings of a future leader…. Some of the qualities that are indicative of future leadership potential are: initiative, results-orientation, solid interpersonal skills, emotional intelligence, etc.

—Soojin Kwon Koh, Michigan (Ross)

Choosing Your Story

Accomplishment has been usefully defined as, "An event or situation in which you successfully exerted a high degree of influence resulting in a sense of personal satisfaction that allowed you to learn something about yourself." That's a pretty broad definition, but it accurately reflects the scope schools are willing to give you. In choosing which of your stories to wrap around this definition, start by asking yourself three questions:

1. What am I—off the record and in all candor—truly proudest of?

2. When have I had the greatest tangible impact on an organization (or individual)?

3. When has a positive experience in which I played a key role *changed* me or *taught* me the most? (See Put Yourself on the Couch on the following page for more questions.)

Defining *accomplishment* as loosely as possible, sift through your memory, scrutinize your résumé, interview your friends or colleagues. Chances are you'll find a story in which the depth of your impact was substantial and concretely, externally visible; one whose lessons you're still applying today; and one you still look back on with a quiet sense of pride. If you do, you have the makings of a killer accomplishment essay. If this brainstorm exercise generates too many candidates, revisit the self-marketing themes you created in Chapter 1. Which of your accomplishments best supports your application's themes?

Put Yourself on the Couch

These questions may help you uncover the reasons why a particular accomplishment is or should be important to you:

1. Did the accomplishment help you learn a skill you didn't know before? Which one?

2. In what ways did accomplishing this achievement require you to take initiative, step out of your defined role, or perform above expectations?

3. Did the accomplishment give you firsthand exposure to the values that matter most to business schools, such as leadership, team play, communication skills, strategic vision (among others)? How so?

4. Did you view yourself or did others view you differently after the accomplishment? Describe that change.

5. Did you perceive any change in your role in the organization following the accomplishment?

6. Did it lead to opportunities or responsibilities that you didn't have before?

7. Was the accomplishment something that earlier in your life you didn't imagine yourself capable of?

8. Did you do anything during the accomplishment that looking back now actually surprises you?

9. In what ways did this accomplishment require you to think creatively or be innovative? What did you do that wasn't "by the book"?

10. Did this accomplishment teach you anything that made other, later accomplishments possible?

Finding exactly which one of your stories has the potential to make admissions officers sit up and actually feel enthusiasm will sometimes be hard to gauge. Becoming general manager at 25, producing your own award-winning indie film, winning a Fulbright Scholarship, toiling in the White House, co-leading a $150 million initial public offering at 26, earning a spot on an Olympic team—the standout accomplishment can take a surprisingly wide variety of forms. Usually, however, such "wow factor" accomplishments combine distinctiveness in the actual attainment itself with a special zest, depth, or personality in the telling and analysis. Try to give admissions committees both.

Wow factor or not, the strengths that your accomplishment illustrates should corroborate the strengths you emphasize across your application. If your post-MBA goals, recommendation letters, and other essays market you as a global person, you may want your "greatest achievement" to have an international dimension.

Also be sure to calibrate the accomplishment you choose against the school's self-image or marketing message. An accomplishment that subtly communicates that you thrive most when independently pursuing your entrepreneurial vision may not go over well at a school that prides itself on its community and team culture. In fact, try to avoid discussing professional accomplishments that don't involve a team component. Save your solitary accomplishments for other essays or sections of the application.

Finally, as discussed in Chapter 1, consider your accomplishment story in light of the school's other essays. The same school that invites you to discuss either a professional or personal achievement may also give you a separate essay for discussing community involvement or your personal background. Consider focusing your accomplishment essay on a professional success—you may have no other chance to.

Case Study: In Pursuit of Gravitas

If Maria had been an opera singer, she would have been a lyric coloratura. Though 25, her high-pitched, candied voice suggested 16. Possessed of a distinctive profile—South American roots, accomplished artist, unimpeachable "globalist" credentials—Maria's application nevertheless had issues: a 660 GMAT score, par-for-the-course career progression as an investment analyst, and an unwillingness to settle for less than Harvard or Stanford. After failing to dissuade Maria from her quixotic quest, I got to work helping her. Since her GMAT score was what it was, her only hope was convincing the admissions gods that there was much more here than an analyst with a sing-song voice. And, it turned out, there was. Aside from leadership accomplishments in her high school and college, Maria had consistently found ways to burst past the tight functional rein of her analyst roles, innovating cost savings in her first IB role and then, at an investment fund, single-handedly devising a new emerging-market equity fund that won her CEO's endorsement. Acknowledging that big achievers can indeed come in small packages, Harvard wisely admitted her.

Structure

Merely describing an achievement is only a partial response to an accomplishment essay prompt. In fact, the "what" is only one of four components common to most effective accomplishment essays.

The Context and Challenge

The opening paragraph or two of a good accomplishment essay ought to draw the reader into the essay in an engaging, vivid way. It should "set the scene" by providing a rough timeframe for the action and just enough context so the reader understands the enormity of the challenge you faced. It should also directly state what the challenge was.

The Achievement

Most applicants devote prodigious swaths of their essays to meticulous accounts of their achievement experience: "I did X..., then I did Y...." The true payoff of the accomplishment essay comes at its end, however, so it's essential that you minimize your treatment of the achievement to the key events, with special emphasis on the variety of ways in which you tackled (or inspired others to tackle) the challenge.

An accomplishment essay is after all a story, and if you can give it the drama of a good story, you'll lift it above the crowd. The use of plot twists or complications, unexpected detours, and moments of self-doubt or uncertainty add texture and interest to your essay, transforming the tedious exposition of a career data point into the kind of human-interest story admissions officers will remember. (Indeed, for several years MIT Sloan has asked applicants to "describe in detail what you thought, felt, said, and did"—great advice for any essay for any school.) So, if you experienced some initial missteps before you experienced success, don't be afraid to describe them and how they made you feel. They'll give your accomplishment true grit by showing you have the maturity to own up to errors and overcome multiple obstacles.

The Outcome

A clear statement of the ultimate result of your achievement gives your story closure and provides the hard evidence to back up your claim of success. As we discussed in Chapter 1, expressing that outcome in quantitative terms will lend concreteness and objectivity to your story, thereby magnifying your accomplishment's impact.

What the Schools Say

Impact is not something that we define and put into buckets; it's something that depends on the situation, the environment, and the person. Moreover, each person will describe impact differently from the next. That's one of the things we're interested in knowing—how you define impact and when you've had it. We can only evaluate the quality of your experience in context, and that's what we're interested in. Next, we compare that to the quality of the experience of the rest of the applicant pool.

—SOOJIN KWON KOH, UNIVERSITY OF MICHIGAN (ROSS)

The Significance

Business schools value the subjective lessons you draw from your accomplishments at least as much as their "objective," bottom-line impact. But not just any subjective evaluation will do. The specific significance you place on your accomplishment tells schools how thoughtful or self-reflective you are, what you value (e.g., personal benefits versus team benefits), and how deeply you learn from new experiences.

Fortunately for many applicants, the emphasis that schools place on your subjective evaluation of accomplishment gives you the leeway to turn unimpressive bottom-line achievements into fabulous tales of personal growth and inner challenge. Deeply insightful analysis of your achievement's value may pull you "equal" to a star achiever who merely phones in the takeaways.

Avoid any lesson learned that smacks of superficiality: "It was my most significant achievement because it led directly to my promotion four months later and a nice bonus." Mention of external personal benefits, like raises and promotions, is the business of your outcome statement (the essay's third section). The significance statement should aim for deeper payoffs. Also avoid asserting lessons that sound like what you think schools want to hear: "This experience was profoundly invaluable to me because it offered me the humbling privilege of giving back to my deserving community in a meaningful way." This reeks of insincerity, whether the writer meant it or not. (Avoid extreme adjectives as a general rule. If you've successfully communicated your accomplishment's significance, then such thesaurus words aren't necessary; if you haven't, then they won't help.)

Your accomplishment's significance, the life lessons it has taught you, must be genuine and personal to you. The only way to make them so is to be honestly introspective and really explore the experience's impact on you. Then describe that as directly and un-self-consciously as you can. Remember, even if the school does not ask you to discuss the significance of an accomplishment, you should always provide it.

ACCOMPLISHMENT ESSAYS: WHAT *NOT* TO DO

1. Write about an accomplishment that isn't your own, either because it's really a *team* accomplishment in which your role was not distinct or because it's actually someone *else's* achievement (because you misunderstood the question).

2. Fail to be strategic about the accomplishment you write about. If your other essays focus on your professional life, you may want to devote your accomplishment essay to a community or personal story, even if it means you must relegate one of your greatest work-related achievements to a recommendation letter, your résumé, or the application data sheet.

3. Write about ancient accomplishments. Focus on something within the past two or three years (sometimes the schools require you to).

4. Select accomplishments involving your family, friends, marriage, or romantic relationships—unless your story is truly distinctive, your impact truly substantial, and you can write vividly about both.

5. Describe the accomplishment but fail to explain why you value it or what you learned from it.

LEADING AND FOLLOWING: LEADERSHIP AND TEAMWORK ESSAYS

"Five or six years after you receive your MBA," INSTEAD dean Dipak Jain once noted, "80% of your responsibility is managing people." Graduate management schools are about leadership, and one way they find it is by directly asking applicants for their best leadership stories. At the same time, schools also know that for many twenty-somethings, professional leadership is as much a work in progress as an accomplished fact. The leadership essay lets them extrapolate future managerial prowess from the hints and foreshadowings of lowercase leadership moments.

Teamwork is another matter. According to the *Wall Street Journal*, corporate recruiters rate the "ability to work well within a team" as the second most important attribute of business school graduates—"leadership potential" ranking only sixth. For recruiters and business schools alike, there's no such thing as "teamwork potential." If you don't already have it, business schools probably won't want to give you the chance to pick it up between your finance and marketing classes. The teamwork essay lets schools judge that as a teammate you're already primetime, capable of synergizing with classmates from day one.

What the Schools Say

Leadership is best demonstrated when candidates show us they had follow-ship! We want more than just your title or position—we want to see evidence of how you rallied others to act.

—SHERRY WALLACE, UNIVERSITY OF NORTH CAROLINA (KENAN-FLAGLER)

What Schools Ask

"Pure" leadership and teamwork essays unambiguously invite you to write about specific experiences or skills:

- "Give us an example of a situation in which you displayed leadership." (Berkeley Haas)

- "Describe your key leadership experiences and evaluate what leadership areas you hope to develop through your MBA experiences." (Kellogg)

- "Discuss your most meaningful leadership experience. What did you learn about your own individual strengths and weaknesses through this experience?" (Dartmouth Tuck)

To elicit more revealing answers or to focus your response in a certain direction, other schools phrase the question more unconventionally:

- "Tell us about a time when you built or developed a team whose performance exceeded expectations." (Stanford)

- "Tell us about a time when you motivated others to support your vision or initiative." (Stanford)

- "Please describe a time when you coached, trained, or mentored a person or group." (MIT Sloan)

- "Tuck defines leadership as 'inspiring others to strive and enabling them to accomplish great things.' We believe great things and great leadership can be accomplished in pursuit of business and societal goals. Describe a time when you exercised such leadership. Discuss the challenges you faced and the results you achieved. What characteristics helped you to be effective, and what areas do you feel you need to develop in order to be a better leader?" (Dartmouth Tuck)

Stanford's first question clearly calls for an example in which you were the formal or informal leader, whereas its second question could be satisfied with an example in which you were a mere team member but showed initiative or entrepreneurial vision. MIT's prompt is clearly interested in leadership defined as mentorship or coaching, while Tuck's seeks an example that highlights your "visioning" skills (with a hint that it wouldn't mind an example with a social impact dimension).

Finally, some schools combine the leadership and teamwork essays into one. For example, London asks: "Give a specific example of when you have had to test your leadership and team working skills. Given this experience what role will you play in a first year study group?"

This last hybrid group underscores a crucial fact: leadership and teamwork experiences are often two sides of the same coin. Indeed, you can often find both leadership and teamwork experiences in the very same accomplishment. As we'll see in the next section, it's often just a question of emphasis.

Choosing Your Story

Choosing the best leadership or teamwork story starts, naturally enough, with knowing what leadership and teamwork are. Note that schools usually let you define the terms, since part of their purpose is to see how much thought you've given to the idea of leadership. So don't assume that leadership can only mean "telling people what to do" or that teamwork must resemble some corny rah-rah sports scenario. The upside of the interpretive freedom these essays give you is that you don't have to occupy positions of great formal authority or work in huge and diverse groups to impress schools with your leadership and team play. The downside is that you must show the schools through the way you execute these essays that you have given serious thought to what leadership and teamwork really mean and have found multidimensional ways to demonstrate them.

Leadership

Leadership can, of course, mean holding a traditional command-and-control position involving direct reports, sharply delineated hierarchy, and budget and profit and loss authority. But on the broadest level, leadership simply means assuming personal ownership of something in a group situation in order to create a positive result that would not have occurred without you. "In a group" is essential; on some level your leadership example must show you influencing the actions of others. At a minimum, then, leadership implies initiative, doing "more" than others, being proactive, not reactive.

Business School Thought Leaders on Leadership

Business schools don't ask for leadership essays in order to test your command of management theory. On the other hand, if the subject of leadership interests you, business school faculty have generated volumes of material on the practice of management that—even if you don't refer to it in your essay (a risky strategy)—may help you find fresh ways of framing or analyzing your leadership stories. Here are some classics:

- *Handbook of Leadership Theory and Practice*, by Nitin Nohria and Rakesh Khurana (Harvard Business Press, 2010).

- *John P. Kotter on What Leaders Really Do*, by John P. Kotter (Harvard Business Press, 1999).

■ *Managing,* by Henry Mintzberg (Berrett-Koehler, 2009).

■ *On Becoming a Leader,* by Warren G. Bennis (Basic Books, 1989).

What do leaders do? Everything from motivating through personal example, establishing and uniting people behind a vision, and training and mentoring to balancing short- and long-term goals, leading in crisis, and knowing when to let people go. What values do leaders demonstrate? Everything from charisma, initiative, decisiveness, and discipline to empathy, supportiveness, and selflessness. The longer you look, the more encompassing you'll find the idea of leadership to be. It can be approached in terms of traits (self-confidence, integrity), situational environment (boardroom, classroom, football field), functions (organizing, mentoring), or modalities (transaction-based power, information-based communication), and so on. What this means for you is that, even if you have no formal supervisory role, leadership's wide definition will more than likely enable you to find examples and angles of attack that can help you project yourself as an effective leader.

Case Study: A Reapplicant Ups His Game

Before retaining me, Jagdeep had made it as far as an interview with Texas McCombs, but the verdict of all six of his schools was ultimately unambiguous: not ready for primetime. In providing ding feedback, one school had even gone so far as to list fourteen areas for improvement!

Jagdeep had his work cut out for him. He was a technology guy from India, with a 710 GMAT, a telecom engineer's business card, and no direct reports, the thoroughly predictable goal of transitioning into finance, and no current extracurricular leadership. The GMAT was fine, and we knew Jagdeep had little control over his workplace advancement. That left goals and extracurriculars as our makeover focus. Noting that Jagdeep's finance goals were vague and unconvincing, I pointed out that a health-care theme ran persistently through his life, from his physician family members and medical volunteering in India to his health-care–related work in grad school and first job. Had Jagdeep ever considered an entrepreneurial career that united his health-care and telecom themes? Now that you mention it …

But there was still the leadership problem. Acknowledging that his extracurriculars were the one part of his life he could clearly control, Jagdeep strategically postponed his applications to the second round to give himself time to ramp up his nonwork leadership. Months later, Jagdeep was growing a self-initiated local alumni group, led a team of volunteers for a local charity (health-care–related, of course), and managed a medical research study for a university grateful for his project skills. Lo, a leader was born. Duke and Virginia snapped him up.

Starting from college, put the microscope to all your group experiences—work, academic, extracurricular, community, personal—asking questions like these:

- When have you been specifically praised for your leadership?
- Have you ever been elected by a group of people for a position of responsibility?
- What methods do you use to motivate people?
- Do you have a philosophy of leadership? Has it changed over time?
- Have people ever followed your lead?
- Which leader do you most respect and why?
- Have you persuaded others to pursue a certain course of action?

Follow these questions (see Put Yourself on the Couch below for others) wherever they lead. Unless the school's essay question limits you, don't shackle yourself by searching only for work-related leadership stories. Because most applicants are still relatively low on the professional totem pole, their best leadership examples may well come from community or personal activities. Indeed, community leadership can often be more impressive because you're leading volunteers who don't have to follow you (or even be there) and frequently interacting with people at a more senior level than you would at work.

Put Yourself on the Couch

These questions may help you flesh out your leadership or teamwork stories:

1. Were the objectives your team pursued clearly established from the outset or left partly undefined?

2. How did you go about solidifying these team objectives? How did you communicate them to your team?

3. What specific methods did you use to ensure that the project was proceeding apace?

4. What steps did you take when (if) the project fell behind the expected pace?

5. Do you recall moments when you deliberately modified your leadership style to deal more effectively with specific obstacles? How did you determine which tactic to try, and were these tactics successful?

6. Did the project ever require you to "manage up"—that is, get superiors to sign on to your methods or goals? How did you earn their buy-in? Why do you think your techniques worked?

7. Which types of interpersonal interaction proved most effective for you? One-on-one meetings or group meetings?

8. What specific tactics did you use to motivate people, and did you apply them on an individual basis or across the team as a whole?

9. What is the one aspect of your leadership during this project that you would change if you could? Why do you think you got it "wrong" this time?

10. Think about the teammates with whom you work most effectively. Name the three personality traits that make them so easy to work with. Now consider the teammates you work least effectively with—what personality traits pose the biggest obstacle in these relationships?

Teamwork

At the risk of sounding glib, the difference between leadership and teamwork experiences is often a matter of a pronoun. The very same accomplishment will often work well as a leadership or a teamwork essay by shifting the focus from "I" to "we." The project that you said you led effectively through mentoring, delegation, or goal-setting skills was by definition also a team experience whose dynamic you can also capture by focusing on diversity, cross-functionality, personality issues, and the like. (If your job title is manager, however, it becomes harder to spin an example of your teamwork when your team had to do your bidding.) Moreover, the traits that make a great team player—empathy, integrity, selflessness, adaptability, communication, and so on—are often the same as those that make a great leader.

Teamwork can take as many varied forms as leadership, from playing the peacemaker, the right-hand man (or woman), or the jack-of-all-trades to being the cheerleader, the diligent worker bee, or the savvy politico. Likewise, you can find valid teamwork experiences in the workplace or classroom, in your church or community center, in sororities or on athletic fields, or even in the family. Which story you choose will depend on which one shows you understanding and empowering teams best. But as with every essay, you must choose topics strategically so that all your strongest stories find their way into each school's essay set.

Structure

Leadership and teamwork are inherently people-centered topics, yet many applicants overload their essays with project-specific and procedural details instead of zeroing in on the human relationships. The four-part structure recommended here avoids this trap by encouraging you to devote as much space to the lessons learned as to the essay's "plot."

The Challenge

In this first section, provide just enough context—the timeframe, the story's "dramatis personae," and your role—to orient the reader to the scene you're about to bring alive. Begin spelling out the leadership or teamwork challenge as soon as possible, as well as the specific obstacles you or your team faced in overcoming that challenge.

It's fine to explain that your challenge was that a $5 million project was now three months over deadline and $1 million over budget, but the essay's *leadership*- or *teamwork*-specific obstacles should stem from people issues. Perhaps you were new to the project, two of your teammates were feuding, a new-hire's learning curve was steeper than expected, or the client manager seemed to have walked right out of *The Office*. Emphasize the differences and issues between people, not just the functional loggerheads and technical hurdles. Turn it into a human-interest story from the start.

Your Response

Here's where you show how you addressed each of the challenges or obstacles spelled out in the first section by deploying several of your leadership or teamwork skills. Think in terms of both traits and tactics. What three leadership/teamwork traits or qualities did you demonstrate in helping the group rise to the challenge? What were the tactical things you did to overcome people issues? They don't have to be epochal. Taking the time to listen to a teammate or changing your personal style to steer around differences (cultural, functional, gender, age, racial, etc.) with another teammate are worth mentioning. Always describe the small human-level things you did to assuage egos, show gratitude, move people forward. These are the details that (together with the lessons learned) make leadership and teamwork essays work. If it's a leadership essay, show the school through mini-examples *how* you lead—inclusively? intuitively? analytically? If it's a teamwork essay, show the admissions committee how readily you can cede power or visibility when doing so helps the group.

If you have a leadership or teamwork philosophy, consider stepping back from the story for a moment to show schools that you can be reflective about leadership and team play. Naturally, avoid sounding superficial, jargony, grandiose, or inauthentic.

What the Schools Say

Most people have had the chance in their work experience or even school background to demonstrate leadership. Even if you have not had direct reports, most people have led teams and projects. All leadership experiences are valuable.

—ISSER GALLOGLY, NEW YORK UNIVERSITY (STERN)

The Outcome

This element of the essay may be as short as a sentence, but it does help "prove" that your leadership had the positive impact you claim it did. Quantitative facts do this very effectively, but, again, because leadership and teamwork essays are people-focused, qualitative and human-level impacts are also valued: saving someone's career, turning a dysfunctional team into bosom buddies, and so on.

Lessons Learned

As always, schools want to see you step back from the Sturm und Drang of experience and give evidence that you're the sort who learns from experience. Many applicants will slot in a few deep-sounding sentences and call it a night. Unfortunately, adcoms know that any reasonably intelligent person can snatch the latest leadership/teamwork jargon off a school Web site. To overcome their skepticism, you need to show how such leadership and team lessons stem organically from the details of your story. Such takeaway statements show that you are reflective and self-aware about leadership and teamwork, that you have thought about what they mean, and that you are conscious of how to practice them.

One way to make your lessons learned seem organic is to show how your essay's central experience changed your idea of leadership or teamwork. Your essay could begin, for example, by stating that you used to believe that leadership meant, say, managing resources efficiently. After narrating a story in which you learned that leadership is about inspiring others to excel, you would then close the essay by referring back to your now obsolete idea of leadership.

LEADERSHIP AND TEAMWORK ESSAYS: WHAT *NOT* TO DO

1. Write about a group accomplishment in which your role was indirect or nonexistent. Likewise, trying to force a leadership example to work as a teamwork essay will misfire if you were clearly the person in charge or if you show yourself interacting with teammates authoritatively rather than collegially.

2. Focus on the team's accomplishment rather than your interaction with the group. Yes, you must establish context and results, but team dynamics and what you did to shape them are much more important than blow-by-blow project details.

3. Fail to be specific and credible about the leadership or teamwork skills you possess. Drill down into your story to find the specific tactical leadership or teamwork skills it illustrates, and only then worry about extrapolating a general principle or lesson.

4. Forget to analyze the leadership or teamwork accomplishment or draw a lesson from it. The bare facts of the story itself are worthless if you don't analyze them to point out the types of leadership or teamwork you demonstrated and the appropriate lessons you drew from them.

5. Draw obvious or clichéd lessons from your example or state obvious or clichéd types of leadership lessons. Don't say you learned that leadership means "taking initiative and showing vision." Dig deeper than such umbrella words to find a more personalized message.

SAMPLE ESSAYS

The ten sample essays that follow are evenly divided between five essays about accomplishments (whose authors were admitted to Harvard, Stanford, and Wharton) and five essays on leadership or teamwork topics (written by successful applicants to Tuck, MIT, Stanford, Harvard, and London Business School).

Sample Accomplishment Essay 1: Anand R. (Admitted to Harvard Business School)

What are your three most substantial accomplishments and why do you view them as such?

"Making Up"

I am a Board Observer for Nature's Bounty (NB), a Summit portfolio company that is the fastest growing color cosmetics company in the mass channel. Over the six months in which I was the sole Associate working on Summit's $60 million investment in NB, I developed a deep understanding of the $7.8 billion U.S. women's color cosmetics industry from niche brands like Neutrogena to high-end department store brands like Revlon to mass market brands like Cover Girl and Maybelline. After completing the deal, I was invited to join NB's Board as an Observer. I am the only Associate in my office with Board responsibility and one of only 3 worldwide. [←*Always insert differentiating details like this if your career has progressed atypically.*] I now attend quarterly meetings and share my ideas and perspectives, sometimes providing tangible analyses that influence operational and strategic decisions. For example, I have discovered and evaluated several acquisition candidates, presenting definitive opinions on their strategic fit within NB. Additionally, I am identifying and evaluating potential exit opportunities, although an exit would not close until after I leave Summit. Board selection validated my efforts to master the industry beyond expectations and to contribute to Summit's and NB's success beyond my defined role. This experience built my credibility within Summit, signifying my transition from deal contributor to industry director. [←*Anand smartly starts with his strongest professional accomplishment, which shows he is already a "star" and taking on significant responsibility.*]

Finding Billion Dollar Deals
[Section titles, while not necessary, can add flavor]

Though it never came to fruition as I would have wished, I was involved in sourcing and pitching what would have been the largest deal in Summit history. Acting upon my own initiative, I found and researched a large private household products company, and convinced the CEO of that company to meet with my team. My diligent preparation and persistence paid off when, despite his initial aversion to raising capital, he found my arguments to be persuasive. Many productive meetings led to a letter of intent to acquire the company for $1 billion. Although the deal ultimately fell through due to valuation, I felt proud to have guided the firm to the brink of the largest deal in its history. Nor did my dedication go unnoticed; I became known throughout the firm as someone able to identify large, high quality investment opportunities for Summit, and received direct positive feedback from the CEO and CFO concerning my professionalism and sophisticated approach. This experience demonstrated, to others and me, the clarity of my business vision and my ability to shape a significant deal. My next goal is to get such a deal across the finish line! [←*Justifies the risk of focusing on a deal that ultimately failed by showing that his boldness was rewarded by his firm.*]

Usha's Legacy

October 29, 2002 was the worst day of my life. I lost my youngest sister, Usha, to leukemia. As painful as this was, I came to understand that Usha's personal gift to me was a promise that I made to myself—and in my heart to Usha—that I could help others battle cancer. Starting while Usha was still hospitalized, I financially supported a 35-year-old man, who couldn't pay for his cancer treatment, living accommodations, or transportation home. I also co-hosted a bone marrow drive with SAMAR to add over 100 South Asians to the National Bone Marrow Registry. Since Usha's death, I joined a friend, who had a brain tumor, in the Relay for Life to raise money for cancer research and, currently, am organizing a fundraiser for the Leukemia & Lymphoma Society through Team in Training, a marathon fundraising organization. I also am a "Buddy" at Lucille Packard Children's Hospital assisting child patients. Finally, the best result of my promise is my partner-ship with Usha's bone marrow donor (whom I met after Usha died) to establish Positive Television, a television station that will focus on celebrity charity events/fundraising. I carry Usha in my heart, thanking her for her blessings in my life. Her death is not in vain. [← *Anand closes powerfully with a distinctive story of loss that not only humanizes him to the committee but becomes a platform for describing an impressive range of closely related volunteer activities.*]

Sample Accomplishment Essay 2: Annie S. (Admitted to Stanford GSB)

Tell us about a time when you made a lasting impact on your organization.

When I applied to the UN online volunteer program in 2009 and matched with The Foundation for Contemporary Music Cambodia (FCM Cambodia), I was thrilled at my assignment: help FCM Cambodia develop a grant proposal. After the first conference call, however, I discovered that FCM Cambodia was feeling devastated from two previous failed attempts to win a grant. [←*Opening para-graph quickly establishes that this will be a distinctive accomplishment with a social impact theme.*]

I believed that learning to develop proposals would bring confidence to FCM Cambodia. So, working from Dallas every Saturday morning, I commit-ted four hours to educating Sinn and Meng, FCM Cambodia's co-directors, in utilizing materials from MIT Entrepreneurship Center's online library such as the Proposal Development Toolkit.

FCM Cambodia at first resisted MIT's business terminology. I tried repeatedly to show them a successful nonprofit proposal, even arranging a conference call with my co-worker, Patricia Pratt, who externed at the Taproot Foundation, a nonprofit strategy consultancy. Gradually, FCM Cambodia grew more receptive and added new perspectives of their own. Through the one-and-a-half-year weekly effort, we shaped FCM Cambodia's "Creative Perspective Initiative," which consists of three major programs: Music Fest Phnom Penh, Karaoke Lunch with the Musicians, and Ramvong Meets Ramkbach. [*←Paragraph provides a lot of meaty detail that lends credibility to the story and shows the depth of Annie's involvement.*]

Finally, on June 18, 2010, FCM Cambodia received a grant of 18 million Cambodian riel through the International Music and Arts Foundation. Cambodian newspapers trumpeted the success under headlines like "We Are Ready To Support Arts" and "FCM Seeks Public Involvement In Arts." [*←The outcome statement.*]

In July I moved excitedly to Phnom Penh to set up the roadmap and execute the early phase of the program. I'm proud not only to have helped FCM Cambodia gain a one-time grant but to have instilled the solid belief that FCM Cambodia can succeed when they do their best, and to have trained its leaders to win proposals independently in the future. This August Sinn and Meng were granted additional funds from the Asian Cultural Council without my help. Furthermore, leveraging their success story, FCM now advises individual musicians in how to draft proposals for small grants. [*←Annie closes effectively by showing that her accomplishment has achieved sustainability—a legacy.*]

Sample Accomplishment Essay 3: Dirk B.
(Admitted to Harvard Business School)

What are your three most substantial accomplishments, and why do you view them as such?

Living may not sound like much of an accomplishment, but in my case it is. On June 18th, 2000, I swerved to avoid a piece of wood flying toward my windshield and sent my Isuzu Rodeo rolling down a ravine. I soon learned that I had broken my neck at the C–5 level and was paralyzed from the chest down. I spent four months in Denver's Exempla Hospital clinging to life through a ventilator. I was only twenty years old, and thinking about the future filled me with terror. [*←Grabs reader's attention with harrowing personal experience that sets up the three accomplishments that follow.*]

Rather than surrender to despair, I decided I would live a full life. I began working, with the unwavering support of my fiancée Nikki and my family, to breathe again on my own, wean myself from tube feeding, and attack the challenges my injury had imposed on me. In the 11 years since, I have stayed true to that choice. In 2003, Nikki and I married, contradicting every statistic about quadriplegia and relationships. By "compartmentalizing" my injury, we enjoy a private, assistance-free life. Moreover, I never gave up on my career, and despite paralysis, continue to realize my ambitions. It is because I persistently defy my injury that I consider living my life fully to be a substantial accomplishment. *[←Dirk's courageous response to his injury clearly counts as a significant accomplishment; the romantic happy ending is icing on the cake.]*

Succeeding professionally is my second most substantial accomplishment. My disability prevented me from writing or driving an automobile, so instead of returning to school, I created a niche building computer systems for individuals and small businesses. Soon thereafter, I learned HTML and switched my focus to designing websites. Within six months, my major clients included Solar Fiber Optics, the Coors Racing Team, and Neon Amusements.

By 2003, the huge potential of Internet retail was obvious. A business associate and I each invested $80,000 to form Sun10.com, an online clothing boutique targeting young adults. As CEO, I did everything from work with suppliers, negotiate terms, and present our business plan to potential investors to oversee and implement web design, supervise our ten employees, and meet with strategic partners. Our Web site was soon receiving over a million unique visits monthly and generating encouraging revenue. Suddenly, stifling competition and a lack of competitive advantage hammered us, and in 2006 we decided to terminate Sun10.com. *[←Ultimate failure of Dirk's business hardly matters given its initial success and the evidence he provides that his injury will not hold him back.]*

After returning to UC Denver and earning my bachelor's degree, I began applying the lessons I had learned about vision and planning at Boeing. Aside from the millions of dollars my analyses have saved Boeing, I have become my manager's go-to right hand for training and supporting fellow analysts, and now advise two to five people daily. My professional history shows my refusal to allow my injury to excuse me from anything less than the highest standard of performance. *[←Success at Boeing proves Dirk is a professional winner whose injury does not impede his leadership potential.]*

My third significant accomplishment is the connection I make with severe spinal-cord injury patients at Exempla Hospital's Acute Spinal Cord Injury Rehabilitation Center. After Exempla Hospital awarded me its Eagle Spirit Award for my injury-defying achievements, a therapist asked if I would serve as a counselor for young patients who experience similar injuries. As Peer Ambassadors, my wife and I have met with over forty patients and their families to help them work through the initial disbelief toward realistic but hopeful attitudes. We offer emotional support, but never sugarcoat the challenges they will face.

Recently, Joe, a teenage spinal-cord injury patient who had refused to participate in support discussions, grudgingly attended one of my group sessions. After hearing my story, he could not stop asking questions, most quite personal and sensitive. Bob Preston, Joe's social worker, later confided to me that he could not believe how well I connected with the group; Joe's participation was a real breakthrough. By sharing my own post-injury accomplishments, I help Joe and other patients believe in the possibility of high-quality life, if they are willing to fight for it. [←*Dirk rounds out his personal and professional successes with a community accomplishment that has obvious personal meaning to him.*]

Sample Accomplishment Essay 4: Brock H. (Admitted to Wharton)

Give us a specific example of a time when you solved a complex problem.

How do you transform a college that consulting firms ignore into a consulting industry feeder school? That was the daunting challenge I faced when I founded the Indiana Consulting Club (ICC) as a senior. [←*Launching the essay with a question effectively pulls the reader in.*]

After struggling with my first consulting job interview, I realized that, compared to other Big Ten schools, Indiana offered fewer resources to help its students prepare for consulting careers. In fact, most consulting recruiters bypassed Indiana because our students lacked awareness of the industry and the case interview method, resulting in five or fewer consulting job offers annually. I founded the Indiana Consulting Club to address these challenges, knowing it would be an uphill climb to convince stakeholders, train students, and woo recruiters. I needed to make progress quickly. [*Directly and efficiently states the context, his accomplishment, and the challenges he faced achieving it.*]

I first tapped the most accessible resources, by building a partnership with Indiana's MBA program, the Kelley School. Leading a team of four interested classmates, I created seminars with strategy professors like Professor Michael R. Baye and panels with Kelley students from consulting backgrounds to provide greater insight into the industry. These early initiatives attracted over 80 members. To improve members' case interviewing skills, I then persuaded members of the Kelley Consulting Club to pair with our members for weekly practices. For more rigorous training, I engaged outside experts—including Mark Asher, author of the popular "Vault Guide to the Case Interview"—to conduct presentations and workshops on effective frameworks for solving case problems. Asher's landmark talk not only advanced members' interviewing proficiency, but also raised our profile and attracted more than 60 new members. [*Brock's accomplishment deepens with each concrete example of his creativity and initiative.*]

The biggest hurdle was putting Indiana on recruiters' radar. I knew that many firms chose to forgo travelling to Bloomington because of its remote location, so I created virtual on-campus events—bi-weekly conference calls where club members could interact directly with current consultants from BCG, Booz & Co., and others. My team and I even persuaded PricewaterhouseCoopers and Monitor Group to purchase $10,000 for advertising space in "Complete Consulting"—a compendium of recruiting best practices and case studies we created. Their sponsorship paid for the creation, publication, and free distribution of the guide to our members. *[An impressive sponsorship coup shows that this was no ordinary collegiate achievement.]*

Since graduation, I have remained involved in ICC as the Alumni Chair. After moving to Vancouver, I formed a sixteen-member Indiana consulting alumni network throughout Canada that is helping current ICC members build connections and uncover consulting opportunities abroad. *[←Brock's continued involvement enhances the accomplishment by showing how much it really matters to him.]*

My strategy of engaging multiple stakeholders and marshalling available resources produced immediate and lasting impact, translating an idea into an institutionalized and still-growing solution. By my graduation, ICC had 180 members (230 today), and the number of Indiana students receiving consulting offers has jumped fourfold since I founded the club. Indiana is now a core recruiting school for the top consulting firms. *[←Provides a concrete, significant outcome statement.]*

Last year, BCG Manager Sue Knappe commented to ICC's board: "Since the Club was started, I have personally noticed an increase in the preparedness of students interviewing, in terms of both case skills and industry understanding." *[←Quoting a senior's praise further validates Brock's accomplishment.]* Knowing that an organization I founded and still guide has unlocked opportunities for so many students is an accomplishment I cherish.

Sample Accomplishment Essay 5: Jennie Z. (Admitted to Harvard Business School)

What are your three most substantial accomplishments and why do you view them as such?

I

One of my greatest accomplishments was developing a sustainability strategy for Medicines for Humanity (www.medicinesforhumanity.org), AlixPartner's first pro-bono client. Medicines for Humanity (MFH), a nonprofit providing basic medicines and health-care to underdeveloped communities with high child mortality, relied exclusively on donor contributions and sought to increase sustainability in its Dominican Republic site near the poverty-stricken town of Consuelo.

We ultimately recommended a partnership with a microfinance institution, Esperanza International, to improve MFH's sustainability. Esperanza's microfinance clients would gain access to basic health-care and medicines through MFH for a subsidized fee of $1 per month, which would provide MFH with a reliable income flow. I initiated conversations with Esperanza's founder to gauge interest in a partnership, introduced MFH, and coordinated talks with program directors on both sides. The project has been successful beyond our client's expectations and the organizations are now in talks to implement a pilot program near Consuelo.

By driving this project I helped set in motion a partnership between two amazing organizations that will help close the socioeconomic gap in one of the world's poorest regions. Through the provision of better health-care and small loans for family businesses, the impact of my work will improve the lives of thousands in the Dominican Republic.

[Opening essay with pro bono consulting engagement not only enables Jennie to highlight her impact and leadership, but also establishes a social impact theme that aligns with her goals and unifies her entire essay set.]

II

For the past two years I have been actively involved in Inspire (www.inspire-inc.org), a nonprofit consulting organization. Run entirely by pre-MBA junior consultants from top firms who volunteer their time on top of full-time jobs, Inspire works with nonprofits that support child education and development. As Case Team Leader, I managed a team of four associates in an Inspire engagement to develop an expansion strategy for Science Club for Girls (www.scienceclubforgirls.org).

Science Club for Girls (SCFG), a Cambridge-based after-school program that supports girls interested in math and science, sought to understand growth opportunities and implications of expansion in surrounding areas. I worked one-on-one with Connie, SCFG's executive director, managed the primary and secondary research campaigns, directed the team in analysis of industry benchmarks and organizational structures, and led my associates in developing a sophisticated yet user-friendly model that illustrated the financial implications of expansion.

This was the first time I managed a project without any higher supervision, and not only did we deliver outstanding products—which Connie now uses as supportive materials when speaking with funders—my own team commended me for leading the project effectively and for creating an open and collaborative working environment. *[Jennie complements the opening professional accomplishment with a purely extracurricular one that shows she can lead teams while further reinforcing her social impact credentials.]*

III

My third and perhaps most significant accomplishment is being a role model for my family. The eldest of seven children, I put pressure on myself to lead by example, whether it was scouring the town to find my sister when she ran away from home or making seven plates of spaghetti for dinner when my parents worked late. *[←Personal details humanize Jennie for the committee.]*

During high school I strived to lead by example through strong academics and participation in extracurriculars, including theatre. In college, I maintained leadership positions and multiple jobs—babysitting, washing dishes in the cafeteria, paid internships, work study, a restaurant gig—to help pay for school. The day I graduated college, I was moved when my grandmother, who never went beyond 6th grade, kissed my diploma with joy.

Nowadays, I'm proud to see my "runaway" sister writing for *InStyle* magazine, my brother excelling in organic chemistry while working his way through college, and the twins who watched my high school musicals now performing in their own.

Being someone for my family to look up to is a continuous process; it requires discipline, thoughtfulness, and passion to inspire. The greatest accomplishment is when my siblings look to me and think, "I can, too." I see that, and it feels extraordinary. *[Shrewdly rounds out her professional and community achievements with a purely personal one that nevertheless shows her in a leadership role.]*

Sample Leadership/Teamwork Essay 1: Cheng X. (Admitted to Dartmouth Tuck)

Tuck defines leadership as "inspiring others to strive and enabling them to accomplish great things." We believe great things and great leadership can be accomplished in pursuit of business and societal goals. Describe a time when you exercised such leadership. Discuss the challenges you faced and the results you achieved. What characteristics helped you to be effective, and what areas do you feel you need to develop in order to be a better leader?

Strive Schools, a national after-school program, was on the verge of losing Goldman Sachs (GS) as its key Illinois apprenticeship sponsor because no one had stepped forward to lead it. *[←Cuts right to the chase and then explains the inspiration for his leadership.→]* I was so impressed by the apprenticeship, which teaches financial concepts to underprivileged students through weekly educational projects on our trading floor, that I decided to form a team to revive the abandoned program and enable Strive Schools to expand the GS program to additional Chicago area schools. In order to revitalize our apprenticeship, I championed the program throughout our office and recruited Paul, Catherine, and Bruce to teach the spring apprenticeship with me. However, when our first class discussion of "client confidentiality" was met with blank stares, we recognized that our curriculum needed to be more relatable to our students. [←*Describing the obstacles he encountered ultimately highlights Cheng's leadership by showing how he copes with adversity.*] We devoted that semester to improving the standard curriculum, and at the end of the semester, I encouraged my team to consider creating a more interactive program. Although rewriting an entire curriculum would require months of additional work, I motivated my team to dedicate extra time by emphasizing that this new program would be ours to design. [←*Specifically addresses Tuck's request for an example of inspirational leadership.*→]

I encouraged my colleagues to be creative in designing our new hands-on apprenticeship. After weeks of brainstorming, we devised a new "Portfolio Manager" apprenticeship that would incorporate middle school math skills in teaching students how to manage stock portfolios. When we introduced the students to trading stocks, their faces lit up as we explained that they could buy and sell pieces of companies they recognized, like Starbucks and Nike. Our "Portfolio Manager" apprenticeship has been so successful that Strive Schools intends to expand it to other apprenticeships nationwide next year.

During the last year of our apprenticeship program, my volunteers were working 70-hour weeks and I knew that if the program became too burdensome they would drop out. I also realized that although it was important to address everyone's ideas, we needed to balance creativity with decision-making to move forward. [←*Again highlights Cheng's team-sensitive leadership.*→] To provide this direction, and relieve some of the burden, I did the legwork after each brainstorming session to facilitate quick decisions from the team. By addressing details like coordinating transportation for our students and obtaining donations, I was able to minimize distraction and enable my team to focus on leading the program.

Even though I assumed most of the administrative details, such as drafting agendas and coordinating Strive Schools staff, I was careful to allocate planning and teaching responsibilities to each member of my team. This sense of ownership engaged my team and enabled each person to contribute his/her special abilities. By relying on Paul's practicality, Bruce's charisma with the students and Catherine's financial expertise, we made our weekly classes even more effective. [←*By naming and characterizing his teammates Cheng makes the story real.*]

The importance of our team having fun together was more crucial than ever during this year's unprecedented market turmoil. I was struck by my team's camaraderie and commitment when we learned that both of the middle schools we mentor had lost all of their after-school sports due to lack of funding. Eager to get involved, my team volunteered to plan a GS Community Sports Day to raise funds for our students' sports programs. Coordinating 150 community supporters, our September event raised nearly $4,000 to fund boys and girls sports in Naperville for the school year. [←*Shows multiple concrete outcomes of his leadership.*→]

Most importantly, the enthusiasm our team brought to the program inspired new interest within our office and three more GS colleagues joined our team last month. I believe that I have been an effective leader because I kept my team focused on results. From improving the existing program to developing a new curriculum and an annual fundraiser, we took responsibility for the program and achieved specific improvements. A shared vision was essential in motivating the team to devote extra time and effort, while the importance of creating a cooperative and friendly team dynamic cannot be underestimated. [←*Adequately analyzes his leadership, including how it could be improved.*→]

I recognize that I need to develop a more confident personal leadership style and an ability to effectively delegate to my team instead of simply addressing tasks myself. Additional team leadership experience would be instrumental in helping me develop these skills.

In our classes, we teachers call out, "Future…", and the students cheer "Leaders!" I believe that this sense of responsibility can inspire change in any situation.

By demonstrating commitment to our community and empowering students to make a difference in their schools, my team's involvement has not only been personally rewarding, but it has demonstrated the "snowball effect" of taking action in a disadvantaged community. As we became more involved, others were inspired to participate along with us and our impact became exponentially greater. With a shared vision and a desire for real results, our volunteer team has been effective in achieving our objectives while developing great friendships.

Sample Leadership/Teamwork Essay 2: Niels F. (Admitted to MIT Sloan)

Please tell us about a time when you executed a plan.

In summer 2009 I conceived the ultimate New Year's sailing cruise: "bare-boat" chartering a 52-foot sailboat with 10 of my closest friends to cruise the Caribbean's Leeward Islands in search of Jimmy Buffett. [←*Unusual scenario immediately grabs reader's interest.]* Since as captain I was responsible for 11 people's safety and enjoyment, not to mention a $600,000 boat, my planning had to be meticulous. *[←Establishes context of his leadership responsibility.→]* From charting the course and ordering the supplies to researching proper procedures for entering foreign waters, I delegated the tasks that others could handle to my planning team, and handled the rest myself. My friend Jordan was responsible for researching specific activities on the six islands we would visit, and was particularly excited about visiting St. Kitts and Nevis, 36 miles south of St. Bart's.

After leaving the protection of Oyster Pond harbor on December 30th, 8- to 12-foot rollers straight from the African coast battered us for the entire two-hour passage southward. Five of my "crew" became seasick, and I made a mental note to watch the weather and my friends' stamina closely. By New Year's Eve Day, we were safely anchored in Gustavia harbor, St. Bart's, where our intelligence told us Buffett himself would be sailing in a regatta. As we gathered at the Baz Bar with 100 locals near midnight, Buffett suddenly appeared. Positioning my party strategically next to the band, I seized the chance to discuss the regatta with him, before sitting back to greet the New Year hearing Buffett play eight of the tunes he'd made so famous. *[←Brushes with celebrity can be effective essay elements.]*

I was getting ready to congratulate myself for planning and executing such an idyllic adventure when our plans suddenly went awry. *[The plot thickens, intensifying the reader's interest; Niels' leadership will be tested further.]* On the day before our planned departure for the two far islands Jordan wanted to see, I began to have doubts. The forecast indicated heavy seas, and a local captain had advised us it would be a very rough sail for a boat that was basically a short-distance cruiser. Moreover, witnessing my friends' misery on our first 12-mile sail, I wondered whether it made sense to spend six-plus hours trying to keep down breakfast through large rolling waves and high winds, just to do it all again on the voyage back. Wasn't the point of the trip to have fun?

When Jordan heard that I wanted to abandon the part of the trip he anticipated most, he heatedly reminded me of how important it was to him and how much he had helped in the planning. I began doubting myself. Was I just backing away from a challenge I wasn't sure I was up to? Then I recalled how Kayla and Jeff, who had little experience in open-ocean sailing, had spent the first day vomiting over the rail and thought of the planes we all had to catch the day after returning, leaving us no margin for error. Reaffirming my decision, I told Jordan that I was the captain, and that while I hated disappointing him, it was my job to watch out for everyone. My decision was final. *[←Though this essay is about a "fun" experience, the leadership context is real (lives at stake), and this strong assertion of leadership drives home the point that Niels had the leadership required.]*

Abandoning our original plan was difficult but wise. Most of my friends later told me how relieved they were to know our trip's potentially dangerous last leg was off. Today, when Jordan and I discuss the cruise, it's Jimmy Buffett we remember, not the islands we never saw. [*←Nice close.*]

Sample Leadership/Teamwork Essay 3: Omar G. (Admitted to Stanford GSB)

Tell us about a time when you motivated others to support your vision or initiative.

When I transferred to McKinsey's San Francisco office in 2008 from Cairo, I was surprised to see that the San Francisco office conducted pro-bono cases two to three times a year versus two pro-bono cases in five years for the Cairo office. Upon returning to Egypt, I decided to improve this ratio by forming "Impact Cairo" with junior consultants. [*←Pro bono theme establishes Omar's interest in causes larger than himself.*]

At our first meeting, only two people (including me!) showed up. I learned that management was unwilling to let consultants accept more pro-bono work because of the office's high workload. To enlighten management on the value McKinsey's global offices place on community work, I contacted 47 overseas divisions and found that they averaged ten times more community service than the Cairo office. Even after sharing this in an office-wide meeting, management questioned whether volunteer activity was worth doing. I didn't quit here. I found a McKinsey Australia case study showing that employee attrition declined 9% after pro-bono activities are increased. [*←Omar shows he can roll up his sleeves and make a compelling "business case" when his ideas are challenged.→*]

To confirm this, I interviewed transferees from the Australia office and surveyed the Cairo office. Fully 78% of respondents replied that community activity would make them more likely to stay, and 80% replied that they felt greater motivation and loyalty the more socially responsible they perceived their employer to be.

Bulls-eye: management had been struggling with employee morale as the recession accelerated. Finally gaining management's support, I easily motivated junior consultants to join by emphasizing that Impact Cairo would give them bigger roles than were possible in normal casework.

In three months "Impact Cairo," now fifteen members, obtained a case load and budget. In our first case, we helped Cairo National University's museum increase quarterly revenue by 30%. Moreover, Impact Cairo has changed McKinsey Cairo's culture regarding community work. Recently, I learned that McKinsey will dedicate a regular resource to our probono case for Egypt's National Pension Corporation. [*←Omar shows he can overcome cultural differences through his persistence and ability to understand others' point of view, creating a legacy for himself as a result.*]

Sample Leadership/Teamwork Essay 4: Elana T. (Admitted to Harvard Business School)

What are your strengths and weaknesses as a leader?

My leadership philosophy defines long-term strategic vision as the paramount responsibility of board level executives. Effectively managing the change necessary to drive the organization towards that vision is a leadership challenge requiring fortitude and emotional intelligence. [←*Elana's serious, high-minded opening sets a high bar: will the leadership example she provides be impressive enough?*]

My primary strengths as a leader are foresight and determination. I demonstrated these qualities during the attempted leveraged buyout of Nixon Polymers Group ("NPG"), a specialty plastics manufacturer. The decision-making process at Black Rock is structured so that junior professionals study a potential investment first, and then advocate its merits to the senior professionals if warranted. Navigating through this process as a junior professional is comparable to a leader implementing his vision throughout an organization.

My investigation into NPG revealed a long-term substitution trend whereby the plastic building materials that NPG produced would replace traditional wood in residential housing. Through foresight, I concluded that Black Rock as an organization should invest in this new market direction. Accordingly, I was determined to convince the internal investment committee of my vision for NPG. A senior partner on the committee was initially hesitant to go along with my assessment. He worried about the rising cost of raw materials used in manufacturing plastic. As questions continued to surface, I performed cogent analyses to mitigate his concerns. Despite pressure from this reluctant superior, my persistence encouraged the buyout process forward for four months. Ultimately, we spent approximately half a million dollars performing due diligence, and submitted a final round bid. [←*Elana shows her ability to do the analysis to defend her ideas and convince seniors despite their resistance.*]

As illustrated above, I am adept at crafting a vision and pursuing it doggedly, but my weakness as a leader is communicating that passion clearly. While my enthusiasm for NPG was appreciated, a more enticing presentation may have inspired the senior partners to increase our final round bid and thereby win the auction. [←*The weakness Elana chooses is credible (not a strength disguised as a weakness) because she admits that the auction ultimately failed as a result of it.*]

Recognizing this weakness, I take proactive steps to place myself in situations that improve my leadership skill of persuasion. For example, when a scheduling conflict prevented the senior partner from traveling, I stepped forward to visit a management team that wanted to run a company that Black Rock considered purchasing. This experience sharpened my ability to facilitate business partnerships. I also frequently volunteer to be the sole Black Rock professional representative at private equity conferences. These events are an important way for Black Rock to generate proprietary buyout opportunities. Coincidentally, I can practice presenting a message and forming mutually beneficial relationships. [←*Ably compensates for her weakness by showing the believable ways she is working to address it.*]

Sample Leadership/Teamwork Essay 5: Qiaoqiao W. (Admitted to London Business School)

Please describe your experience of working in and leading teams, either in your professional or personal life. Include any specific challenges you have faced. Given this experience, what role do you think you will play in your first year study group?

At MacroDatex, over the last five years, I have built and led a diverse team of 8 representing 6 nationalities (including Brazil, Italy, and Korea). [←*After establishing that she leads a large and diverse team, Qiaoqiao immediately begins documenting the specific ways in which she empowers it.→*] I used rotational leadership where each team member would assume the team lead role cyclically to maximize on each member's strengths. I introduced the concept of "story points" in which the velocity of the team toward our deadline was measured weekly by assigning a certain number of points to each completed feature, bringing a healthy sense of competition among team members to "win" more points. I also announced a weekly "product vision" meeting where each team member was given the opportunity to step out of their narrow roles and express their opinions on our product's overall vision. I established demonstrations that gave a different team member each week a chance to show the project's status to management, enhancing each member's visibility with management and their own sense of ownership. To promote collaboration, I introduced a different "culture week" for the group each week so team members would appreciate each others' cultures. And I always scheduled team-building activities including monthly potlucks and "Friday frolics" as well as outdoor getaways when a goal was completed. As a direct result, my team performed under intense deadlines: developing a voice interface for our products that opened a whole new market and winning our biggest customer (United Technologies with 50,000 users) by integrating travel booking with expense reporting into our product. [←*Impressive list of specific leadership techniques gives ring of truth to Qiaoqiao's leadership claims.*]

My team leadership has also been shaped by my community experiences. In 2006, I joined the 5,000-member China Young Professionals Association (www.cypa.org) in San Jose and noticing that all CYPA's members were employed professionals, I proposed to CYPA's president that we start a mentorship group to help college students build professional networks.

[←Transitioning to a community example shows that Qiaoqiao can lead in multiple environments.] Though the board agreed, after a year my mentorship group had only eight mentors serving twelve students. Seeing a solution, I recruited 7 volunteer CYPA ambassadors to identify the appropriate student club at each Bay Area university that could best publicize our mentorship program on campus. *[←Example shows her initiative, creativity, and marketing skills.→]* On the mentors' front, I partnered with CYPA's professional/networking committees to find more volunteers, designed criteria to match mentors and mentees, and held regular programs to train mentors. By the end of 2007 we had between 40–50 mentors mentoring nearly 200 students at 8 campuses, including colleges in Los Angeles and San Diego. It was a powerful lesson in the importance of maximizing existing networks and organizations and in the "force multiplier" effect of effective delegation. I also learnt how to motivate busy people to help a cause on a volunteer basis as well as the role of mentors in realising one's goals. *[←Draws appropriate lessons learned.]*

My leadership experiences at MacroDatex and CYPA will enable me to directly enrich my LBS study group. I will suggest we try rotational leadership methods, schedule fun cultural awareness activities, elect an alumni or faculty mentor to maximize our study group's learning opportunities, and partner with other study groups for some learning sessions. *[← Qiaoqiao avoids a generic closing paragraph by mentioning specific tactics she will explore with her LBS study group.]* Since my study group will consist of highly talented and motivated individuals with broadly different experiences and perspectives, I will be a follower during group assignments that emphasize skill areas outside my own experience.

CHAPTER 4

Getting Personal: Self-Revelation Essays

You must remember that you are unique. Your choices throughout life are unique. Just be yourself and tell your story.

—Kris Nebel, Former Michigan (Ross) Admissions Director

In one form or another every business school essay question is trying to get you to open up and reveal yourself to the admissions committee. Are you the sort of person whom this most exclusive of exclusive clubs, the top-drawer business school, really wants as a member? What will you be like chatting it up after study group, floating opinions in class, officially representing the school as an alum? More directly than any other topic, the essays in this group try to answer these pivotal "fit" questions. With them, biting the bullet of self-revelation is not optional.

With self-revelation essays your goal is not to *sell* the admissions committee on the viability of your goals, your ardor for their program, or the grandeur of your accomplishments, but simply to *be* yourself. These are the worst possible essays in which to tell schools what you think they want to hear. No matter how facile a writer you may be, admissions officers have spent their entire careers reading between the lines, sifting the real from the bogus. If you try to fake them out, you will not win. Be real.

The self-revelation essay can take a great variety of forms—essays about your background, key experiences, passions and interests, uniqueness or diversity factors—in short, anything that might provide a glimpse behind the résumé and into the real you. For the purposes of this chapter, we've boiled all these possible topics down to six basic clusters:

- Pure "Who Are You?" essays and essays about passions

- Diversity and cross-cultural international essays

- Self-evaluation and strength/weakness essays

- Creative, visual, and multimedia essays

- Failure and mistake essays

- Growth and learning essays

THE REAL YOU: "WHO ARE YOU?" AND PASSION ESSAYS

Essay questions of this type come as close to any in directly asking you to, "Tell us about yourself":

- "What matters most to you, and why?" (Stanford)

- "Describe the ways in which your family and/or community have helped shape your development." (UCLA Anderson)

- "Please tell us about yourself and your personal interests. The goal of this essay is to get a sense of who you are, rather than what you have achieved professionally." (Columbia)

- "When you join the HBS Class of 2013, how will you introduce yourself to your new classmates?" (Harvard)

- "You are the author for the book of Your Life Story. Please write the table of contents for the book. Note: Approach this essay with your unique style. We value creativity and authenticity." (Cornell)

- "If you could imagine a life entirely different from the one you now lead, what would it be?" (HEC)

They are a varied lot, but they share one potential trap: the sheer breadth of potential subject matter they could inspire you to disclose. The danger is that you'll try to show who you are in so many different directions that your essay will become a grab-bag of events, significant others, and personal and community experiences loosely strapped together with a blanket theme. An essay that tries to chew off too much will lack the detailed stories that really communicate your unique life experiences (note that even Cornell's table of contents approach can include running text). Honing in on a limited number of personalized themes and luminous, vividly etched moments is your salvation. Identify key experiences, qualities, or interests of yours, and then drive them home with anecdotes that illustrate your theme.

For Stanford's legendary "what matters most," avoid if at all possible topics like "my family," "becoming the best person I can be," "leaving the world a better place," unless you know you have unusually powerful material and can find a personalized way of stating these tired themes. For all of these essays, think outside the box. The risk of getting dinged for blandness vastly outweighs the risk of choosing a topic or approach that's too off the wall (do vet it with someone who's seen a few of these essays, of course). These essays are all about letting your creativity run free.

Case Study: A Remarkable Story from an Unremarkable Applicant

Andrew wanted to get into Stanford, but I told him he wasn't being realistic. His 700 GMAT was fine, but didn't compensate completely for his submediocre GPA in college, his hardly electrifying profile (IT guy with a major consultancy), and his fine but unremarkable extracurriculars. Then Andrew told me his story. Raised in one of America's poorest and least educated counties by an alcoholic father, Andrew had watched in horror one night as his mother wrestled a gun from his raging father's hands. Traumatized by his home life, he had imploded academically in college, until his junior year, when he met a studious and traditional Asian student, who simultaneously stole his heart and set him straight. Gradually, Andrew's life began to turn around, academically, professionally, and extracurricularly until, by the time I met him, he felt he had earned the right to call an MBA his best next step.

Andrew's finished essay read like the treatment for an especially moving Hollywood romance—and every word rang true. By getting the admissions committee to focus on his remarkable life rather than his unremarkable profile, Andrew earned admission to Stanford GSB.

Some schools' self-revelation topics helpfully force you to narrow your focus:

- "What event or life experience has had the greatest influence in shaping your character and why?" (UCLA Anderson)

- "People may be surprised to learn that I...." (Kellogg)

Never forget that these essays are often sandwiched between more prosaic essay questions where your professional or less personal material will feel more at home. So wherever possible focus these self-revelation essays on the extracurricular you. After all, the odds that an admissions committee member would be truly surprised to learn that you do great liquidity risk models are remote, and claiming that the IMS Health LBO you worked on had the "greatest influence in shaping your character" will sound a tad shallow.

What you spend your free time doing says more about you than what you do in the workplace, where your choices are often decided by someone else. People who sustain deep personal involvements outside their work lives—particularly unusual ones—are simply more interesting than those who spend their off hours vegetating. Moreover, the history of your involvements tells schools something about your commitment and focus. Whether you enjoy volunteering as a dance instructor, collecting antiques, weight training, or working as a math tutor, your extracurricular involvements prove you are not all work—you have "a life."

Since most extracurricular interests involve other people, learning about your nonwork passions also tells schools how you will respond to the many formal and informal group activities that define the business school experience. And since many B-school applicants are too young to have gained significant leadership experience at work, schools also look to these extracurricular essays to find evidence of leadership. If your nonwork commitments entail helping your community, especially in a leadership role, you'll be demonstrating the other-directedness that admissions officers like to see in students and alumni.

Demonstrating an intensive enthusiast's knowledge of an obscure subject and/or dramatizing your passion through a specific memorable experience can produce essays with grit, credibility, and distinctiveness. You may also consider focusing on interests that offset the negative stereotypes every profession drags behind it. If you're a computer programmer, writing about your love of math puzzles may feed social-skills concerns, but an essay about your leadership of a deep-sea diving team will surprise schools in the best possible way.

As always, it's not enough to simply describe the experience, interest, or passion. You must also address the why, by, for example, explaining the context that brought you to the experience or interest in the first place, how it makes you feel, and any broader impact it has had on you or the world. Has the experience or passion changed you or taught you anything about yourself or life? Better yet, if the experience or interest has enabled you to benefit others or improve an organization, say so and provide substantiating evidence.

Admissions essays that lack passion can be damaging; "passion" essays that lack passion can be disastrous. Whether you are writing about a defining personal moment or your love of cosplay (costume + play), you must make the reader experience your genuine enthusiasm, and you must make her understand why you feel it.

Prying into your personal secrets is never the goal of a self-revelation essay, so don't write defensively or guardedly. The schools want to discover whether you're interesting and likable, so an engaging tone is crucial. If your own life seems boring to you, imagine how it will sound to the admissions committee.

WHO ARE YOU? AND PASSION ESSAYS: WHAT *NOT* TO DO

1. Forget that the focus should be you. Self-revelation essays are about getting you to spill the beans about your values, interests, and life experiences. Make sure that your response provides information unavailable elsewhere in your application and insights about you that corroborate the themes of your application as a whole. Don't waste unnecessary space on information that is not ultimately connected to who you are.

2. Choose inappropriate material. Not everything revealing about you is essay fodder. Some, such as relationships, is too personal. Others—religion, politics—are rife with danger because of their inherent controversy. If such risky topics are essential to who you are, frame your essay so as to defang them of their offensive potential. For example, focus on what your faith or political career have enabled you to do for others, not on doctrinal issues.

3. Fail to admit weaknesses. Failing to acknowledge that you have negatives when a question invites you to discuss them or palming off a disguised strength as a weakness damages your credibility with the admissions committee.

4. Write passion essays that lack passion. Because self-revelation essays always come down to you—someone you presumably are vitally interested in—yours has failed if it portrays you as a person not enthusiastically engaged in your own life.

5. Bite off more than you can chew. Since many self-revelation essays leave the scope of your answer up to you, your urge to communicate all your strengths may tempt you to spawn a kitchen-sink essay packed with three-sentence generalities about scattered shards of your life but bereft of examples and a unifying theme. Resist temptation.

VIVE LA DIFFÉRENCE: DIVERSITY AND CROSS-CULTURAL ESSAYS

The uniqueness that makes you who you are and the element of diversity you could add to an MBA class are obviously related, so some schools cut right to the chase with pointed diversity prompts like these:

- ■ "Tuck seeks candidates of various backgrounds who can bring new perspectives to our community. How will your unique personal history, values, and/or life experiences contribute to the culture at Tuck?" (Dartmouth Tuck)

- ■ "How will your background, values, and nonwork activities enhance the experience of other Duke MBA students and add value to Fuqua's diverse culture?" (Duke)

- ■ "At the McCombs School of Business, you will be part of an active and diverse community. How will you use your personal strengths and unique experiences to enrich the McCombs community during your two years in the program?" (Texas McCombs)

- ■ "Describe what there is about your background and your experiences that will contribute to the diversity of the entering class and enhance the educational experience of other students." (Indiana)

Don't just tell us about yourself, these prompts seem to say; tell us how who you are will enhance our program's diversity. Likewise, diversity and contribution are two edges of the same sword: you may have a truly distinct profile, but how exactly will it contribute to our class?

This emphasis on diversity stems from admissions committees' conviction that we learn more from those we differ from than from pale reflections of ourselves. As a result, typical top-tier programs boast everything from art dealers and zookeepers to plastic surgeons, TV anchors, and helicopter ski guides. And the variety only deepens when geographic origins, cultural backgrounds, and personal pursuits are tossed in the pot.

Because the word *diversity* still carries an affirmative action tinge, however, many applicants assume that they're out of luck in the diversity department unless their grandmother was Mohican. Though it's true that schools show special favor to applicants from U.S. underrepresented minority groups—namely, African Americans, Hispanic Americans, Native Americans, and Pacific Islanders—class profiles prove beyond a doubt that schools define diversity much more widely than ethnically.

The increase in international representation at business schools is perhaps the most obvious way in which schools have diversified the MBA experience in recent years. None of the top ten U.S. MBA programs today has fewer than 32 percent non-U.S. students, and the top European schools all boast international populations of 86 percent and higher (IMD comes closest to "perfect" diversity at 98 percent). Schools value international exposure not only because new perspectives deepen the classroom learning experience, but because global experiences often go hand in hand with personal growth, tolerance, and enhanced professional value. Of course, being international no longer automatically confers diversity points, as many outstanding Indian applicants have discovered to their chagrin. Applicants from well-represented countries or those who have modest cross-cultural profiles can offset this with vivid, detailed, compelling descriptions of their international stories and through the depth of insight and reflection they bring to their analysis of them.

In the diversity essay, admissions committees are inviting you to help them sculpt the class of maximum variety they seek. The pressure is on you to "prove" your diversity, to convince the schools that you can enhance your classmates' experience more profoundly than the next applicant. But how you accomplish that is left mostly up to you. What do *you* think makes you unique, the diversity question asks; what do *you* think your distinct contribution to your class will be?

However they are worded, the shared intent of schools' diversity questions is to coax you into highlighting the aspects of your profile that will add the most flavor to your class and benefit to your classmates. Most schools give you maximum leeway by asking broadly about "personal history, values, and/or life experiences," but one important variant of the diversity essay tries to determine your potential contribution by narrowing your focus to international or cross-cultural experiences:

- "Describe any significant experiences outside of your home country. What did you gain from these?" (London Business School)

- "Have you ever experienced culture shock? What did it mean to you? or What would you say to a foreigner moving to your home country?" (INSEAD)

- "Tell us about a time when you had to adapt by accepting/understanding the perspective of people different from yourself." (Wharton)

- "An effective leader for business and society is one who is able to hear, understand, and communicate with people from all segments of society. In order to educate such leaders, Yale SOM is committed to promoting diversity and creating a community that cultivates a wealth of perspectives. In this spirit, describe an instance when, as part of a team, you played a role in bringing together individuals with different values or viewpoints to achieve a common goal." (Yale)

Because the range of stories that diversity essays allow you to tell is potentially so wide (what does "personal history, values, and/or life experiences" exclude?), deciding what to write about is the first stumbling block in crafting a standout essay. How can you know which aspects of your profile are really "diverse" or can actually constitute a "unique contribution" to future classmates? One way is by simply inventorying your life, as discussed in Chapter 1. Start with the narrow, conventional definitions of diversity—ethnic background or gender. If you are an underrepresented minority, then consider discussing that fact to whatever depth captures its importance to your life. Next, look at socioeconomic, cultural, and geographic types of diversity. If you overcame an economically disadvantaged childhood, identify strongly with your family's cultural roots, or come from a foreign country or a U.S. region underrepresented at your target school, these are diversity factors you will want to expand on in your essay.

Your education may have been unusual (e.g., your school's location or affiliation, your major or scholarships), your religious or spiritual life may be significant and unusual, your post-MBA goals may set you apart, even your sexuality or specific family dynamics (if handled properly) may convince the schools that you'll contribute a distinct perspective. Skills or areas of expertise, unusual or challenging life experiences, even personal qualities or traits such as the gift of humor are all valid, potentially fruitful diversity topics.

If after drawing up your personal diversity inventory you still think you're too unexceptional, don't fret. A diverse class doesn't mean a class filled with demographic outliers; it also means one that includes a good number of strong applicants with traditional, "middle-of-the-road" profiles. If you feel that's you, then tell your "normality" tale as engagingly and vividly as you can. Your charm and winning presentation can themselves create the sense of potential contribution that schools look for. Personality, in other words, can be a "diversity factor." Many qualified applicants who believed schools eliminated them for "diversity" reasons actually eliminated themselves at the start by assuming they had none. Your diversity elements may not be terribly unusual taken individually, but together they may well make you memorably distinct.

What the Schools Say

We define diversity much more broadly than some people do. For us, the academic environment is enhanced when you're challenged and confronted by a multiplicity of perspectives. Students have a lifetime to be around people like them in their same industries, so an MBA program is a time to really confront your own values.

—MAE JENNIFER SHORES, UCLA (ANDERSON)

Aside from the content you choose, what can you do to ensure that your diversity essay really convinces admissions officers that you can make a significant contribution? First, you must provide vivid details and concrete examples that automatically individuate you because they're specific to your life. Since the general phrases or themes you will use to label your uniqueness have probably been used before, it's your examples that will give your diversity essay its real singularity. Make sure they have color and bite.

Second, it's not enough to simply name your diversity factors and drop in a few examples. You must also address the diversity essay's contribution component (sometimes stated in the question's wording, sometimes not, but always implied). That is, explicitly state how your diversity or uniqueness factors have benefited or educated you, what they've added to your life, and how they will benefit classmates. For example, what life lessons or insights did you gain from growing up in Mozambique or abandoning your budding career as a rock musician or chasing your passion for Tang Dynasty antiques to Nepal? And in what ways will you share these lessons or insights with your future classmates? By joining the African Students' Club? By playing for classmates during orientation week? By explaining antique auction bidding theory in class? In other words, show schools that you've already begun envisioning how to share your special traits and interests within their program.

THE DIVERSITY ESSAY: WHAT *NOT* TO DO

1. Assume that diversity can be defined only in terms of certain underrepresented races or that uniqueness is limited to tales of being raised by cannibals or overcoming obscure medical conditions. Schools define both terms loosely.

2. Use "unique contribution" material that really isn't all that singular—being a mother, being Canadian, making your high school's varsity basketball team. Dig deeper.

3. Focus on questionable, inappropriate, or negative uniqueness factors, such as your psychic gifts or your weekend recruiting work for underground terrorist cells. Stay positive and within bounds.

4. Try to cram too many uniqueness factors into your essay, thus producing a bland, all-inclusive porridge unsubstantiated by examples. Focus on three or four diversity themes.

5. Waste space informing schools how great diversity is. They know this; that's why they asked the question. Talk about how great your own diversity is instead.

ANALYZE THIS: SELF-EVALUATION AND STRENGTH/WEAKNESS ESSAYS

This group of questions gets at who you are by asking you to evaluate yourself and your strengths and weaknesses, or to discuss how others do so:

- "Give a candid description of yourself, stressing the personal characteristics you feel to be your strengths and weaknesses and the main factors, which have influenced your personal development, giving examples when necessary." (INSEAD)

- "Assume you are evaluating your application from the perspective of a student member of the Kellogg Admissions Committee. Why would your peers select you to become a member of the Kellogg community?" (Kellogg)

- "What are the 2 or 3 strengths or characteristics that have driven your career success thus far? Do you have other strengths that you would like to leverage in the future?" (North Carolina)

Self-evaluation essays give you another slot in which to insert stories that flesh out the committee's picture of you while they run a reality check on your self-awareness. Do you have a mature, balanced understanding of yourself? Do you see the same strengths and weaknesses the adcoms have started to notice, or do you live in perpetual denial? These essays also offer you a chance to gain credibility by simply being honest. If you come clean in these essays, admissions officers will be more willing to lend credence to your positive claims about yourself.

The strengths you discuss in this essay must complement (if not entirely overlap) the strengths your recommenders cite and your application as a whole communicates. Naturally, all business schools value skills like leadership, team skills, integrity, analytical ability, communication skills, and cultural adaptability, but each school broadcasts its own peculiar mix of valued traits (e.g., Haas's innovation, Chicago's iconoclasm), which you should be well aware of before mapping this essay. Ideally, your essay will blend "obligatory" business school strengths, such as leadership, with strengths that are really personal to you, like artistic ability, spontaneity, or adventurousness.

Moreover, since *leadership, team skills,* and the like are broad terms that encompass many distinct traits, try to give your essay individuality by finding the particular traits that best capture you. Avoid strengths like "persistence" and "dedication." They're not only vague and clichéd, but they will paint you as a worker bee rather than a dynamic leader.

The laziest and most common structure for self-evaluation essays is to take up each strength or weakness in turn, illustrate it with an example, and then awkwardly transition on to the next: "My second biggest strength is my …". To avoid this, find some common element or quality that your strengths share and weave your essay around that, or, better yet, find a single story (a work project, for example) or activity (your salsa class) that will illustrate all your strengths and weaknesses in one fell swoop. It's awfully hard to be original when discussing traits you likely share with most of humanity, so remember that in this essay your creativity and uniqueness will derive from the special combination of strengths you cite and—most of all—from the stories you tell to illustrate them. If you can, draw explicit connections between your strengths and the specific B-school forum (class, study group, etc.) in which you plan to leverage them.

For most applicants, the minefield at the heart of the self-evaluation essay is the weakness section. This is not because most applicants have an embarrassing number of weaknesses—the vast majority don't—but because they refuse to admit they have any. Thus admissions officers must trudge through a purgatory of "good weaknesses": perfectionism, workaholism, impatience with people with low standards, and so on. Such "strengths in disguise" may actually have worked 30 years ago when adcoms first encountered them, but trotting them out today only shows unimaginativeness, immaturity, and dishonesty—not especially becoming traits. True weaknesses, the kind schools want to hear about, are personal characteristics that most of us suffer from and that can be reversed with sufficient awareness and effort: poor time management, procrastination, indecisiveness, and so on.

Do more than merely "cite" your weakness. Give a brief example or explanation of how it has affected you, what specifically you are doing now to rectify it (classes, mentoring, etc.), and—if relevant—which specific B-school resources can help you purge this Achilles' heel for good. You don't want the self-evaluation essay to read like a static report card but as a snapshot of confident self-transformation—a savvy, evolving person working on her flaws, deepening her assets.

Put Yourself on the Couch

A self-evaluation essay should not be a no-holds-barred exercise in self-recrimination—the essay must still advance your candidacy. But to give these essays the ring of truth it's a good idea to start with genuine self-analysis. The following questions may help:

1. Pull out your performance review from work. What strengths have your supervisors or peers consistently identified? Which weaknesses?

2. Which of your strengths is most uncommon among your professional peers?

3. Name two important ways in which you differ from your professional peers. Name two ways in which you differ from your two closest friends.

4. When people misunderstand you, what do they normally get wrong?

5. What do friends like about you? What do colleagues admire most about you? Are these two lists mostly the same, or mostly different?

6. In what single respect or characteristic have you changed the most since your teen years? Since your college years?

7. Which of your weaknesses do you suspect will never change? Which ones are you optimistic you can eventually address?

8. If you could be someone else (someone you know personally), who would it be? What personal trait do you most envy or admire in that person?

9. Name the one personal or professional accomplishment that best captures who you are as a person. What three characteristics or qualities does that accomplishment illustrate?

10. Name the one characteristic or trait of yours that you believe will be most affected (positively or negatively) by your business school experience?

PRETTY PICTURES: CREATIVE, POWERPOINT, AND MULTIMEDIA ESSAYS

As applicants have become savvier both about the importance of the admissions essay and strategies for writing effective ones, some business schools have turned to less verbal methods to accomplish the underlying purpose of the self-revelation essay: to expose the real you.

What the Schools Say

Essay Three lets people stand out and talk about who they are. If you've worked in banking and your GMAT is average, then Essay Three lets you stand out and show how you're different. We get collages, recipe books, photo albums. Now we have size restrictions. We say, Think outside the box, but it has to fit in the box.

—ISSER GALLOGLY, NEW YORK UNIVERSITY (STERN)

Creative Essays

NYU Stern pioneered the nontextual approach with its "Describe yourself to your MBA classmates" personal expression essay more than a decade ago. By allowing applicants to use "almost any method" to communicate their uniqueness, Stern gives applicants a daunting creative challenge since the only submissions it currently excludes are perishable items (a blow to chefs everywhere). The trick is turning the intimidation factor around and viewing it as a potentially fun opportunity to unleash your creativity and truly differentiate yourself.

What the Schools Say

A successful Essay three is one in which an applicant is able to share aspects of himself or herself that are not otherwise highlighted in the application, such as a unique experience, specialized skills and strengths, or a personal passion. The most memorable nontext submissions often use their creative form to dramatize what an applicant will bring to the Stern community. For example, applicants who have a passion for cooking—or who are self-proclaimed "foodies"—have submitted a menu or recipe book that blends some of their favorite dishes with various aspects of their lives. Applicants who have lived in or traveled to many parts of the world have created a custom-made passport or constructed a mini-suitcase with memorabilia and photos. We have even seen applicants represent their lives in the context of the NYU Stern brand—by making their own personalized Stern brochure.

—ALISON GOGGIN, NEW YORK UNIVERSITY (STERN)

Don't let Stern's invitation to abandon prose make you feel guilty about submitting text—a substantial percentage of all Stern applicants do wind up submitting written essays. Just make sure it gives ample insight into your personality and character. If you do decide to eschew words, be sure your idea—whether it's a photo collage, a product you worked on, or a meticulous Lego replica of your childhood home—truly captures who you are. Creativity for its own sake usually comes off as gimmicky; creativity that expresses your passion is much less likely to miss the mark. Nontext ideas tried in the past have included:

- An Excel-based Jeopardy game in which each answer category highlighted an aspect of the applicant's life—clicking on a cell revealed the answer.

- An eight-page autobiographical Web site featuring 52 photos and a humorous Fun Facts section that the enterprising applicant had professionally printed and bound as a book.

- A giant world map on which a globe-trotting applicant pasted photos of herself in places like Sudan, Sri Lanka, and Macedonia and accompanied by captions explaining what she had learned in each location.

- A set of manga-style game cards, each emblazoned with the image of the applicant revealing one of his particular skills (skateboarder, chef, guitarist).

- A personalized scrum board festooned with sticky notes showing the tasks, "in-progress" projects, and goals of 15 years, from learning Spanish to earning a patent.

- Postcards from all the locations an international applicant had lived, with descriptive text inserted on the back of each card and the whole series artfully bound together into a booklet.

- An Excel spreadsheet that carried the reader through a multiple-choice compatibility test with the applicant (and allowing the admissions committee to score their results: "WOW! We are exactly alike!").

If you decide these inventively visual approaches just won't work for you, there is still significant room for creativity using the 500-word essay format. Aside from the photo collage approach, applicants have submitted:

- A self-penned article from the applicant's school newspaper in which he decried classmates' obsession with business school admission. The text accompanying the submission cleverly elaborated on the theme of "maturation."

- An autobiographical essay illustrated by multicolor comic-book cells created by the applicant himself, and introduced by an anecdote about his childhood love of comics and books. (See sample essay on p. 136.)

Text-based essays without visuals can also be very effective, whether it's a poem (only if poetry is important to you), a eulogy, a (brief) chapter in your autobiography (but don't just drop in your Booth PowerPoint or Cornell "Life Story" essays here), an imagined media interview with you once you're successful, a vivid description of a typical day, and so on. Stern will probably have seen many of these before, but it's always the execution, personality, and honesty that make a creative essay work—the metaphor, idea, or framework is just the starting point. If your description of yourself sparkles with personality and joie de vivre and the stories you focus on show you've led an interesting life, the admissions committee will forgive you for not writing it in crayon or iambic pentameter.

In 2010, Stern expanded the range of possible submissions it would entertain to include multimedia essays (it had previously nixed anything that had to be "viewed or played electronically"). The inspiration for that decision was the adoption of digital and multimedia essay formats by schools like Chicago, UCLA, and Notre Dame, which we discuss next.

PowerPoint or Slide Essays

Chicago and Notre Dame's "slide presentation" essays are not really refinements of Stern's "(almost) anything goes" approach in that they curtail rather than expand the potential range of creative responses. Despite both schools' openness to PDF submissions, PowerPoint has quickly established itself as the standard format, and before you could say "spontaneity be damned," a de facto "best practice" emerged: applicants began using each slide to capture a different aspect of their profile (professional on one slide, community on another, and so on), with some content-strapped applicants using the first slide as a "cover slide" that introduces the set.

Some applicants thrived within these constraints; some reverted to clichés: timelines, bar charts graphing applicants' personal "return on assets," and company logos and generic clip art proliferated. Some ideas mercifully failed altogether, such as submitting four slides completely devoid of visuals and reiterating information readily available elsewhere in their application.

PowerPoint Essay Ideas

■ *Shoes:* Slides featuring images of shoes: high heels representing the applicant's ambitious career goals; flip-flops to capture her down-to-earth nature; Chinese slippers reflecting her passion for travel.

■ *Story of passions:* Slides showing the applicant's Radio Flyer wagon, from which he used to sell watercolor paints door to door, his grandfather who inspired his interest in finance by helping him buy Marvel Comics stock, and an image of a world map with pushpins indicating the places the applicant had traveled.

■ *Furniture entrepreneur:* The first slide showing a screenshot of the homepage of the applicant's future furniture business, followed by a slide showing all the challenges the business faces, next a slide describing his future entrepreneurship goals, and ending with a slide of longer-term goals, from earning an MBA and starting a family to launching another business.

■ *Dictionary.com:* A screenshot of the dictionary.com home page, showing the applicant's name as the search term. The following slides show the five resulting definitions, including "An engineer who works 107 hours in a week to meet a tight deadline"; "One who strives to master the field of culinary art"; "One who shotguns a beer in three seconds and is fond of drinking wine."

■ *Travel brochure:* All four slides re-create a professionally designed tour brochure, with the applicant's life rather than a destination as the subject. Tour tips include: "Hikes and tours involve an upward career trajectory. Please come prepared to tackle challenging elevations."

What the Schools Say

To me this is just four pieces of blank paper. You do what you want. It can be a presentation. It can be poetry. It can be anything. … You can tell when someone figures out how to work with the ambiguity and really embraces that, rather than saying, "I'm going to play it safe and regurgitate what is in my application already."

—ROSEMARIE MARTINELLI, UNIVERSITY OF CHICAGO

The best "slideware" essays are those that focus on some distinctive aspect of the applicant's life not discussed elsewhere, and then find some creative (as opposed to gimmicky) way to link each slide through a governing metaphor (as Sergei does with his "Top Secret" conceit in the PowerPoint sample on p. 139). A pronounced emphasis on images, with text used primarily for page titles and captions, and an ability to create a sense of an unfolding visual story from slide to slide also work well. Be strategic. Since PowerPoint slides can be decisive in close-call cases between similar applicants, use them to work against type:

■ If your career is or will be in finance, steer clear of charts, text, and timelines showing career progression (let all your IB competitors work that cliché).

■ If your career is or will be in marketing, avoid the "I'm a brand" gymnastics that your rivals will trot out. Focus instead on some substantive hobby or activity (perhaps one that bolsters the analytical, quantitative, or leadership parts of your profile).

As with Stern's creative essay, capturing who you are and standing out from the pack will always trump unimaginative content, no matter how polished and gussied up that content is. One applicant's PowerPoint essays featured nothing but book covers (including a cheeky *Multiorgasmic Man*) and ended with a slide of an empty bookshelf, captioned with, you guessed it, "The Future." Though this essay failed to show a single photo of the client and clearly did not take much effort or creativity, it accomplished what ultimately matters more: (1) it captured who the applicant was, and (2) it differentiated him through a unique approach. Chicago admitted him.

Don't get so caught up in finding snazzy visuals or devising a creative metaphor to unify your essay that you forget the essay's purpose: to introduce yourself truthfully to the school and your classmates.

Multimedia Essays

The ultimate twist on the creative essay is the multimedia essay, which has evolved from UCLA's one-minute audio essay (with a 250-word text-based option for those "unable" to go digital) to Anderson's current multiple-choice, multimedia invitation to "respond to the question by recording an audio or video response (of no more than 1–2 minutes)."

Although the potential prep time required for a one- to –two-minute audio or video essay makes the PowerPoint format seem like a walk in the park, UCLA's multimedia format has proved popular, with some 70 percent of applicants choosing the video or audio versions over the text-only versions (indeed, Anderson claims that the new format came at applicants' request).

The potential advantages of videos to schools are obvious: in addition to gauging the same skills—ability to be introspective and to communicate—that the traditional written essay measures, the video also gives schools insights into "applicant personality, sense of humor, intonation, verbal skills," according to Anderson admissions dean Mae Jennifer Shores. Call it an interview before the ultimate official interview. UCLA audiovisual essays have employed a variety of production approaches, themes, and content:

- One applicant employed a soundtrack of music and battlefield sounds to describe his entrepreneurial resourcefulness in gaining critical intelligence from Iraqi civilians while serving as an Army Ranger.

- An Asian applicant overcame a strong accent through a smiling and poised self-presentation and the sophisticated use of establishing and face-the-camera narration shots, professional scene transitions (cross-fades, iris wipes, etc.), embedded live-action video, and clever zooming and panning techniques over still photographs of his extracurricular passions.

- An avid golfer described how he recovered from a triple-surgery shoulder dislocation to resume his beloved pastime, deftly drawing on still-shots of his shoulder X-rays and action shots showing the applicant in physical therapy and sinking putts on the fairway.

Purely audio essays (featured on UCLA Anderson's Web site and YouTube) have taken the following creative forms:

- A former bassist for a California punk band responded to UCLA's "surprise" prompt with a relaxed and bemused narrative about his rock star days ("that's right, a *punk* band") and a brief snippet of his greatest hit.

- An Asian analyst who moonlighted as a break dancer used a hip-hop soundtrack to unfurl an essay highlighting not only his artistic side but his leadership (he led his college's dance group) and social impact (his dance group offers community outreach classes).

- An urban professional revealed his inner country boy and guilty love of rodeos and country music with a well-written piece about a childhood spent "scratching my showpigs' bellies and manicuring hooves" at the county fair. A tour de force.

- A former comedienne who performed on late-night talk shows, taught improv comedy, and produced shows in Hollywood deftly connected the "make people feel good" impulse behind her comedy career to her current career in the nonprofit space.

- An editor for a book publisher explained how she was approached by agents for a book deal (*I Am Neurotic*) when she started a blog featuring peoples' most interesting neuroses.

Some of UCLA's multimedia essays are quite polished and professional; others are decidedly folksy and unrefined. But the ones that work rarely do so because of their sophisticated presentation. Rather, they are effective because the applicants (1) project themselves in an authentic, relaxed, engaging, and even humorous manner and (2) focus on material that genuinely matters to them and reflects a significant involvement in their lives (the more off the beaten path, the better). If your audiovisual essay can manage these two, your production polish or lack of it won't matter a whit.

That said, multimedia essays will require equipment, preparation, and practice. As with an interview, you want confidence, poise, plenty of smiles, and eye contact. Since you have the added benefit of being able to edit, your finished product should be devoid of nervous twitches, pets leaping across the picture frame, car horns, and other distractions. On the other hand, don't practice it so much that you come across like a talking manikin.

As with a written essay, start with an outline and then develop it into a script. Once you have a solid idea of what you'll say (directly to the camera and in your voice-over narration), create a storyboard or visual map showing the content and timing of each scene. The elements that make written essays work will also serve your audiovisual essay well: providing context, using specific examples, and including reflective passages where you tell the viewer how you felt or what an example or event means to you, and so on. And, as with a written essay, edit, revise, edit, and edit again. The multimedia essays' strict time limits will force you to be concise, but you must balance your concision with the need to maintain a conversational spoken voice. Never speed up your narration just to fit the content into your time limit.

Once you know how many words you can comfortably and naturally speak in the one- or two-minute window given you, begin work on the visuals that will illustrate your essay. As a general rule, your essay should strike a balance between scenes in which you directly address the viewer and illustrative scenes where you narrate over the visuals of your story. Your goal will be to achieve a natural rhythm between scenes in which you directly address the camera and illustrative visuals.

You need not start the essay with an opening scene in which you address the camera, but you must introduce yourself and indicate your theme ("Though I am an IT consultant by day, even my friends are surprised to learn that I spend my off-hours high-wire walking between Chicago's skyscrapers"). Early on and then occasionally throughout the video, you should return to these direct-address scenes in which you face the camera. Why? Because the purpose of these essays is to introduce and personalize yourself to the admissions committee, so committee members must see you and be addressed by you. On some level, visual essays function as interviews in which the admissions committee can evaluate you for raw verbal skills, poise in spoken delivery and body language (eye contact, smiling, etc.), and general personableness.

Your transitions between direct-address scenes and illustrative visuals should be continual but measured, avoiding both frenetic cutting and long static scenes of inaction. If you integrate still images in your video, experiment with gradual pans or zooms within the image to create the impression of movement (à la documentarian Ken Burns). Effective videos continually work to hold the viewer's attention and sustain visual interest (as a rule of thumb, a one-minute video might entail 12 to 15 shots).

Only when you have fleshed out your video's basic rhythm of direct-address scenes and voice-over visuals should you concern yourself with snazzy video techniques like fades or wipes for transitions, pans and zooms for still images, and so on. And don't try to tackle all this alone. Ask people who know you to evaluate whether your script captures you well and to help you with the actual filming. This is, like it or not, a major undertaking.

What the Schools Say

A lot of business schools have concerns about authenticity. [Our multimedia essay] was a way to get a more authentic view of a candidate.

—Mae Jennifer Shores, UCLA Anderson

CREATIVE, POWERPOINT, AND MULTIMEDIA ESSAYS: WHAT *NOT* TO DO

1. Feel obliged to submit a nonwritten essay if you feel you can't create a good one. Text-based essays that are straight from the heart, well-written, and creatively framed/presented can still equal or surpass most visual essays in effectiveness.

2. Forget that visual essays are a hybrid form of essay-interview: your face and/or voice will be front and center, so if you're bashful or disinclined to smile when a camera is pointed at you, you won't have written words to hide behind.

3. Try to oversell your devotion to the school. Avoid devoting an entire PowerPoint slide to Chicago's lovely Hyde Park campus or photos of its brilliant faculty. Eschew video essays in which you do cartwheels in UCLA's Marion Anderson Courtyard or get interviewed by your best friend dressed as a Bruin.

4. Employ clichéd or goofy ideas: PowerPoint essays that use bar graphs or video essays in which you become a superhero or perform stupid pet tricks for the admissions committee.

5. Forget that creative and visual essays live or die to the extent that they (1) communicate some passion or experience that's deeply important to you and (2) show you to be an engaging, world-directed, socially skilled achiever. Everything else is just smoke and mirrors.

NOBODY'S PERFECT: FAILURE/MISTAKE ESSAYS

No one likes to fail—least of all achievers with the smarts and drive to aim for the best business schools. For you, the only thing worse than failing might be having to admit mistakes to complete strangers whose admissions verdict can decide your professional future! Yet however counterintuitive it seems, an increasing number of business schools expect you to be able to admit, analyze, and learn from a real blunder.

Your ability to admit and coolly dissect a personal foul-up evinces maturity and humility, qualities that business schools in our scandal-plagued era value dearly. Conversely, pretending you can outfox the admissions committee by slipping them a success wrapped up as a failure immediately announces immaturity—in (1) trying to pretend you've never failed and (2) thinking you can hoodwink admissions officers who've seen it all.

Moreover, failures are classic obstacles, and how you overcome difficulty says a lot about your character, resilience, and willingness to change in response to the feedback reality gives you (as we'll see in the next section of this chapter). Like anyone, admissions officers also love to hear "come-from-behind" tales in which the hero (you) overcomes her tragic flaw to redeem herself in the closing minutes. *Failure → understanding → redemption* is a traditional pattern in all storytelling; use it in this essay to rouse the reader's interest and sympathy.

Failure also often says good things about those who strive for the brass ring but miss. Ambition, boldness, innovation—these and other positive traits usually cling to those who "dare mighty things." Finally, responding to the failure question honestly will pay dividends all across your application. Once the schools see that you've been aboveboard about your failures, they'll be much more inclined to take your word about your successes.

What Schools Ask

- "What have you learned from a mistake?" (Harvard)

- "Describe a failure that you have experienced. What role did you play, and what did you learn about yourself?" (Wharton)

- "Describe a time when you wish you could have retracted something you said or did. When did you realize your mistake and how did you handle the situation?" (Chicago)

Though "mistake" and "failure" are unambiguous terms (they don't mean "setback" or "disappointment," for example) many applicants react to them like cornered ferrets. Defensively denying that they could be anything less than flawless, they narrate "failures" that are really 80 percent successes, team failures in which they played a marginal role, or moments of adversity in which their only lapse was being victimized by fate. Think again. *Failure* means you personally were to blame; *setback* only means things didn't turn out as you wished. Even though Wharton's question does not require the failure to be yours (it could be your team's), looking for examples that allow you to shift the blame really defeats the nonsinister purpose of these essay questions.

Frustrated by the evasions such straightforward failure questions elicit, some schools have softened the question to situations where you disappointed your standards as in INSEAD's "Describe a situation taken from school, business, civil, or military life, where you did not meet your personal objectives, and discuss briefly the effect." But the intent remains the same: they want a screwup. Always read carefully to determine whether the question allows you to draw from failures in any part of your life or only from your professional or academic life.

When brainstorming for the "perfect" failure story, remember that an *ideal* example will meet four criteria:

■ It was clearly your fault because you, for example, let someone down, conspicuously and unexpectedly failed to achieve a reasonable target, or misread or misreacted to a situation.

■ It sheds light on an activity or experience not treated elsewhere in your application.

■ It is no more than five years old but is not so recent that you haven't yet applied the lessons it taught you.

■ It reflects some positive aspect of your personality, such as initiative.

These aren't conditions that all effective examples will meet, of course, but they are an ideal to shoot for. Popular topics for failure essays include failed start-ups, being laid off, academic reversals, athletic failures, and rookie mistakes at work. But the best failures are often doozies of misadventure for the very reason that exceptional individuals often attempt things that others avoid, or they rise to positions where their mistakes are magnified by the scope of their responsibility. If you have experienced a truly distinctive, outsized failure, this may be just what the adcom ordered. After all, if you must come clean about a real failure, there's something to be said for failing big (provided your failure didn't bring down the entire subprime mortgage market). So don't give them some milquetoast peccadillo—choose a blunder that only a big risk-taker swinging for the fences could manage.

Case Study: The Blunder of a Lifetime

Taylor had always been a good kid—maybe too good. An outstanding student, athlete, and volunteer, when I met him Taylor was building a quietly impressive career as a strategy staffer at a Fortune 100 firm. But he had a dark secret. In college, his unobtrusive ability to get along with just about everyone had almost done him in. Accompanying two friends home from a party one night, Taylor watched in astonishment as they began systematically vandalizing campus property, causing thousands of dollars in damage in a matter of minutes. Taylor never physically intervened to stop them or even attempted to flee, and when his friends later told him to stay quiet he submissively acquiesced. Even when campus security interrogated him, Taylor loyally clammed up. Only when witnesses finally came forward and fingered Taylor and his friends did he finally admit his involvement.

Taylor's months of silent loyalty cost him a suspension and almost a felony charge. Fortunately, he learned his lesson, as he proved when he later rebuffed a senior colleague who ordered him to doctor data. Most applicants lack failure stories this lurid and egregious. By candidly sharing it, his takeaways, and his redemption with Wharton's admissions committee, Taylor earned himself an acceptance call.

Structure

Since schools ask you to "describe a failure," many applicants mistakenly burn through three-quarters of the essay's prescribed length detailing the ins and outs of their fiasco. The failure itself, however, is perhaps the least important section of the essay. At least as critical are your analysis of the failure, the lessons it taught you, and the ways you applied those lessons later on.

Context and Failure Statement

The first section of the essay, the context and failure statement, should give just enough information to pique the reader's interest and clarify that your failure was a real one, was indeed your fault, and had specific consequences. Since being able to stand up and admit failure is a key reason why schools pose this topic, your statement of failure should be unambiguous. You blew it.

But the failure statement should also be short and sweet. Avoid trying to wring pity from the admissions officers, but also stay away from orgies of self-recrimination. As we noted in Chapter 1, the tone of your entire application should be positive; so keep this part of the essay factual, mature, and above all brief.

Analysis

The analysis section of the failure essay exists only to demonstrate that you have the self-awareness and analytical skills to dissect the causes of your failure. Don't use this brief section to try to shift the blame to someone else, rationalize your failure away, or strain toward a happy ending. Focus objectively and succinctly on what you did wrong and why. The only place for emotional expression in this essay is in stating your deep regret for the negative impact of your failure on *others.* No whining or wheedling.

Lessons

If you've played your cards right you'll have reached the essay's halfway point (or thereabouts) with the pungent details of your blunder safely behind you and plenty of room still remaining for the essay's positive payoff: what your failure taught you. Aim for multiple takeaways to show how conscientiously and exhaustively you examined this "teachable moment" to identify where you went wrong and how. Generally, the greater the magnitude of your initial failure, the more lessons you should be able to glean from it. Avoid banal, generalized lessons like, "I learned that leadership means taking responsibility for your mistakes." This should be implicit in the much more specific and personalized lessons you draw.

Much better are lessons like failing to turn to others for help; failing to listen; mishandling stress, conflict, or team dynamics; delaying a decision until you had more data; or failing to correlate ideal objectives with hard realities. What steps did you take to ensure that you will not have to learn these specific lessons again?

If the lesson you learned was that you lacked sufficient self-knowledge about your skills, strengths, or career goals, you can actually leverage your failure to advance your case for needing an MBA.

Lessons Applied

If your failure has a happy ending, it should come in the essay's last section, where you show yourself redeeming your earlier lapse. This part of the essay answers the essay's implicit questions: What do you proactively do after you've realized you failed? What corrective actions do you take? Brainstorm for a specific subsequent occasion when you encountered circumstances similar to those of your failure but in which you responded differently and effectively because of the lessons your failure taught you.

FAILURE/MISTAKE ESSAYS: WHAT *NOT* TO DO

1. Write about a failure that isn't one. To say you "failed" because INSEAD dinged your application last fall or because you once reduced costs by 15 percent instead of the 25 percent you intended is to misunderstand what schools mean by *failure.*

2. Describe a trivial failure. Recounting the time your fraternity's barbecue imploded may shed light on your skills as an organizer (or cook), but it doesn't meet the significance level business schools expect.

3. Reveal a failure that exposes inexcusable flaws in your character. Getting fired for sexual harassment or committing a hate crime are true failures, no doubt, but they're far too egregious for schools to overlook.

4. Write too much about the failure itself. If you overload your essay with every gory detail of your lapse, you won't have enough space for the section that can redeem you—the lessons learned and applied.

5. Choose a failure that's more than, say, five years old or whose subject matter is otherwise inappropriate. Failing to make your high school's chess club may well have scarred you, but its antiquity may cause the schools to assume that you're evading the question. Similarly, failed relationships are too personal and common.

THE EVOLVING YOU: GROWTH, CHALLENGE, AND LEARNING ESSAYS

- "Reflect on a time when you turned down an opportunity. What was the thought process behind your decision? Would you make the same decision today?" (Wharton)

- "Tell us about a time in your professional experience when you were frustrated or disappointed." (Harvard)

- "Discuss a time when you navigated a challenging experience in either a personal or professional relationship." (Wharton)

- "Master Classes are the epitome of bridging the gap between theory and practice at Columbia Business School. Please provide an example from your own life in which practical experience taught you more than theory alone." (Columbia)

- "Discuss the most difficult constructive criticism or feedback you have received. How did you address it? What have you learned from it?" (Dartmouth Tuck)

In a sense, growth and learning essays seek the same thing as failure or mistake essays but from a different angle: evidence that you have experienced challenge in your life and have the self-knowledge to analyze and grow from it. Rather than invite evasion and prevarication by asking you about a failure, these essay questions take a gentler, more positive approach to get at the same information: your ability to change once you realize things are not as they ought to be.

Where Tuck asks you about external feedback you received and responded to, Wharton's "opportunity" question asks about a decision you made and its ramifications in your life. And like Tuck's prompt, which cares less about the feedback than your reaction to it, Harvard's interest in your frustration or disappointment is limited: it's really after your response to it.

As a general rule, growth, challenge, or learning essays should have three sections. The first is the description of the context: the initiating "feedback" event itself or the moment when you received criticism (Tuck), realized you faced an opportunity or challenge (Wharton), experienced frustration or disappointment (Harvard), or learned that your "theory" (or starting assumption) was invalid (Columbia).

The second is the analysis: your personal acknowledgment of a growth opportunity—your frank, direct analysis and confirmation of your need to act on the feedback, reject the opportunity, respond positively to the disappointment or challenge, or revise your initial assumption or theory. This should be the essay's pivot point and most personal moment, where you set the describing and positioning aside and get real about your internal response to the self-learning moment.

The third section is your growth-in-action moment: the concrete steps you took to heed the criticism; build on or move past the disappointment, challenge, or rejected opportunity; or apply your newly revised "theory" in the real world.

Don't expect the power of the moment or the feedback to speak for itself. Admissions committees want you to walk them through the lessons and subsequent life changes. As much as possible, let the reader inside. Candidly describe your emotions in response to the event and your thought processes while coming to grips with it and moving on from it. A good growth or learning essay will convince the admissions committee that you are an evolving, self- and world-aware person rather than a superficial achievement engine perpetually cocked to fire.

SAMPLE ESSAYS

This section of sample essays contains fifteen examples: five self-revelation essays (written by applicants accepted by Harvard, Stanford, Wharton, Columbia, and Tuck), two self-evaluation essays (whose authors were admitted by Harvard and Kellogg), three creative or multimedia essays (from admitted applicants at NYU and Chicago), three failure examples (written by successful applicants at Harvard, Columbia, and Wharton), and two growth or challenge sample essays (whose authors were admitted by Columbia and Tuck).

Sample Self-Revelation Essay 1: Jack B.
(Admitted to Harvard Business School)

What do you wish the MBA Admissions Board had asked you?

"What does it means to be a Pinball Arbitrage Wizard?" [← *Enticingly offbeat lead grabs reader's interest by the lapels.*]

In one of my mother's first recordings of me as a child, I can be heard belting out The Who's "Pinball Wizard." I still have fond memories of pinball time I shared with my father at a local arcade. When my wife, Ellen, and I began dating, we would often cap a date with a few rounds of Earthshaker at the local Golfland. All these memories seemed threatened by the harsh reality of my accident, [← *Jack refers to a life-changing accident he describes in another Harvard essay.*] until Ellen suggested that we purchase an Earthshaker as a form of physical therapy. We enjoyed the game so much that a year later we added a second to our collection. By then, I had insinuated myself into the online pinball community, and learned how to repair machines, locate parts, and participate in auctions. Not content with simply battling my fellow collectors for machines at the monthly auction, I scoured the globe via the Internet for deals. Finding two in New Zealand, I bought them for $1500 and sold them three months later for over $3700. Encouraged, I began my search for larger quantities. [← *Jack's obvious passion for his unusual hobby sends just the right message to admissions readers.*]

I focused on Europe, where pinball machines are not considered collectibles. Using a crude, but effective, text translator, I established relationships with three German suppliers who were willing to send twenty-foot cargo containers to the United States. [← *Jack's resourcefulness and thoroughness are obvious, but his essay's insights into an industry the adcoms are unlikely to know also win him points→*] In exchange for strategic benefits (free circuit-board repair, a secure warehouse, discount parts), I partnered with a local amusement game company and agreed to split each container load and cost. I handled all aspects of the transaction, and negotiated the machine assortment, price, shipping, and wire transfer of funds. Soon, we were receiving a container every three months, and I couldn't refurbish the games fast enough to meet demand! On an average transaction, I would more than double my $15,000 investment. [← *Not just an obsessed hobbyist, Jack's a good businessman as well.*]

In 2001, my pinball importing adventure came to an end. Competition had driven prices up, and dwindling supply only yielded battered, overplayed machines. It was an exciting time while it lasted, and it taught me valuable lessons about enterprise, building a business, and arbitrage. Most of all, having my pick from each shipment helped me expand my collection, which I am proud to say now stands at ten of the most sought-after machines ever made. Now, if I can just figure out how to apply the principles of arbitrage to Texas Hold'em Poker! *[←The closing line sustains the engaging and humorous tone that distinguishes the entire essay.]*

Sample Self-Revelation Essay 2: Lena W. (Admitted to Stanford GSB)

What matters most to you, and why?

Color: A phenomenon of light that enables one to differentiate otherwise identical objects. (Merriam-Webster's). The most important thing for me is to find in every person their color, to help develop that color to its full luminosity. *[←The dictionary definition introduction is not original, but where Lena starts to go with it pulls the reader in.]*

My adopted sister, Hannah, three years younger than me, first opened my eyes to color in this context. In 2000, my parents volunteered in Zambia and, becoming her guardians, helped her to start a new life in Germany. German society, however, turned a cold shoulder to Hannah. I was appalled to find that classmates teased her, and parents of her friends forbade their children from hanging around Hannah because she came from a poor country and could not speak German. She eventually quit school and fell into despair. *[The second paragraph establishes Lena's distinctive cultural background, and her protectiveness of her adopted sister humanizes her for the admissions committee.]*

Our family cherished Hannah, but I was convinced that she could not turn around unless she cherished herself first, by understanding her core value— she needed to find her own color. *[←Repeats color theme to sustain essay's unity.]* One day when traveling to Dresden, I noticed Hannah latched onto my camera. For the rest of the day Hannah continuously shot pictures of Turkish Gastarbeiter, whom German society also discriminates against. I noticed the glow in Hannah's pictures, which showed hurting people in a warm light. This otherwise nearly suicidal girl found her purpose behind the lens of a camera.

I scrounged my money together and bought Hannah a used Leica. Deeply touched by Hannah's growing self-confidence through photography, I committed myself to showing her works to her classmates and their parents to banish their prejudice. I posted her works in subway stations and on high school homepages. In 2005, I was thrilled when Hannah was awarded the Kulturrat (German Cultural Council) Award in a national cultural contest for students, becoming the pride of our town. She is currently working as a photographer in an artist-in-residence program in Istanbul.

[Lena's efforts for her sister ensure the reader's empathetic identification with her unfolding story.]

What would have happened to Hannah had I not bought her that camera eight years ago? My experience with her changed my understanding of myself, making me realize I can make a difference in another person's life. The fulfillment I discovered influenced me to continue to discover colors in diverse ways, including mine. *[←The essay's pivot: repeats color theme to show that the lesson Lena learned in helping change her sister's life changed her own as well.]*

My situation resembled Hannah's, when before college parents, teachers, and friends asked me, "Do you really plan to give up Technische Universität München after passing through the Abitur?" Through my eighteen years of life, I had thought of nothing but becoming an engineer, following my father, a celebrated inventor and entrepreneur. I wanted to be adored by my parents and was terrified that doing otherwise would disappoint them.

And yet as I helped Hannah find and inhabit her color, something in me started to change, to open. I shed my own prejudices about the marginalized in my society. And I looked at myself. I had learned in math class the hypothesis that elements in a set are all equal, and realized that our society does not mirror the ideals of mathematics' equality, with some living in discomfort.
I understood that my path was not engineering, but changing society through social work. *[←Business schools respond positively to candid and self-knowing admissions of one's capacity to change.]*

Finding is one thing; inhabiting my color was long and treacherous. *[←Lena's deft phrasing—"inhabiting my color"—shows a sense of writerly style that further individuates her essay.]* My gymnasium, renowned for sending students to technical universities, strongly resisted my transfer to liberal arts. It was uncomfortable for those around me, even my parents, to accept my leaving engineering. To apply for the social sciences, I studied sociology and science, and on my own studied economics, politics, and history, sleeping four hours a day, and even studying while eating. Despite no one supporting me, I believed in myself. I took the entrance exams, placing in the top 0.5%, and was accepted into Heidelberg University's Faculty of Economics and Social Sciences. I was the very first female student specializing in science at my gymnasium to enter Heidelberg's Economics and Social Sciences faculty. When these results were published, my parents hugged me tightly and congratulated me on my new path.

Looking back, I realize that changing programs was the first step towards illuminating my own color, enabling me to take the next steps with assurance.

Having learned the importance of eliminating fear and facing what I really want to be, I now consider it a mission to help others find their own colors. I have advised students facing such struggles at Heidelberg University's career placement center and supported McKinsey consultants by organizing a McKinsey careers conference. I will continuously commit myself to finding diamonds in muddy ground. *[←Lena's essay skillfully uses the color metaphor to trace her personal redirection and the expansion of her focus on personal change from her sister, to herself, to others in the wider world.]*

Sample Self-Revelation Essay 3: David B. (Admitted to Wharton)

Is there anything about your background or experience that you feel you have not had the opportunity to share with the Admissions Committee in your application? If yes, please explain.

Have you ever had a Greek child named after you? *[Leading the essay with question directed at the reader commands attention.]* I hadn't either, so at first I was overwhelmed by the honor that Stefano—my college roommate, best friend, and basically brother—extended to me in naming his child "Christos David Kounelis." How I, a 25-year-old American, managed to convince Stefano to break his family's age-old tradition and use my name rather than Stefano's father's as Christos's middle name is, even to me, a strange and fascinating story.

Stefano arrived early one morning in my freshman year after travelling all day from a small town in Southern Greece I'd never heard of. For the next six months, we shared a room the size of a shoe-box and didn't speak the same language. But quickly we found a common interest: The Jerry Springer Show. Then one night, Stefano's English clicked and I discovered that he's absolutely hilarious. I learned that he comes from a long line of aristocrats and resides in a large villa overlooking the Aegean Sea. So I obviously was ecstatic when he invited me to stay at his home, Amorgos, the next summer. *[Pithy details of dawning friendship ensure the reader's empathy and interest.]*

Amorgos is a true paradise. It's the sister Island of Naxos but much more authentic in that it's not flooded with tourists. When I first arrived there that summer, I was the classic disgusting American: baggy clothes, poor manners, and an impatient guzzler of frappé (Greeks savor them slowly). Despite my rough edges the town welcomed me warmly. Stefano introduced me to all his friends, who quickly became great friends of mine. The people of Amorgos were so wonderful I wanted to be a part of their world! So each summer for the past 10 years I've traveled to Amorgos, accumulating so many great experiences I could fill a book. For example, there's "To trelo dēpno" (the crazy dinner), a monthly ritual in which the guys have an evening of food and wine but no girlfriends, and fill the air with songs like "Stekoumeni pēsēni" (bottoms up). Or my hilarious lunches with Stefano's mother, who I incorrectly nicknamed "metera olis tis elladas" ("mother of all Greece"), who, hearing that I'm vegetarian, served me squid, clams, and prawns because they're clearly not meat! [←*David's cultural insights and obvious passion for Greece lift this paragraph above the ordinary.*]

These rich experiences made me feel part of Amorgos. In return for Amorgos's hospitality the least I could do was open my home to it. So each winter a different Amorgoan spends two months with me in America. Out of our friendship and mutual curiosity, we have created our own de facto exchange program.

I wish I could say I created a wonderful charity for orphaned Amorgoans or helped its poor fishermen improve their business skills, but it wouldn't be true. But what I have done on Amorgos is something I'm just as proud of. I've created a real Greek family for myself at whose center is my best friend—my "adelfós"—Stefano. When his first son was born Stefano wanted me to be the godfather, but since I live too far away he decided to break a tradition and make Christos's middle name "David" rather than Nikos, after Stefano's dad. It's an honor I'm a little embarrassed about, because I can never be worthy, but it also makes me extremely proud. [←*Touching ending ends the essay on warm "human interest" note: readers feel they know David as a person now.*]

Sample Self-Revelation Essay 4: Leopoldo V. (Admitted to Columbia Business School)

Is there any further information that you wish to provide to the Admissions Committee?

While I am very proud of my academic career and personal growth, I grant that my background is not typical. I am using this essay to address any question marks that my academic and personal history may raise. [*Though Leopoldo used this self-revelation story for Columbia's optional essay, it was his core personal story that appeared in one form or another in every application he submitted (he also gained admission to Wharton.)*]

Growing up in Tallahassee, Florida, I lived in daily fear of my alcoholic and abusive father. As the only son, I protected my mother and two sisters from my father's rage by taking the brunt of his anger on myself. This painful environment led to a struggle with depression that evolved, during my early teens, into alcohol and marijuana use as a form of escape. The cliché about liquor and pot leading to harder substances is true, and by my sophomore year in high school I was rarely attending class. My only priorities were drugs, alcohol, and the punk rock music that gave me a way of understanding my life. [*Gripping story holds reader's interest. How will this tragedy turn out?*]

After countless fights with my family I eventually left home at the age of 16. It was more than two years before I saw any family member again. While most kids my age were taking Advanced Placement classes and dreaming of admission to prestigious universities, I was living on friends' couches with no possessions but my skateboard and the contents of my backpack. With no financial support, I simply struggled to survive and attended high school only occasionally, more to see friends than to attend class. If not for the grace and support of the Assistant Principal, Mark Posner, I am certain I would not have graduated. *[This third paragraph takes Leopoldo's tale to new lows, bringing us to the pivot point.→]*

It was shortly after I finished high school and before my 19th birthday that I realized the pain I was running from was nothing compared to the pain my own actions were creating in my life. I could no longer blame my past for what I had become. In friends dying, going to jail, or simply wasting away, I saw my own future. Depressed and alone, I realized I had only two choices: continue on my path of self-destruction, or change everything and move in a direction determined not by my past experiences, but by my potential and my will. *[←Dramatic wording seems fully earned; Leopoldo's brave epiphany locks in reader's empathy.]*

Having encountered Alcoholics Anonymous at various points in my life, I recalled the serene confidence of its members. With nowhere else to turn and desperate for a chance at life, I took the step that forever changed my world. At my first A.A. meeting I met my sponsor, Andy Molitor, though we all called him "Tony Soprano." A teacher who had lost his home, job, and family to alcoholism, Andy, 52, had been sober for more than 20 years through A.A. when I met him. My only friend during my first year of A.A., Andy encouraged me to remove myself from my destructive friends (many of whom I had grown up with) and literally start from scratch. *[←Introduction of Andy brings believably human mentor-savior character into Leopoldo's story.]*

Andy taught me how to live, how to follow my dreams, how to work hard and leave the rest to faith, but most importantly how my recovery would depend on giving selflessly of myself to my A.A. peers. Andy encouraged me to study music at Tallahassee Community College (TCC), the only school open to me given my academic record, and walked with me every step of the way as I rebuilt my life.

Though my break with my old life was clean and total, my new—real—life was anything but easy. Still living away from my family, I worked as a waiter (rising to assistant manager) and a door-to-door home security salesman to support myself and to pay for TCC. School, something that had never been my focus, was incredibly challenging given my high school experience. I spent countless hours at the library, met with professors every chance I could, and took remedial math and English classes for no credit simply to build my knowledge. In short, I persevered with a determination that overwhelmed any skill I may have lacked.

Thus it was that at the age of 22, after taking three years to complete community college, I was accepted at Duke University. Since then, my life has continued to be an adventure into a world I nearly missed. I apply to Columbia Business School having learned that it is only through service to others and personal challenge that I can find my deepest potential.
[Leopoldo's skillful telling of his harrowing tale transforms his journey into a powerful asset that will color the admissions committee's entire evaluation of his application.]

Sample Self-Revelation Essay 5: Lynn S. (Admitted to Dartmouth Tuck)

Tuck seeks candidates of various backgrounds who can bring new perspectives to our community. How will your unique personal history, values, and/or life experiences contribute to the culture at Tuck?

Growing up, my family devoted much of our time together to working in our garden and orchards. I remember sunburns and chapped hands after weekends of helping my parents pull weeds, prune trees, remodel our house, and repair our old car. No matter how intimidating a project may have been—from remodeling a kitchen to taking apart an engine—I learned to finish it through sheer determination, sometimes with varied results (I recall nearly getting electrocuted while re-wiring the living room). I appreciated the sense of ability and self-sufficiency my family's work ethic bestowed, and I believe it enabled me to create opportunities where others might have found the outlook uninspiring.

Principled, strictly religious, and thoroughly pragmatic, my parents had a self-sufficient bent, supporting my five younger siblings and me on limited means and avoiding what they considered to be a materialistic American lifestyle. They emphasized pride in manual labor and disdained valuable possessions, even vacations. They taught me not only a tough work ethic, but also a sense of personal responsibility for my future that continues to motivate me to make the most of every situation. *[Lynn effectively establishes the values that defined her childhood and adult self.]*

Unwilling to send my four sisters, brother, and me to the troubled public schools in our Sacramento neighborhood and unable to afford private education, my parents insisted on teaching us themselves. They valued learning—ours was a home of reading, music, and political debate—but they rejected the formal educational system.

Although mostly self-directed, my education was nevertheless rigorous and included parochial coursework and classical music, philosophy, and literature. This unique arrangement, and the fact that we had to pursue extracurricular activities on our own initiative, inspired a sense of self-sufficiency. My education became my own responsibility.

Aware of my family's financial circumstances, I also assumed responsibility for my own expenses, other than food and housing, from a young age. I began working for myself at age 12, teaching a total of fourteen piano students before I took on a second job at age 16. Financially independent by 17, I had four jobs and was working 70–80 hours per week. Even then, I knew that the more I worked, the more tangible my goals would become. [*←Lynn's self-education and resourceful work ethic send very strong signals to the admissions reader.*]

During college, I often began work at 4:30 am managing a coffee shop, racing from there to an internship before busing tables at night. During school breaks, I worked seventy hours per week at construction and service jobs; on weekends, I often returned to Sacramento to work on a day-labor crew. Work—however dirty, difficult, and exhausting—was the mechanism available to me to achieve my dreams of college and career. Managing this schedule to self-fund school was my decisive entrepreneurial experience, and I was proud to be defining my own destiny.

As the first in my family to pursue a four-year degree, I faced resistance from my parents despite my nearly perfect grades in high school. For financial reasons, my parents urged me to attend junior college while working full-time, and although I was disappointed, I focused single-mindedly on making the most of these circumstances.

While working 40 hour weeks, I became a TA for the Economics Department chair, obtained a research internship, and was named Economics Student of the Year at Sierra College. Ultimately, my dedication yielded an amazing opportunity: an offer of admission to UC Berkeley. [*←A theme of bootstrapping determination is continually reinforced.*]

At Berkeley, I thrived in economics and French classes, sorority leadership, and even an unpaid investment banking internship in the evenings, all while working odd jobs like scrubbing the sorority house's kitchen at 5:00 am each morning to pay for books. I authored an econometrics honors thesis, and at graduation, I was one of several honors candidates nominated for class speaker. Even more rewarding than I had anticipated, my experience at Berkeley was the realization, through determination, of my long-held ambitions. This accomplishment deepened my confidence in my potential.

[*Transition to surfing is a bit abrupt, but Lynn has established her bona fides in the preceding paragraphs; all she needs now is to coast home to the close.→*] Feeling the spray of icy water off Marin's coast, I now patiently scan the horizon for the next perfect, glassy wave and recall the many times I've searched for opportunities in challenging circumstances. To me, optimism—like surfing—is the ability to both visualize opportunity and take the initiative to make the most of it, and I think that this optimistic determination and appreciation for every opportunity will contribute to the collaborative culture of the Tuck program. I believe that my personal values of personal excellence and integrity will reinforce the values of the Tuck community. More than simply a business school, Tuck presents the experience that I believe will position me to pursue my lifelong ambitions.

Sample Self-Evaluation Essay 1: Hla T. (Admitted to Kellogg)

You have been selected as a member of the Kellogg Admissions Committee. Please provide a brief evaluative assessment of your file.

In reviewing Hla T.'s file, what immediately jumps out is her dramatic and powerful personal story, from her family's harrowing escape from Myanmar to her ability to overcome poverty and her mother's abandonment to achieve academic and professional success. Hla's remarkable story says much about her character that's relevant to our decision today. Her commitment to family and personal integrity, her unfailing dedication and sense of responsibility, and her volunteer contributions all make her an exceptional fit for Kellogg's program. Which is why I believe Hla is applying to Kellogg: our commitment to the Kellogg "family" mirrors the values that Hla has lived her whole life. *[Hla is smart to lead with her childhood refugee story, which is vividly detailed in another of her essays: it's one of her key assets.]*

To understand Hla's academic potential, it's important to see the full context. Hla overcame the disadvantages of attending a public high school with a 13% drop-out rate, frequent race riots and school fights, and the near total indifference of students and teachers to gain admission to Purdue University. Her transcript there shows a strong GPA of 3.34, with an upward trend as Hla switched from Pre-Med to the College of Business. Within the Business School, Hla demonstrated strong performance in both quantitative and analytical courses and made the Dean's Honor List for five out of her seven semesters, all while working 20 plus hours a week. Her undergraduate record indicates that Hla can handle Kellogg's academic challenge.

Hla's GMAT scores are lower than our average, though not by a large margin. In her last GMAT exam her qualitative percentile rose to a very strong 96 and her quantitative to an improved 57. Is Hla's Quant score indicative of her analytical abilities? I don't believe so. First, her undergraduate transcript reveals that while she did not excel in Pre-Med Calculus, she showed great improvement in the Business School's calculus course and excelled in statistics and programming. Second, her professional experiences as a programmer and performance tester have required significant quantitative abilities, such as developing mathematical models to predict server capacity. Moreover, as Hla has helped implement Finance packages she has had to design test data to simulate and evaluate Accounts Payables, Accounts Receivables, General Ledger, and their applicable charges. Third, Hla's SAT score was 1050, yet she was top 15% in her high school and thrived at Notre Dame, where the average SAT is 1250.

This, together with her GMAT score, suggests that Hla may be the kind of candidate whose performance on standardized tests does not reflect her actual abilities. *[Well-handled discussion of GMAT issue; Hla doesn't pretend it away or argue defensively.]*

In her work experience Hla has done exceedingly well in IT consulting for one of the top consulting firms. From her first days as Systems Analyst, Hla was on an accelerated promotion path, gaining three levels in her four years with A.T. Kearney Consulting. The variety of roles she's been given indicates the confidence that others placed in her ability to manage many aspects of a systems implementation, from analysis and design to development and testing. She was rated in the top two performance brackets every annual review (placing her in the top 15% of her peer group), and after just five years she was assigned a management role building a development team from scratch and managing the application development of over 300 development objects and over 18 developers, a role usually assigned to someone with over seven years of experience. Hla's transition from IT consulting to the educational sector at the UC Berkeley fits into her overall theme of redefining herself, and though she's only been there three months she appears to be making the same kind of unusual impact she made at Kearney. Hla's career profile is clearly an impressive, atypical one. *[←Hla must be careful not to rehash too much of the career progress section from her Kellogg goals essay.]*

Hla's desire to meld her diverse work experience in finance, manufacturing, and customer relationship IT implementations into a career as a product manager for an emerging-markets-focused consumer goods company makes logical sense and is attainable with a Kellogg MBA. Her long-term product development entrepreneurial goal stems naturally from her lifelong interest in consumer products. To make this kind of career transition, however, Hla clearly needs a foundation in marketing, operations, and entrepreneurship, and few schools are as strong in these areas as Kellogg. *[←Again, some of this material might best be presented in the goals essay.]* In addition, her international background and her desire to support humane investment in third-world countries will make her a strong candidate for the Global Management Initiative where Hla would not only provide insight into the impacts of foreign investment in Southeast Asia but would also contribute as a lead for the GMI: Vietnam initiative. Hla's goals will make her a valued asset in the Kellogg Social Impact Club whose Net Impact network and Innovating Social Change Forum will enable her to network with others who are also intent on promoting socially responsible business.

Hla's five years as a "road warrior" for Kearney and her unusual pressure to support her family (which it's possible to view as her "community service") explains why her involvement in community activities is not as deep as we might like. We should note that while she was on the road six days out of the week, Hla remained involved by sponsoring local events such as Hope House and Toys for Tots while she was in Rockford, IL. She also maintained her involvement in Kearney volunteer activities such as "Impact Day: Century High School" and leading the Women's Initiative Education program. It is notable that as soon as Hla landed an "in-town" project in Altamont, California (90 miles from her home), she took the opportunity to get involved on a more hands-on and consistent basis. As a volunteer for Project Angel Food and a big sister for Christopher James (through Bay Area Big Brothers and Big Sisters), she demonstrated that she has the same dedication to community as to her personal and professional lives. I believe she will be a valuable asset to our Business With A Heart program. [←*Makes a strong case for her social impact credentials—she is a Kellogg "type."*]

Throughout Hla's essays runs the theme of commitment to family, which is precisely why she feels an affinity for Kellogg's family spirit. In reviewing her profile, I believe her unexceptional GMAT score is more than adequately countered by the positives of her undergraduate record, exceptional professional experience, and compelling personal story. Hla's commitment to her community and ability to transform challenges into positive influences reflects an open, empathetic person. Her dedication, maturity, and optimism will make her a valuable asset—even an inspiration—to her Kellogg family. Hla's contributions here should be as substantial as those she has already achieved in her professional career, her family, and her community. I strongly recommend "admit." [*Nothing flashy; balanced and meaty advocacy for her candidacy.*]

Sample Self-Evaluation Essay 2: Ian Y.
(Admitted to Harvard Business School)

Provide a candid assessment of your strengths and weaknesses.

Obviously, some would consider my physical disability to be a "weakness." I depend on an electric wheelchair for mobility and on my wife's help for transportation and personal care. However, in the workplace, a trackball and adjustable desk are the only adaptive devices I require. Sure, I have to wait in the hallway near the elevator during fire-drill evacuations—but this hardly poses a problem (unless there's a real fire!). Seriously, today I am very independent, as I'm sure my recommenders will attest. I have repeatedly demonstrated that my "weakness" is a source of personal strength. [*Blend of humor with candid honesty about his disability gets the reader in Ian's corner, enabling the reader to quickly dismiss concerns that his condition is a valid weakness.*]

Charismatic, effective leadership skills are a strength I rely on every day. As CEO of TextToys.com, for example, it was my job to establish contracts with publishers during the book industry's annual tradeshow. Due to time constraints, many of the meetings we scheduled with distributors overlapped. I developed a meticulous itinerary which allowed our six representatives and me to cover the twenty appointments in small teams, pairing team members to best combine their strengths. At each meeting, I introduced our team and described our company's edge as an online retailer: Web site innovation, warehousing capability, and strategic partnerships. After initiating our review of each publisher's capabilities, I passed the meeting on to the team members, and moved on to the next appointment.

Some distributors were biased against a Web-based retail presence. Undeterred, I distributed handouts detailing our strengths, and used a laptop to demonstrate a virtual shopping experience at our store. This tenacious, hands-on approach combined with our professionalism and dynamic presentation enabled us to close contracts with eight distributors, including two who had initially refused to entertain our proposals. Jumpstarting TextToys.com taught me how to delegate authority and manage groups under intensely stressful conditions, increasing my self-confidence as a leader. *[←Impressive example of Ian's entrepreneurial leadership.]*

My ability to communicate honestly with people is another of my strengths. I appreciate "straight talk" from others, and I always provide it in turn. This doesn't mean I'm curt, cold, or rude; I couch my message so it is received as genuine and direct, but encouraging. Many of the students I mentored at Brown expressed that they appreciated how honestly I warned them of their bad choices, because it showed I was sincerely interested in their success. I do the same when I counsel people with spinal cord injuries. They appreciate my honest answers and my ability to discuss painful topics. It shows I care enough to step outside the comfort zone of commonplace advice. *[Returning to his disability at the end brings closure to the essay.]*

Sample Creative Essay 1: Kamal R. (Admitted to NYU Stern)

Please describe yourself to your MBA classmates. You may use almost any method to convey your message (e.g. words, illustrations). Feel free to be creative.

My fascination with books—from comics to novels—began during the summer of my twelfth year. *[Kamal's self-created illustrations outdo the typical "photo collage" approach of many applicants and link directly to the love of books illustrated by his first paragraph.]* The only way to satisfy my insatiable thirst for reading material was to rent books from libraries, which were at least

3 miles from my house in Imbaba, Cairo. Since most of the comic series came out with new bi-weekly editions during the summer, the demand from teenagers like me was so great the libraries ran out. The summer I turned fifteen, I therefore decided to start my own summer lending library! Knowing my savings would not cover the 150 comic books I envisioned, I partnered with two friends, Tarek and Reyad, to open a library out of Tarek's home. During our first year we had about 40 members and money flowed in. But while Tarek and Reyad wanted to use profits on candy and fancy school accessories, I wanted to reinvest in the business. We parted ways, and I launched my own library out of my home. By promptly responding to waitlisted book demands, by giving comic hero stickers and posters to loyal members and free books on birthdays, and by minimizing defaults by rigorous follow-up, I attracted two-thirds of the original library's membership. By my sixteenth year I owned the only surviving library in Imbaba. *[Shrewdly links his personal experiences to NYU activities he'll get involved in.→]* I can't wait to share my love of knowledge and entrepreneurship with you all through NYU's Entrepreneurs' Exchange Club.

The Ragab family's textiles business, Al Nada Co., was the largest textiles distributor in Imbaba. During my final undergraduate year (2005), Egypt's new export-import policy opened our market to inexpensive Chinese imports, sending Al Nada's sales into a tailspin. Postponing my career plans, I used my technical skills to streamline Al Nada's manufacturing process, reducing unit manufacturing costs by 6%. Since our business was volume driven, this translated into huge savings. I then increased cash flow by 25% by identifying and selling non-performing assets. Moreover, by suggesting we use Al Nada's waste material and existing infrastructure to manufacture low-cost textile products, I compensated for the 35% profit loss of our primary product line. When Al Nada's recovery seemed secure, I moved to Canada for my master's. Eighteen months later, Al Nada was breaking even and today its subsidiary, Salah Salem Textiles, is Imbaba's largest distributor of raw cotton. *[Kamal's second anecdote deftly establishes his business credentials.]*

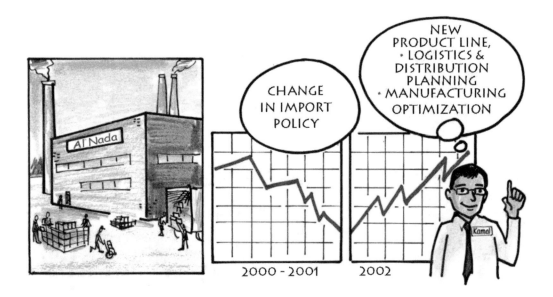

When my manager at DynaGenomics unexpectedly resigned in July 2008, I was shocked. Seeing an opportunity to help the company, the next day I proposed to my VP of Product Development that, though I was the group's youngest scientist, I had the background and the track record to assume leadership of DynaGenomics's three most-challenging drug development projects: for obesity, anxiety, and erectile dysfunction. When he agreed, I spent nine months driving a team of 12 cross-functional professionals in completing the product development, clinical trials, and regulatory framework for submission to Health Canada. By prioritizing resources, delegating tasks, and reinforcing team morale, I led all three products to very positive clinical trials and official filings at Health Canada. If they are approved in 2–3 years, these drugs will generate at least $200–250 million in annual revenues. For my efforts, I was given a 22% raise and appointed to lead the product development group's steering committee. I will bring this same initiative, creativity, and leadership to NYU's Part Time Leadership Forum and Stern Pharmaceutical Students Association. *[Though Kamal takes a risk in focusing this personal essay topic on two business stories, the creativity of his art redeems him.]*

Sample PowerPoint Essay 1: Sergei U. (Admitted to Chicago Booth)

In four slides or less please answer the following question: What have you not already shared in your application that you would like your future classmates to know about you?

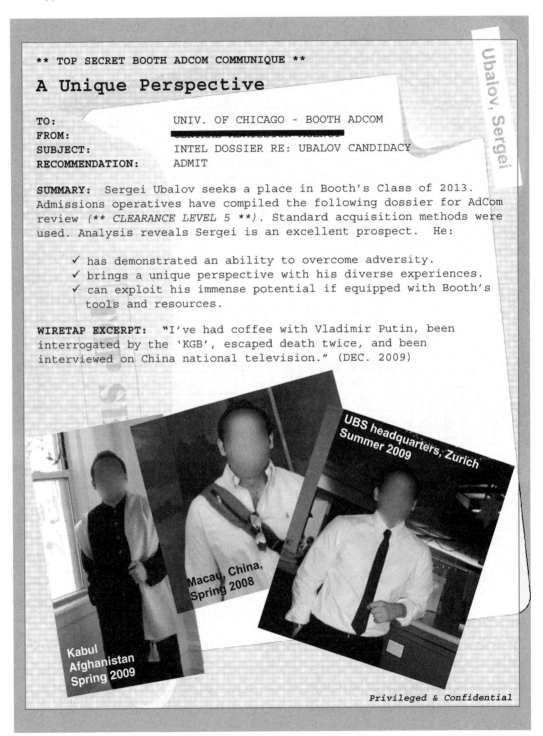

** TOP SECRET BOOTH ADCOM COMMUNIQUE **

A Unique Perspective

TO: UNIV. OF CHICAGO - BOOTH ADCOM
FROM: ~~CENTRAL ADMISSION AGENCY~~
SUBJECT: INTEL DOSSIER RE: UBALOV CANDIDACY
RECOMMENDATION: ADMIT

SUMMARY: Sergei Ubalov seeks a place in Booth's Class of 2013. Admissions operatives have compiled the following dossier for AdCom review (** *CLEARANCE LEVEL 5* **). Standard acquisition methods were used. Analysis reveals Sergei is an excellent prospect. He:

- ✓ has demonstrated an ability to overcome adversity.
- ✓ brings a unique perspective with his diverse experiences.
- ✓ can exploit his immense potential if equipped with Booth's tools and resources.

WIRETAP EXCERPT: "I've had coffee with Vladimir Putin, been interrogated by the 'KGB', escaped death twice, and been interviewed on China national television." (DEC. 2009)

UBS headquarters, Zurich
Summer 2009

Macau, China,
Spring 2008

Kabul
Afghanistan
Spring 2009

Privileged & Confidential

Ubalov, Sergei

Overcoming Adversity

(Photo Evidence)

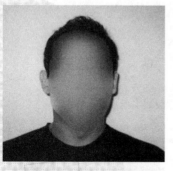

Feb. 6, 2004 - Violently Mugged - London, UK. Sergei was mugged at knifepoint on LSE's campus by 6 men. He was left on the ground, bloody and unconscious. £13 and 2 train tickets were taken.

Left: Still bruised and swollen but unbowed a week after the attack.

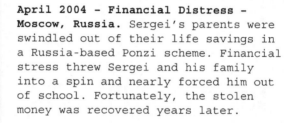

April 2004 - Financial Distress - Moscow, Russia. Sergei's parents were swindled out of their life savings in a Russia-based Ponzi scheme. Financial stress threw Sergei and his family into a spin and nearly forced him out of school. Fortunately, the stolen money was recovered years later.

Left: Sergei's parents, Ivanna and Ilya, now reside in Geneva.

April 2006 - Illness - London, UK. Sergei was hospitalized for 6 weeks with a life-threatening intestinal infection - causes unknown. Risky surgery was performed that removed one foot of intestine. Released a day before graduation, Sergei walked in his graduation ceremonies with a 3" long surgical wound in his belly. He is now fully recovered.

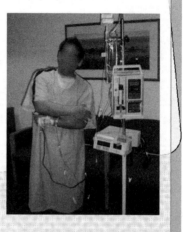

Right: Sergei, post-surgery, smiling and still alive at Royal London Hospital.

Privileged & Confidential

Ubalov, Sergei - pg. 3

Distinctive Professional Experience

(Photo Evidence)

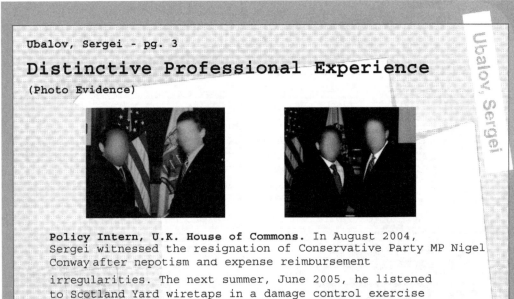

Policy Intern, U.K. House of Commons. In August 2004, Sergei witnessed the resignation of Conservative Party MP Nigel Conway after nepotism and expense reimbursement irregularities. The next summer, June 2005, he listened to Scotland Yard wiretaps in a damage control exercise for MP Ian Hain.

Above: Sergei with MPs Nigel Conway and Ian Hain.

Senior Specialist, UBS. In August 2007, Sergei developed a predictive regression model for the wealth management division's trading revenue ($2B/yr), which led to a division-wide review of forecasting.

Senior Strategy Analyst, Galaxy Entertainment Group. Sergei played a major role supporting negotiations that won construction approvals for Galaxy Macau resort.

Below (left-to-right): Marketing materials, Galaxy Macau, "the endless neon sea" of Macau's casino district viewed from the top floor of Sands Macau.

Privileged & Confidential

Ubalov, Sergei - pg. 4

Extraordinary Personal Experiences

(Photo Evidence)

Dec. 31, 2003 - Coffee with Putin - Moscow, Russia. Sergei meets with President Vladimir Putin at his official residence for an hour. The meeting was arranged by a personal advisor of Putin's who was impressed by Sergei's knowledge of Russia's internal Chechyan threat at a dinner for Russian expatriates.

Above: With Pres. Putin at the Kremlin, Moscow.

Oct. 12, 2009 - Interview on China National Television - CCTV News.
The morning of Putin's 2009 visit to Beijing, Sergei was sought out by China Central Television producers for a live interview.

Above: Screenshots of Sergei's live interview with CCTV News Channel.

Privileged & Confidential

Sample PowerPoint Essay 2: Haitao L. (Admitted to Chicago Booth)

In four slides or less please answer the following question: What have you not already shared in your application that you would like your future classmates to know about you?

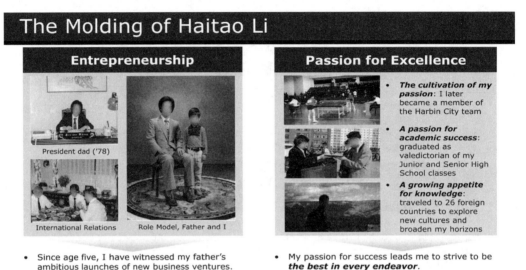

The Molding of Haitao Li

Entrepreneurship

President dad ('78)

International Relations

Role Model, Father and I

- Since age five, I have witnessed my father's ambitious launches of new business ventures. Today, he heads China's largest electronics importer, importing cameras and computers.
- *Immersed in the entrepreneurial spirit from childhood*, I now aspire to found my own company and pioneer new ventures.

Passion for Excellence

- *The cultivation of my passion*: I later became a member of the Harbin City team
- *A passion for academic success*: graduated as valedictorian of my Junior and Senior High School classes
- *A growing appetite for knowledge*: traveled to 26 foreign countries to explore new cultures and broaden my horizons

- My passion for success leads me to strive to be *the best in every endeavor*.
- Visiting new places refreshes my spirit and rejuvenates my motivation. Experiencing new cultures helps me gain insights into myself and *rekindles my aspiration to succeed.*

My Core Values as a Professional: Unflagging Ambition & Relentless Determination

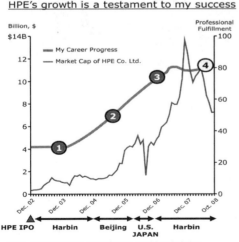

HPE's growth is a testament to my success

Billion, $

Professional Fulfillment

- My Career Progress
- Market Cap of HPE Co. Ltd.

HPE IPO   Harbin   Beijing   U.S.   Harbin
                              JAPAN

Note: Exchange rate (6.8 Yuan/USD) is used for calculation
Source: HKSE data: 1133

(1) **A Rapid Ascent**
- Recruited into Harbin Power Equipment Co.'s (HPE) management training program
- Developed innovations to transform HPE into an industry leader

(2) **Pioneering New Territory**
- First management trainee recruit to receive an overseas assignment
- Developed and launched outsourcing business, earning the annual "Most Creative Employee" Award

(3) **Advent to Leadership**
- Youngest employee to be promoted to Team Leader in HPE's history
- Spearheaded unification programs to align subsidiaries with HPE's corporate vision

(4) **Future Ambitions**
- '10-'12: Student at Chicago Booth
- '12-'16: Manager at a global technology firm
- '16- : Chief Finance Officer at a high-tech company

Personal Values: Compassion & Understanding

Inspirations for my Personality

"Caring for the happiness of others is how our soul retreats to heal; it is the principal source of success in life."
                    Ping Xue, my mother

Music has always been a part of my life; my sisters are classical musicians.

My travels have further reinforced my values.

Leadership Through Service

- Harbin Children's Hospital Volunteer: **encouraged** a terminally ill patient to overcome her demobilization

- Mentoring: **Accepted responsibility** for counseling adolescents as they face challenges in their lives

- A love of music cultivated **my empathetic understanding** as I acquired the skills of listening

- Organized HPE's cultural activity club, which evolved into the "Harbin Yes!," North China's first online service for sharing music and art experiences

- **Exposure to a variety of cultures** has helped me approach sensitive situations with a clear perspective and view issues from a broader global context

A Perfect Fit for Chicago Booth

What Haitao Has

- Carrying **the torch of entrepreneurship** passed down from my personal role model, my father

- **Played an integral role** in HPE's unprecedented innovations and bold endeavors, aiding our **growth from a venture startup into a global player**; Forbes ranks HPE as the 5th-best global performer in power plant equipment

- Taking the time to appreciate the things we take for granted is the foundation of **compassion**. This principle has allowed me to **help others see the strengths hidden** within themselves, just as **an artist** can reveal the hidden meaning behind another artist's work.

What Chicago Booth Wants

- *"My M.B.A. from Chicago Booth has given me a **complete package as an entrepreneur**."*
                    Michael P. Polsky

- *"The qualities that contribute to the success of our graduates can be found early in their careers; **a track record of success, resourcefulness**..."*
  Chicago Booth Admissions Committee

- *"I began to realize that my ability to **serve and be philanthropic** – and, equally importantly, my ability to **influence others to serve and be philanthropic** – grew exponentially as I moved up in my career."*
  Karen Parkhill, '92, Young Alumni Award

Sample Failure/Mistake Essay 1: Amber M.
(Admitted to Columbia Business School)

Please provide an example of a team failure of which you've been a part. If given a second chance, what would you do differently?

It's not the wasted hours and lost weekends that hurt when a deal fails; it's knowing that you could have prevented the failure. In March 2007 I was only two months into my new opportunity in M&A execution at Apollo Advisors but was already close to executing my first official closing. A 100% IRR on Apollo's acquisition of "BuildingCo" seemed realistic, and I was excited.

As the junior member of my seven-person deal team, I had been tasked with the grunt work, from data-room mining and financial modeling to coffee runs—whatever it took to help the team. Manuel Estevez, our team's partner, was familiar with BuildingCo's industry and showed us their management team's impressive résumés and strong track record of operating and integrating companies. As we performed our due diligence he encouraged us to rely on the management team's expertise and familiarity with their company. Following procedure, we perused documents that seemed untroubling in seconds and spent days on documents that hinted at issues. *[Amber does a nice job of establishing the context of the failure.]*

The BuildingCo deal did have issues. We knew their manufacturing facility in Tijuana, Mexico, had trouble retaining quality employees, for example, and it was relying on daily busloads of employees from San Diego to manufacture product. But when Manuel raised the issue with BuildingCo's management, they showed us a detailed plan that would, they said, rectify the issue within three months. Because Manuel seemed receptive to their plan I decided not to comb through the thousands of pages of corporate documentation, including Board of Director minutes, in the data room. *[Amber hints at her shared responsibility for the failure we sense is coming.]*

There were other worrisome issues, but it was impossible to read every document and, following Manuel's lead, we relied on the assurances of BuildingCo's management. *[←Details show the complex difficulty of the impending failure—blame is hard to assign; circumstantial pressures are enormous.]* Four months after Apollo acquired BuildingCo, focused analysis by our operating team determined that the unreliably staffed Mexican facility was a lost cause and that a large customer contract BuildingCo had boasted about would vanish when we took the company in a new direction. *[←The failure statement.]*

As the team's partner, Manuel took the blame for the disappointing investment. It was ultimately his responsibility to set the proper tone for the due diligence effort that would have revealed these issues. At the same time, with or without his guidance, we all knew what good due diligence was and we failed to deliver it. Only later did I read a document from the board meeting transcripts I had failed to read that showed BuildingCo had been struggling unsuccessfully with its retention problem for three years. [←*Amber wisely and maturely accepts some of the blame (accepting none or all of it would feel "off").*]

If I were to do it all over again I'd focus substantial skepticism on BuildingCo's story. I should have approached management's claims and projections with the total lack of confidence I now bring to all deals. I should have analyzed a larger percentage of the documents in the data room and specifically tried to visually tie the financials to BuildingCo's current and historical operational environment. [←*Amber's "second-chance" statement seems credible, not forced.*]

Luckily, BuildingCo was my first deal, and I've been given multiple second chances. In September, when a hot tub manufacturer's management assured us their customers were loyal, I proactively ran credit checks on their top 20 customers and numerous red flags appeared. [←*A brief redemption story shows that Amber learned her lesson, which she restates at the essay's close.→*] After all, apathy due to lack of responsibility is no excuse when you're part of a team.

Sample Failure/Mistake Essay 2: Gustavo V. (Admitted to Wharton)

Describe a failure or setback that you have experienced. What role did you play and what did you learn about yourself?

Amid the chaos following Venezuela's financial crisis in 2009–10, I virtually abandoned my university studies for two months. At this pivotal point when language education was becoming an unaffordable luxury for most of my clients, saving my language-school business became more exciting and critical than lectures. [←*In another essay Gustavo introduced his language business in full, so he only needs to telegraph it here.*]

When my bank closed until further notice, denying me access to my accounts, I panicked. All I had was USD2000 worth of prepaid advertising and my pocket money—which was losing 10–15% of its value daily—to re-animate my language school. I had four employees; we had to keep our clients.

While my classmates were discussing their notes about Organic Chemistry, I was redefining my business's marketing tactics, and pumping up revenues by organizing promotions and designing personalized payment plans to help clients survive until the economy stabilized. Instead of translating texts on liquid dynamics in class, I concentrated on the "dynamics of liquidity," quickly reinvesting my business's cash assets into merchandise and services as the bolivar's value sank. I skipped seminars on Communication Psychology to negotiate barter schemes with suppliers. [←*Repeated comparisons between what classmates were doing and what Gustavo wrestled with create effective contrast between academic security and real-world business lessons.*]

By February, my business was up and running again, but I was behind in most classes at Universidad Central. To restore my grades I sacrificed weekends and sleep for the rest of the semester, relying on the generosity of professors and classmates in helping me catch up. Though both my business and academic transcript survived, I was a wreck as I was extremely exhausted having had no rest and no life outside work and school for more than five months. *[←Since both Gustavo's grades and business survived, he is "cheating" a little by claiming his five lost months were a failure. But his analysis in the next paragraph compensates nicely.→]*

Looking back, my main mistake was that I panicked. This unhinged my priorities as well as my comfort level; I lacked balance. I would have had enough time for my academic study if I had relied more on my language school's team by delegating authority, sharing responsibility, and stimulating creativity. Moreover, if I had prudently diversified my company's assets before the devaluation I would not have reacted in so frenzied a way when the crisis hit.

In March 2010, I restructured my business accordingly, and the increased cooperation within the team resulted in new courses, new payment schemes and a more aggressive promotion strategy. We increased our revenue by 8% despite the unfavorable market conditions, kept client retention at 72%, and I also had sufficient time to attend all lectures.

Sample Failure/Mistake Essay 3: Jeanine B. (Admitted to Harvard Business School)

What have you learned from a mistake?

A couple spun past me on the dance floor in a flurry of high-kicking patadas, the woman's four-inch stiletto nicking my calves as I lurched out of the way. My partner glared. I perspired. This was an Argentinean free-for-all, the center of a storm. It was my first milonga (tango dance party).*[Vivid, crisp writing lends panache and atmosphere to Jeanine's essay, setting it apart from the crowd.]*

My partner pushed me like a shopping cart; I resisted, forcing the steps I learned in class. After our tumultuous attempt at a dance, I sat on the sidelines and watched a couple burn up the floor with amazing coordination. He stepped with graceful confidence; she was a pliant flower in his arms reacting beautifully to every movement.

Watching them, I realized my mistake: to dance a tango well, I needed to be flexible and adapt to my partner, even if he missed a step or guided me into unfamiliar waters. Instead of trying to dance what I felt were the right steps, I needed to be versatile and adjust to each partner's unique style. Once I grasped this, I was able to reinvent myself with each tango and became adept at adjusting to various partners' techniques as they led me into tornadoes of voleos, ochos, and dips. [*Jeanine's decision to use tango as a mistake rather than something "heavier" is shrewd. She has the writing skill to pull off an essay that differentiates and humanizes her.*]

I applied this to professional experiences by identifying how various people and teams work and adapting my management style to lead more effectively. When I was staffed on a project with a new consultant, Patrick, who was rather rigid and combative with the team, I quickly realized that I needed to change my approach. I approached Patrick and explained the tension on the team stemmed from the fact that we were accustomed to collaborating as opposed to a structure where our input was not considered. I gently suggested reorganizing the workplan to give the team opportunities to help drive the project. Patrick was grateful for my frank but tactful feedback and allowed me to reorganize the workplan, giving each associate ownership over a module which resulted in better team rapport, increased productivity, and an excellent end-product. [*Jeanine wisely situates her follow-on redemption story in a more traditional environment, showing that she takes her lessons learned seriously.*]

Through tango I learned to work with and respond spontaneously to various partners and have applied this in professional settings as well. But the tango is a rich, complex, and improvisational dance that is constantly evolving. Just as every partner I dance with has something to teach me, each person or team I work with gives me a better understanding of how to adapt my work and management style, and there is still much I am eager to learn.

Sample Growth/Challenge Essay 1: Christine C. (Admitted to Columbia Business School)

Please provide an example from your own life in which practical experience taught you more than theory alone.

Helping = giving money.

When I first began to realize that the message of service I learned at Saint Bartholomew's could connect with a career in international development, I began to search for the mode of greatest impact. Indoctrinated by well-meaning ads declaring "one dollar can save a life," I believed that giving money is the best way to help the poor. The theory of development I absorbed, even from respected scholars like Jeffrey Sachs, sees the world's poor as passively reliant on a developed world "savior." [*Christine efficiently introduces the guiding "theory" that reality will eventually revise.*]

This was the working "theory" of aid I brought with me to Rwanda in 2007. Working with the nonprofit Catholic World Mission, I traveled across Rwanda with young Rwandan leaders, conducting workshops on nonprofit management and advocacy and volunteering alongside them in five NGOs. From bloated UN programs and international NGOs, to small, but profoundly impactful grassroots organizations working in the heart of the country, I saw my theory of aid at work.

At the beginning my theory was reinforced by what I glimpsed of Rwanda's tragic past: stories of Hutu butchery of up to 800,000 Tutsis; orphaned or mutilated children lining city intersections begging for change; adult survivors of the massacre telling me how as children they had seen their entire families wiped out. Everything I saw made me doubt Rwanda could ever fully recover on its own. *[Her initial theory is still intact.]*

Yet I felt an immediate connection with my Rwandan peers. Communicating through broken English, we took long trips up the Nyabarongo River, playing music together on deteriorating guitars and sharing our passion for a better world. Aimé Samputu, the founder of a grassroots nonprofit, invited me to his home and rural village, a place he had had to run away from simply to attend school.

Neither Aimé nor any of the other young Rwandans I met wanted a Western savior. "We are responsible for our destiny," they told me. They showed me how an economy of foreign aid is destined to fail, how the big international NGOs rarely help the neediest Rwandans, how unintelligent philanthropy only reinforces the divide between the rich and poor. *[Christine's theory begins to crumble.]*

It was in Rwanda that I learned firsthand what Professor Stevens recently wrote in a *Financial Times* article: "fund[ing] government and NGOs to run economic development projects … is not how to end poverty: only the local business sector does that." *[Allusions to scholars like Sachs and Stevens lends Christine's essay greater weight.]* Practice has taught me that what the developing world needs most are jobs, access to opportunity and capital, and sustainable economic growth. *[← Direct statement of the lesson that practical reality taught her.]*

Returning from this "master class" in Rwanda, I had an idea—to found the Rwanda Recovery Organization (RRO) to support development organizations like Aimé's in isolated rural Rwanda. This "simple" idea proved far more challenging than I imagined. I struggled to inspire help from those who had no connection to Rwanda and to juggle my vision with the realities of a 65 hour-per-week job. Gradually, after winning a grant for pro bono legal support from Catholic Charities Legal Services, rallying committed friends, developing a Web site (www.rro.org), and hosting our first fundraiser, RRO was born. *[← Christine's frank admission of the difficulty of nonprofit leadership earn her further credibility.]*

In the two years since RRO sent its first $1500 grant to the Development Council of Kigali, Aimé's nonprofit, we have distributed more than $7,500 in capital to three community ventures, impacting more than fifty Rwandan families through microloans, business training, and agricultural development assistance. Though a modest first step in my social entrepreneurship career, RRO has helped me learn far more than theory alone.

Sample Growth/Challenge Essay 2: Jon T. (Admitted to Dartmouth Tuck)

Discuss the most difficult constructive criticism or feedback you have received. How did you address it? What have you learned from it?

"You have a hole to dig yourself out of." I was stunned, speechless and embarrassed, sitting before two terrifyingly serious partners of the firm. [←*Opening quotation and dramatic language pull the reader in.*] As an analyst only eight months out of college, I was unsure of expectations at my fast-paced investment banking firm and I was not expecting such harsh criticism half-way through my first year.

In retrospect, I realize that I had made careless mistakes by working too fast and not paying attention to detail. I had overlooked basic investment banking analyst protocol in an environment that did not tolerate mistakes. Until that review, I had not fully appreciated the importance of the tasks for which I was responsible as an analyst. The pressure was intense and work weeks often exceeded 100 hours, but there was no room for error in analyses and documents critical to clients' $100 million transactions. [←*Direct, mature statement of culpability—the keystone of this essay type.*]

At the time, the criticism delivered by the firm's partners was such a devastating blow to my ego that I questioned my career choice. I was disappointed in myself, but I refused to dwell on this difficult feedback and instead resolved to dive into my analyst role with renewed passion and intensity. [←*Lets the reader know how he reacted, felt.*]

My new resolution entailed grueling effort on top of an already challenging job: triple-checking spreadsheets, working later nights and longer weekends, and eagerly assuming new responsibilities. I was the first into the office and the last to leave. I was prompt, serious and focused, and I brought a new sense of perfectionism to my work. [←*Jon begins to react constructively to the feedback he's been given.*]

Through determination, hard work and a sense of personal responsibility for my professional improvement, I proved my competence and earned the senior bankers' confidence in me. As I improved, I became more proud of the quality of my work and the caliber of my professionalism. My confidence grew, and at the end of the year, the partners lauded my improvement. "You have become one of our top analysts and your improvement is remarkable. We can see you doing very well in this business in the future," they smiled as they handed me my first bonus check. [←*Direct quotations are always more effective than indirect.*]

Instead of the setback I had initially expected, this criticism catalyzed my evolution into a more polished professional than I would have become otherwise. I saw the realization of my potential that would not have occurred without this critical feedback, and experiencing it early in my career cultivated the high standards I continue to bring to my work.

Even though this performance review occurred three years ago, I value this experience because of the impact it had on the standards to which I have held myself ever since. Now, at Goldman Sachs, I am often noted as much for the accuracy of my work as for my presentation and professional demeanor, all of which I have worked to improve since that first performance review. In fact, having been selected by management to recruit and mentor junior analysts entering the firm, I have been able to help new analysts avoid some of the challenges I faced directly out of school. Of the three summer analysts I have coached, all three have obtained offers to return to the firm full-time. *[←Meaty evidence of Jon's true growth since his feedback moment.]*

There will always be areas for improvement both personally and professionally, and I have learned that feedback is a valuable tool for self-improvement. I have experienced the importance of resisting the temptation to react with frustration or hurt feelings. The challenge is to leverage the opportunity to improve the status quo by responding thoughtfully and effectively.

5

The Required Optional Essay

When is a good time to write an optional essay? Always. Everybody has an interesting story. I love to see what people choose.

—Dawna Clarke, Dartmouth (Tuck)

For most applicants the optional essay is either an afterthought glibly tossed off or a dreaded challenge to defend the indefensible. The deceptive little word *optional* accounts for the first misperception, and the latter stems from the optional essay's traditional role as the place where you explain your F in freshman-year calculus, those six glaring months between jobs, or the reasons why your supervisor won't write a recommendation letter (though he really is your biggest fan).

Admissions officials are all over the map when it comes to the advisability of using the optional essay. Some love them; others speak of them with thinly veiled impatience. Ultimately, it's you who must decide whether adding yet one more essay to the adcom's heap will put you over the top or transform sympathy into exasperation.

What the Schools Say

I would caution you to limit it to stuff that truly adds to your application. Too much additional information might not be viewed in a positive light, as we really do read all of the applications! I would use the optional essay if needed, but try to avoid too much information that is not requested.

—PETE JOHNSON, UNIVERSITY OF CALIFORNIA BERKELEY (HAAS)

WHAT SCHOOLS ASK

Almost every business school allows applicants to submit an optional essay or at least "additional information" of some kind. Some schools narrow the focus by hinting darkly that you should address "areas of concern," "extenuating circumstances," or "aspects that need explanation." A smaller subset steers you toward specific topics that they want to hear about if they're relevant to you. NYU Stern invites you to elaborate on "plans to retake the GMAT and/or TOEFL," for example, and Wharton helpfully offers a grab bag of potential embarrassments: "unexplained gaps in work experience, choice of recommenders, inconsistent or questionable academic performance, significant weaknesses in your application." UNC Kenan-Flagler even provides two optional essays, one to address a low quantitative GMAT score or weak quantitative coursework and a second for anything else.

But the typical business school's optional essay remains an extremely open-ended invitation to talk about exactly what you want to:

- "Any information you would like to add to your application that you haven't addressed elsewhere." (Haas, Georgetown)

- "Anything else you think the admissions committee should know about you to evaluate your candidacy." (Michigan, UNC Kenan-Flagler)

- "Whatever else you want the Admissions Committee to know." (MIT Sloan)

Because business schools range from discouraging optional essays to positively welcoming them, your decision to submit or omit one will need to be highly school-specific.

TO WRITE OR NOT TO WRITE?

Should you write an optional essay? Anywhere from half to two-thirds of business applicants probably do, and it's a good bet that of those who don't, the majority view optional essays as strictly for applicants with "excuses" to give—about grades, test scores, or missing recommendations. Blessedly free of these negatives, pressed for time, and already thoroughly sick of essay writing, these applicants probably don't give the optional essay another thought. This argument has appeal. If applicants are tired of writing essays, imagine how admissions officers must feel about reading them. Why throw away the goodwill you've carefully built up over four required essays by exhausting their patience with a fifth?

That's the "don't write" argument. But as the title of this chapter suggests, there's another, more positive case to be made for writing the optional essay. First, banish the thought that optional essays are only for "extenuating circumstances." The number of schools who hold to that narrow definition is outnumbered by those whose instructions welcome "any other information" you care to give. Second, as for the argument that the optional essay will turn an impatient and bleary-eyed reader against you, the truth is it might, but only if you write a rambling, off-the-cuff, inessential porridge of an essay. The tired-admissions-officer argument is not a reason to avoid submitting an optional essay, just an ineffective one. Committees may be overworked, but they're also professionals who want to discover qualified and distinctive applicants, and the optional essay offers you one more opportunity to show them you're one of those. Third, in recent years business school applications have been trending toward fewer essay questions and/or smaller word limits per question. But MBA applicants are not becoming less multidimensional or accomplished (quite the contrary). So as schools shrink the space available to you to tell your story, the optional essay emerges as an essential opportunity.

Fourth, the more selective the school, the greater should be your presumption that you do indeed have more to tell. Taking these schools up on their offer to skip the optional essay may send the unprepossessing message that you have only a limited number of accomplishments or distinctive experiences to share. Submitting a (good) optional essay sends the opposite message: "There's more where this came from. I've done a lot!" If you're top-twenty B-school material, you really ought to have enough new and important material to add. In risk/reward terms, the potential downside of testing adcoms' patience with an optional essay is greatly outweighed by the upside of submitting an essay that adds one more compelling new component to your profile.

Finally, just as visiting the campus a second time communicates your intense interest in a school, so the optional essay signals that you are willing to expend extra effort to win admission. After plowing through dozens of applications that seem casually tossed off, or, worse, don't even bother to get the school's name right, your extra effort may help you stand out from the pack (if your optional essay is an effective one). View the optional essay then for what it is—a sincere invitation to strengthen your application. Take it.

WHAT SHOULD YOU WRITE ABOUT?

As we've seen, there are two basic categories of possible topics for optional essays—the bad and the good. The bad encompasses all the "clarification" and "extenuating circumstances" topics; the kinds of things you're likely to discuss only because failing to will raise admissions officers' suspicions. The good is everything else—the purely discretionary topics that you choose because they will tell the schools something new and important.

Whatever topic you choose, remember that it's only human nature for the reader to approach your optional essay with slightly less gusto than your first, so be as direct and concise as possible. The added quality you give it can resuscitate the reader's waning attention and overcome natural skepticism about an "extra" essay.

The Fine Art of Damage Control

Allaying admissions officers' concerns about curiosities or weaknesses in your application is the most common use of the optional essay. The two most common ways of doing this "damage control" are (1) making the case, with evidence, that what appears to be a weakness really isn't and (2) acknowledging the weakness but building the case that you've grown past it. Personal hardship is perhaps the most effective single explanation for application weaknesses. Convincingly explaining such hardships may not only get you admitted; with some schools they may also earn you a scholarship.

For damage-control optional essays, brevity is most definitely the soul of wit. Short essays of 100 to 300 words will discuss most application blemishes in all the detail that's likely to do you any good. Get in and get out fast. And try to conclude the essay with an example or two that show that you have overcome or are overcoming the negative, whether it's a low GPA, an employment gap, or even a criminal conviction. In other words, it's not enough to explain in optional essays. You should also show recovery.

GMAT Scores

There's little you can say in an optional essay about a disappointing GMAT score that will help you very much—and nothing that the admissions committee hasn't heard before. Explaining how you couldn't afford the time for a GMAT prep course because you were caring for your sick mother might be worth putting on the table, but it won't change the fact that your GMAT score is unsatisfactory, so keep it short and tell the committee when you plan to retake the test. In describing such extraordinary circumstances, your tone should be direct and unemotional—avoid woe-is-me dramatics.

An explanation for low GMAT scores that may work for some is to prove (not just claim) that there has always been a disconnect between your standardized tests scores and your academic performance. If you can prove this, you may convince the committee that you belong to that small minority whose intellectual aptitude is simply not accurately measured by tests like the GMAT, GRE, or SAT. Note that this "outlier" defense will work only if you can point to a clear pattern of standardized test scores that seems to bear no relation to your high grades. For example, you scored a cumulative 900 on your SATs but earned National Honor Society and class valedictorian honors. If your grades or test scores don't clearly support this argument, avoid it.

Remember, just because you are disappointed with your GMAT score or know it's lower than the school's median doesn't mean you should devote your optional essay to the subject. There often is nothing worth saying. And, of course, if you got a 700 and the school's median is 720, you have no explaining to do.

If your quantitative and verbal scores are out of balance (for example, a 20-point percentile difference, as in 65th percentile verbal score and an 85th percentile quantitative), then you may want to focus your optional essay on providing evidence that the low score should not concern the committee. For example, a low-quant-score applicant could mention all the quant-intensive models she builds and numbers she crunches in her finance job, and a low-verbal-score applicant could talk about all the white papers he writes, presentations he gives, and award-winning Toastmasters speeches he delivers. In their letters on your behalf, your recommenders can also provide their evidence that your GMAT weakness is not what it appears.

Case Study: I Am More Than a Score

Tuan had a 640 GMAT score dragged down by a truly humble verbal score. But he also had a relatively distinctive industry background (automotive), a dizzying variety of community involvements (from the YMCA and United Way to the Alzheimer's Association and the Rotary Club), and an unmistakable fast-track profile as a young project leader already supervising eight employees. The University of Chicago was his dream, and because he was based in the Midwest, its part-time program was feasible for him—significantly improving his odds of admission. Tuan added the following brief note to the end of an optional essay devoted to more positive material: "I would like to clarify to the committee that my disappointing verbal score on the GMAT does not mean my oral and written communication skills are inadequate. I regularly make group presentations to customers, submit written weekly project reports to my management, and have authored five papers on distribution management published in prominent professional journals. I am ready for the University of Chicago Graduate School of Business in every respect." Chicago agreed and admitted him.

Poor Grades

Many applicants think they should use the optional essays to do "damage control" on the lone C they suffered in freshman-year basket weaving. Such minor lapses are too trivial to waste space on. If your weak grades were few in number, not failing, and/or lasted only a semester, state the cause for the lapse (a family crisis, a health issue, a too-heavy course load, etc.) in one or two sentences in a separate addendum or as a note at the end of an optional essay devoted to more positive material (see the next section). Optional essays focusing on grades should be limited to scenarios like:

- A string of Fs and Ds during a bad semester or two or in core business courses.

- A lower GPA in your last two years than in your first two.

- A bell-shaped GPA curve, in which your strongest grades came in your sophomore and junior years.

- A lower GPA in graduate course work in comparison to your undergraduate years.

What explanations for poor grades carry weight? A weak but all-too-common one is the "lack of focus" argument. This only begs the question—why did you lose focus? It's one thing if you struggled because you're the first person in their family to go to college and simply needed time to adjust. It's quite another if you devoted your freshman year to becoming your frat's unofficial kegger king.

The best explanations emphasize concrete factors, preferably those outside your control. If you had unusual and unavoidable family or extracurricular obligations or had to work full-time to self-fund your education, admissions officers will surely cut you slack. Even factors over which you had control can sometimes constitute persuasive explanations. The defense that you viewed college as an opportunity to grow and gain leadership experience through unusually deep extracurricular commitments can work if your extracurricular involvements were, in fact, substantial, sustained, and atypically broad. Use specific numbers to demonstrate your level of commitment.

Whatever your reasons may be, explain them succinctly, objectively, and maturely. In any event, take responsibility, and draw a lesson from the episode: "I learned that I must better balance my outside commitments and study," or something similar. The first explanatory part of your essay should be equaled or exceeded in length by your positive statement about the things you've been doing since then to make a repeat of this scenario unlikely. Give examples that show how you have developed better discipline and a responsible attitude toward work and school. If the problem was time management, consider discussing recent time management feats, such as juggling a full-time job and a master's program.

No Recommendation from Current Supervisor

Many schools recommend that you explain why you have chosen to omit a recommendation letter from your current supervisor. This is not an application weakness in the same sense as poor grades or test scores. The schools simply want assurance that it is not because your supervisor has a low opinion of you.

Most applicants omit a letter from a current supervisor because they don't want to jeopardize their jobs if no business school admits them. Luckily, business schools fully appreciate the delicacy of this situation, and if you've been with your current employer for under a year, an enthusiastic letter from your previous supervisor is an acceptable alternative. In this case, you need not devote your optional essay to explaining. Just insert a two-sentence note in your application stating that you're submitting a recommendation from your previous manager. This frees you to devote the optional essay to more value-added information.

Another acceptable reason for omitting a letter from a current supervisor is that you are self-employed or work for a family business (letters from family members don't carry much weight). In these cases, inform the school that you are submitting letters from clients, colleagues, or vendors who can comment authoritatively on your candidacy. If you're unemployed, devote the lion's share of the essay to what you've been doing during your time between jobs.

What if the real reason you've omitted a letter from your current supervisor is that you're unsure he or she would be enthusiastic? Simply inform the school that the recommenders you are using (say who they are) are exceptionally well qualified to comment on your performance and potential and back this up with evidence—and leave it at that.

Writing Optional Essays: Practical Tips

Play the admissions officer for a moment. Step back from your application—or better yet, give it to an objective friend—and ask yourself whether it all coheres. Is anything missing? Did your friends hand it back to you and say, "I still don't understand why you left Goldman Sachs for Ernie's Carpet Empire," or, "Why exactly did you major in marketing if your goal was always entrepreneurship?" or, "How come your résumé is the only place where you mention your world trophy in archery?" If you or your readers discover such anomalies, you have a potential topic to explore in the optional essay.

Assume that the topic you decide to write about involves clarifying an ambiguous episode or explaining an extenuating circumstance. You must map out the most concise, objective, and mature explanation possible. If the episode is significant enough to warrant an essay, chances are it's a subject you're touchy or even emotional about. You need to eliminate your subjective, defensive take on the situation and describe it as analytically as possible. One way to do this is to banish for the moment the question of how the committee will "judge" the substance of the situation (a bad grade, poor test score, employment gap). Pretend instead that what they're really judging is how succinctly, soberly, and responsibly you can *describe* the situation. Or, alternatively, imagine that you're a CEO evaluating a wayward business unit. You wouldn't be interested in blame or guilt but in the realities of the situation and what you can do to fix it. Adopting this case-study mindset will enable you to describe your "extenuating circumstance" in precisely the kind of clear, compact, and responsible tone the admissions committee expects. And by doing so, you will have set yourself apart from the many applicants who hem and haw, cast blame, and generally sound mealy-mouthed.

Employment Gaps and Weak Extracurriculars

Admittedly, it's hard to spin current unemployment in a positive way, but the circumstances behind your jobless situation can have a mitigating effect and should usually be explained. For most schools, joblessness of under, say, two months need not be given the full treatment of an optional essay. If you were terminated for cause, the details of your particular case will determine whether it's worth explaining in full in an optional essay or just briefly in the "reasons for leaving" space on the application's data section. Don't, however, deny your joblessness on your application data sheet, résumé, or anywhere else.

If you were terminated because of a companywide downsizing in a lousy market, you need not be defensive or apologetic. Many are in the same boat, and while a negative, schools won't regard it as a deal-breaker. Use the optional essay to provide mini-stories about the activities that have been occupying you since the pink slip, such as classes or community involvements.

Business schools have very high standards when it comes to extracurriculars and community involvement. If you're weak in these areas, either draw no attention to it and hope the rest of your application compensates or write a sincere and detailed essay about the intensive extracurricular commitments you had in college when you weren't working 80-hour weeks, the time you've spent mentoring juniors at work, or even examples from your family life that show the same traits as community work, such as taking care of one's child as a single parent or providing an unusual amount of care for family members. If you work ridiculous hours, make sure it's mentioned somewhere in your application, but don't present it as an excuse for poor extracurriculars. The admissions committee won't buy it.

Other Extenuating Circumstances

The range of weaknesses that applicants may need to discuss in the optional essay is hardly limited to grades, test scores, less-than-ideal recommenders, and gaps in employment or community involvement, of course. The impact of visa restrictions on career plans, an abbreviated stay in medical or law school, a transcript showing more than three universities or a six-year undergraduate career, reasons for deferring admission a year ago or for needing a second MBA, even why you as a reapplicant applied in round two rather than the preferred round one—all of these raise concerns that the optional essay can go some way toward alleviating. Just remember that many explanations can be made briefly, thus freeing the bulk of the essay for positive material.

Less typically, the optional essay can help you make the case that, for example, being wheelchair-bound is not an impediment, that the clinical depression you suffered in college is a thing of the past, or that you have been a changed man since those instances of academic or professional censure such as for cheating or plagiarism. The bottom line is the same: schools offer the opportunity to write optional essays not to smoke out negatives but to give you a chance to explain them honestly, succinctly, and positively.

Positive Optional Essays

As we've seen, most schools are quite open to optional essays that don't "explain" anything at all; they just provide new insights into or information not on your application. So what should you write about? One effective strategy is to return to the self-marketing handle we discussed in Chapter 1—the four- or five-theme message you've been trying to convey across your entire application. Have you illustrated all these themes sufficiently in the school's required essays? Perhaps you intended to discuss the weekly advice column you write for the *Quincy Herald*, but couldn't fit it into the available topics. Your optional essay could be the place to highlight this unusual, creative hobby. Perhaps you're trying to offset your techie background by emphasizing your interpersonal and communication skills. In that case, your optional essay could dramatize a work situation in which you worked subtly behind the scenes to build momentum for a key decision. Or it could focus on your rise through the ranks at your local Toastmasters. The range of possible uses is enormous. Just don't repeat a story you mentioned elsewhere in the application, and make sure the activity is strong and/or distinctive enough to warrant an additional essay.

What the Schools Say

The optional essay is your opportunity to tell us anything that you haven't had the opportunity to cover in the other four essays or in your interview. Common responses have to do with explaining extenuating circumstances, hobbies, travel experiences. I definitely recommend completing it.

—Dawna Clarke, Dartmouth (Tuck)

Since the optional essay represents your last chance to market yourself to the admissions committee and you don't want to outstay your welcome, avoid writing about prosaic workplace accomplishments or "football hero" type essays. Look for that one remaining story that only you can tell and that will deepen the committee's sense that you are a distinctive person of many "parts". The more outside the box your story or insights are, the more benefit you may gain. And don't equate effective or unpredictable optional essay topics with exciting ones. An essay about your passion for cooking, the harpsichord, or stamp collecting could enhance your distinctiveness just as much as an essay about skydiving or mountain climbing (both of which the committee will certainly have encountered before).

As a general rule, avoid the glib, loosely structured, "I-dashed-this-off-in-a-minute" exercise. Admissions officers like color and humor as much as the next person, but not as a substitute for having something substantive to add. If your point is that you'll make your future classmates' learning experience fun, then find a story with a beginning, middle, and end that illustrates this.

Case Study: Quiet Leadership

I had to lower my voice when speaking with Michael. His rock band had been his passion and his life since his teenage years. All those amped-up concerts had gradually fried his ear drums, however, until even the sound of the human voice caused him excruciating pain. Not only was he forced to give up music; he had hid himself away at home to avoid irritating sounds, before eventually getting treatment. While the typical applicant might have milked this story for all its adversity potential, Michael did much more. Shocked to discover that there was no national organization for victims of his disorder, he created one, formally registered it, and began fielding e-mails from fellow sufferers. By taking advantage of an optional essay to explain his crusade, Michael won admission to MIT Sloan.

As we saw in Chapter 4, business schools love challenge essays. They admire the character it takes to rise above difficult circumstances, and they sometimes reward it with offers of admission. Ideally, you worked your "obstacles overcome" stories into your required essays—it's the kind of material you will want to highlight. If this was not possible, however, or if you have more than one such tale, the optional essay can help.

Reusing a leftover essay from one school for another school's optional essay is a legitimate strategy but only if you do two things. First, recycle an essay that gives your essay set greater balance. If the required essay topics forced you to devote three-quarters of your essays to professional topics, then you could use one of your leftover essays about community or personal topics in the optional essay. Second, purge any wording that signals that in its former life this optional essay was another school's required essay. You also need to add wording that informs the committee why you are submitting this extra essay. Because optional essays leave the topic up to you, you should clearly state the essay's topic to the committee at the very beginning. Don't make committee members figure it out as they read.

OPTIONAL ESSAYS: WHAT *NOT* TO DO

1. Abuse the length limits or write more than a page or so. Keep optional essays as short as possible. If a school states no limit, then limit yourself to the typical length limit of that school's required essays. If a school has one 600-word essay and three 400-word essays, your optional essay should not exceed 400 words.

2. Go into agonizing detail about the cruel conspiracy or bad karma that led to your D in Introduction to Polymer Science. Even if every word you say is true, the committee may wonder at your sense of proportion. Essays of explanation should never belabor the negative.

3. Lie. Don't even think about explaining your poor GPA by spinning out some fiction about your grandmother being kidnapped by a sect of militant environmentalists.

4. Whine or complain about an unhappy outcome. By all means explain the circumstances of your setback, but take personal responsibility for it. When the admissions officer evaluates how much weight to assign to your weakness, your mature mea culpa will reflect well on you.

5. Repeat any substantial story or anecdote or accomplishment from your other essays. If you devoted two paragraphs in a required essay to your passion for Civil War reenactments, don't elaborate on the story in your optional essay. You've already scored all the points your unusual hobby will bring you.

6. Tell stories that are so personal that they can have no relevance to graduate management study. These usually involve topics such as failed relationships or deeply personal events that would make the committee uncomfortable.

7. Enclose photos of your cocker spaniel, your 700-page treatise on Syncretism and the Epistemology of Being, or a video of your last bowling tournament. Admissions officials will usually welcome one short news-relevant article about (or by) you, but any other creative attempts to stand out will usually come across as manipulative or cheesy (or both).

8. Write epic summaries or cute throwaway stories that provide no substantial new insight or information. Avoid optional essays that consist of disjointed, relatively trivial leftover topics with no unifying theme.

9. Create your optional essay by carelessly cutting and pasting in another school's essay. If your essay starts with "People may be surprised to learn that I …" or, "If I had to choose three people to travel cross-country with …," the committee may wish you luck with Kellogg or Indiana but view your application to their school less favorably. Remember that admissions officials are well aware of what other schools ask.

10. Use the optional essay to explain a negative episode but fail to conclude it with a positive example that shows you learning from or overcoming that negative.

SAMPLE ESSAYS

The following five sample essays (whose authors were admitted by Wharton, Columbia, and Chicago) illustrate both the positive and negative uses of optional essays. The first three demonstrate that the mundane business of explaining "extenuating circumstances" can be done with style and personality. The last two—one the story of a fascinating alternative career; the other a clever overview of an applicant's strengths—hint at the range of "value-adding" topics that optional essays can cover.

Sample Optional Essay 1: Judi S. (Admitted to Wharton)

If there are extenuating circumstances or concerns affecting your application that you feel the Admissions Committee should be aware of, please elaborate here (e.g., choice of recommenders, unexplained gaps in work experience).

Making the cover of the 2006 Duke Blue Devils Women's Basketball media guide was a special thrill for me—surpassed only by making the team as a walk-on and, of course, the Final Four. Being on the cover felt like the last chapter of my personal "come-from-behind" story. In my four years on the Blue Devils only three of us were less than six feet tall, and I am 5'6", on a good day. Each one of my teammates could boast All-American honors from their high school careers; I had only honorable mention All-State honors in Georgia. What's more, 13 of my teammates went on to play professionally. In other words, I was the underdog. *[Vividly personal intro establishes Judi's underdog credentials, while getting the reader firmly in her corner.]*

Being among the very best was an extraordinary experience, but the price I had to pay for that Blue Devils uniform with "Stark" on the back was not small. First, there was the sheer time commitment. In-season training alone required 30+ hours per week, but the commitment was year-round, from fall preseason workouts to spring training and summer conditioning. Between practice, skill work, rehab, game-film study, and weight-lifting in the Duke athletic complex, I rarely saw my dorm room. Moreover, of our 32-game season, half were on the road, which meant a minimum of five Wednesday-through-Sunday road trips. If by good fortune and our hard work we earned a postseason tournament (which happened all four years), our season expanded by another three weeks. Since I was a backup, to maintain my scholarship I had to give 100% to keep my place on the team. The coaching staff gave no handouts, and my coach, Joanne P. McCallie, fresh from coaching the 2006 Olympic gold-medal team, was not one to waste time with "dead weight." *[Rich detail and insights build the essay's momentum.]*

By the spring of my freshman year, the strain of basketball and my premed chemistry classes was taking a toll. Because chemistry labs overlapped with practice, my advisor encouraged me to switch to a major that presented no schedule conflicts. The excitement of Research Triangle Park's technology revolution had been drawing me since my first day, so I switched to Computer Science as my major before the end of sophomore year. This gave me only two years in which to complete one of the most challenging disciplines at Duke University. Since my scholarship would not extend past my senior year, I had no room for grade-inflating electives. Despite many bright spots—an A in "Compilers" and B's in "Matrix Theory and Applications," "Object-Oriented System Design," and "Applied E-Commerce"—my GPA suffered.

Though I wish my GPA had been higher, under the circumstances—relying on an athletic scholarship at a university that gives athletes no special favors—I believe I did fairly well.

Should my disappointing GPA raise concerns about my academic aptitude? I don't believe so. As my transcript shows, in summer 2007–08 I participated in a high school program that enabled me to take three Duke courses, in which I earned 4.0, and in semesters when I was not distracted by basketball, I maintained a 3.42 average including demanding calculus and chemistry courses.

(In fact, I did so well on the chemistry midterm, a human biology major asked me to tutor him for the final.) Finally, I've recently earned A's in two accounting and two statistics classes. My academic aptitude remains strong. *[← Makes a compelling case that her disappointing grades are not indicative of her ability.]*

Nor should my disappointing computer-science grades raise doubts about my career potential. My career at Panasonic has been successful in every respect. I consistently receive performance reviews, with such ratings as "Exceeds Standards" and "Outstanding."

Do I wish I knew at Duke what I know now about time management? Yes. Finally, do I wish I could trade my basketball experiences for a higher GPA? No way! *[Energized conclusion ends essay on a high note.]*

Sample Optional Essay 2: Flavie L. (Admitted to Columbia Business School)

Is there any further information that you wish to provide to the Admissions Committee? (Please use this space to provide an explanation of any areas of concern in your academic record or your personal history.)

Tofurkey. Have you heard of it? If you haven't, then you have not spent a holiday at my parents' house. Christmas, Thanksgiving, Festivus—it doesn't matter, if you visit you will be served a slab of tofurkey. Though it may be the worst food product ever invented, both of my parents grew up in the tree-hugging, peace-loving, organic-eating "Hippie" 1960s and have never quite let go. *[←Personable tone and hippie lifestyle details soften reader up for forthcoming "area of concern."]*

Born in Santa Cruz, they bought their first home and sailed it—a 38-foot sailboat—to Mexico, where they lived for three years, doubtless relying on insights from one of my favorite books on their 70s-era bookshelf: *How to Live on 25 Cents a Day* (yes, cents!). Don't get me wrong. Both my parents worked hard (as a secretary and a carpenter) to provide for my sister, Apple, and me. But money was always tight (needless to say, everything in our house is home-made), so I began working at 13, washing dishes at a family friend's restaurant.

The lessons I learned working 25-hour weeks in high school and being the first in my family to attend university (which I paid for myself) are fundamental to who I am today. UC San Diego was an amazing place to go to school but also an expensive one, and my 30-hour-a-week job did not give me the time to master the fine art of balancing work and academic success—especially for someone raised without career guidance under the philosophy that "everything will work out." *[←After presenting the full context for her failing, Flavie finally admits it—poor study habits, the fallout of her hippie childhood.]* It wasn't until I began to get firsthand experience in the professional world after college that my ambition was truly ignited and I began to pursue excellence, define my goals, and master time management.

When I think about what I've accomplished professionally and where I am today, I'm very proud of what I've done and where I "came from." I wouldn't trade it for any other childhood in the world. As for Tofurkey—maybe my parents were just ahead of their time? *[Humorous close nails down reader's empathy: who could begrudge her a weak grade or two?]*

Sample Optional Essay 3: Peter J. (Admitted to Chicago Booth)

If there is further information that you believe would be helpful to the admissions committee, please feel free to provide it.

I would like the admissions committee to know that my undergraduate GPA is not an accurate measure of my academic abilities. Because my parents could not pay for college and I did not want to take on loans, I chose to work. *[←Leads with his strongest material: he had time commitments that other students did not face.]* My work experiences in college, both at JSM Real Estate and as a Resident Advisor, proved to be excellent and worthwhile experiences. As a real estate associate at JSM, I was able to see the lessons of my business classes applied in real situations. As a Resident Advisor, I was able to gain valuable leadership experience. *[Deftly turns a negative fact into a platform for showing off positive experiences.]*

When I developed the time management skills to balance work and study, my GPA rose and I was able to earn dual degrees, a Bachelor of Arts degree in Russian and Eastern European Studies and a Bachelor of Sciences degree in Accountancy. *[←Provides the "happy ending" that mitigates his weakness.]* My degree in Russian and Eastern European Studies was for avocational purposes. It enabled me to understand my heritage and learn how to read and write in Russian. My fluency in Russian has enabled me to contribute to the Russian community of Nashville by tutoring and mentoring new immigrants. My degree in Accountancy, which led to my licensure as a CPA, was for vocational purposes and has proved to be indispensable to understanding the way businesses function.

I ask the admissions committee to view my GPA in my last three years in college as well as my professional successes since college as the true indication of my ability to participate in Chicago's rigorous program. *[←Respectfully and humbly closes a damage control essay that's actually a highlight reel of his application's strengths.]*

Sample Optional Essay 4: Soonbae L. (Admitted to Columbia Business School)

Is there any further information that you wish to provide to the Admissions Committee?

In the winter of 1994, my uncle Ki-Yon, a professional studio session guitarist, gave me his electric guitar, a Gibson Les Paul, and Led Zeppelin's fourth album for my birthday. Shocked by the thundering sound of Jimmy Page's guitar, I began practicing guitar day and night. In my Seoul high school, I put together a three-person band, Iris, featuring me on lead vocal and guitar. While I began writing and recording my own songs, we became good enough to perform at major school events like school festivals and basketball half-time shows.

After we graduated from high school, my band and I began performing at local clubs in Seoul. By my sophomore year of college, we were the headline act, selling 200 tickets per show. Performing sold-out shows every weekend and interacting with the audience was a sheer joy for me, and I began skipping school to write more songs and perform more shows. As Iris gained recognition, we signed a two-album three-year contract with Music Story Entertainment, a major Korean record label, in the spring of 2002. From that moment, my band members and I began performing as an opening act before crowds as large as 15,000 for famous Korean bands. *[In two paragraphs, Soonbae has skillfully sketched a fascinating rise to musical stardom, Korean-style. Note that he doesn't need to directly state that his rock god ascent affected his grades.]*

In the summer of 2002, a rare opportunity came to me: Music Story Entertainment chose me to be the main producer for the original soundtrack for "Loving U", a 24-episode soap opera (www.kbs.co.kr/end_program/drama/loving) that had an average weekly audience of 5 million on the Korean Broadcast System. For 12 weeks, I led the songwriting, arranging, and recording with a lyricist, studio musicians, an orchestra, and recording engineers. The biggest challenge was not only writing good melodies but arranging the music to fit the action of each scene in the show. Moreover, my deadline to write the main title song was only three weeks! Receiving advice from fellow film music producers, I revised the score over and over again.

The two months of hard work paid off. From the first broadcast, "Loving U" recorded high viewer ratings, and my main theme song, "Loving U," (www.kbs.co.kr/end_program/drama/loving/plus/ost/ost.html) debuted at #1 on Korea's pop charts, became the most requested song on KBS radio, and in December 2002 was named Best Television Soundtrack of the year by KBS. *[Truly impressive achievement.]*

As a result, my band and I became the subject of countless media interviews. Hearing my song playing on screens and radios everywhere and occasionally signing autographs when people recognized me were strange but pleasant experiences. Though I had to devote all my time to rehearsing, touring, and recording, this period was one of the happiest of my life: I was immersing myself in something I was really passionate about. *[←Direct statement of*

Soonbae's joy in music effectively sets up the reversal that comes in the next sentence.→]

Just before going into the studio for a second soap opera project, my father was diagnosed with cancer. As the first son, I was destined to take over the company, but seeing I was headed in a completely different direction, my family and Kokam Co. executives became concerned about the company's ownership and management. Since a portion of my father's share in the business had already been transferred to me, I had to accept the right of management or the family company would be managed by my older cousins. I loved my music career, but I felt I had a responsibility to continue the family legacy—a sacred responsibility in Asian society. Just as my father had had to give up his career as a journalist to continue the family business, so I too decided to follow in his footsteps, without regret. [←*Soonbae maturely faces up to the family obligation he feels so strongly about.*]

It was difficult to walk away from my music career, but I did the right thing. Although my father isn't actively involved in Kokam's management anymore, he still guides me as chairman of the board. I still hold on to my music career as a precious memory and inspire fellow songwriters with my musical ideas whenever I have time. Since October 2008 I have channeled my music passions into conducting the choir of the Southern Californian Woori Presbyterian Church in Anaheim Hills and by giving vocal/instrumental lessons. As Columbia Follies Club officer Galen Thomas explained to me, I can use my music industry experience to play in the band Juranimal, score background music for Follies skits, or record music for the club's music videos. [*Finds way to appropriately integrate his knowledge of Columbia's resources into the essay.*]

Note on Volunteer Work

Since my first Columbia application in June 2008, I have deepened my community leadership. In addition to my music-related work for Woori Presbyterian Church, I also provide transportation (dropoff/pickup) and translation (Korean/English) services for elderly church members. Moreover, for the Istituto Italiano di Cultura, in Westwood, California, I help organize fundraisers and art events by arranging catering, handling invitation mailings, and translating the newsletter. [*Shrewdly uses the optional essay to bolster his case as a reapplicant.*]

Sample Optional Essay 5: Oleg G. (Admitted to Wharton)

Is there anything about your background or experience that you feel you have not had the opportunity to share with the Admissions Committee in your application? If yes, please explain.

[Oleg's intriguingly understated writing style lets the oddness of the scene shine through.→]

It's nice to be out of the cold and sitting down in a warm cozy tea house. Catherine Cui, my Beijing patent attorney, likes oolong teas for the kung fu tea ceremony, so that's what I order. She compliments me on my Mandarin.

"No foreigner speaks better. Honestly."

When she praises my trilingual three-year-old daughter for her Chinese, I try to hide my fatherly pride. Eventually, the topic shifts. Catherine is impressed by my successful UN translator exams in Chinese, English, and Russian. She praises my communication strength.

"Xiexie (thank you)," I say.

"What's the Russian for Xiexie?"

Spasibo.

We sip the fragrant tea.

I thank her for the good work on my patent application for the dynamic presentation board. Catherine says the legal work was straightforward because my mathematical model complemented the blueprints well. Inventors go far in life, she says, because they think outside the box. *[The method in Oleg's madness becomes clear: he's using the optional essay to sum up the well-rounded distinctiveness of his profile, and earning big points for doing it so cleverly.]*

"Creativity and good people skills must have helped you manage two language programs in China," she states. I agree and suggest that leadership and innovation often go together; this reminded me of the time I trained a team of 12 teachers to use my "One, Two, Three" teaching method designed to benefit all types of learners. In this case it resolved an underperformance problem in the Grammar classes.

Knowing that I have lived in China, Russia, America, and Canada, Catherine tells me she envies the exposure I have received from these diverse cultures.

"Modern managers need this cultural flexibility," she says. "Tell me your China story."

I tell her about bicycles, backpacking, leading international teams, a condo mortgage, startups, friends, volunteering, an anti-SARS Marathon, red tape, raising children in Tianjin, meeting President Hu Jintao ...

"Sounds like you will be an interesting MBA classmate—communicative, creative, multicultural, and mature."

"Xiexie," I say. "My essays will need to communicate that!"

"Write about our kung fu tea."

I take her advice.

Credible Enthusiasm: Letters of Recommendation

When I read a really great recommendation the person jumps off the page and they really come alive. I feel like I know them; I know the good, the bad, the warts; if I walked into a room, I could almost pick out this person.

—KIRSTEN MOSS, STANFORD GSB

A balanced recommendation is a beautiful recommendation.

—PAMELA BLACK-COLTON, UNIVERSITY OF ROCHESTER (SIMON)

Sometimes the last item read in an applicant's file, sometimes treated as a pro forma rubber stamp, occasionally the element that saves or damns a candidate—the letter of recommendation occupies a unique place in the business school application. It is the only element in the admissions folder in which a third party, other than you and the school, is given the opportunity to weigh in on your qualifications. Because it is the element over which you have the least control, the letter of recommendation is the application wildcard.

Called by some schools "letters of evaluation," "career progress surveys," or "confidential statements of qualification," recommendation letters by any name are critical to your admission. A detailed, fervent recommendation can sound almost like an endorsement from your organization itself, lending your application an air of credibility that's hard to equal. A supportive recommender can enthuse about you in a way that you cannot, at least without sounding like a raving egotist. And as a more experienced professional with broader managerial exposure, your recommender will have observed aspects of your skills that you aren't likely to see yourself. Recommendation letters can do what no other parts of your application can, so make sure you execute them well.

This chapter differs from every other in that it concerns an application document you should not write. Almost every business school insists that applicants not write their letters of recommendation themselves, even when their recommenders ask them to. Many of these same schools encourage you, however, to proactively help your recommender craft letters that really strengthen your application. This chapter will help you and your recommender do just that.

WHAT DO RECOMMENDATION LETTERS DO ANYWAY?

You're probably thinking, "Why all this fuss over documents that are almost always dripping with praise? How can schools take letters of recommendation seriously?" There's no denying that the vast majority of letters of recommendation are positive endorsements. But consider that anywhere from 10 to 20 percent of the recommendation letters schools receive are actually negative—not lukewarm. Negative. Add to this the sizable percentage of recommendation letters that, though apparently positive, contain one telltale deal-breaking hint, and you begin to see why schools scrutinize letters of recommendation so closely.

The experienced adcom member knows how to read between the lines, to gauge when a negative remark is a legitimate weakness and when it's a ding trigger that will separate the fulsome praise from the hard accomplishment. The percentage of positive recommendations may be huge, but there's a much smaller universe of genuinely enthusiastic and knowledgeable recommendations.

Because schools seek different qualities in their applicants, a good letter of recommendation will mean different things to each school. In general, schools use letters of recommendation to determine whether you can handle their program academically and whether you have the kind of senior management potential to eventually make the school shine. On the broadest level, schools use recommendations letters to learn about your hard (technical, analytical) and soft skills (team play, communication), but also about something more important than skills—your personality and character.

Letters of recommendation also serve a corroborative function. They tell the school whether the people who work directly with you view your contribution in the same way you do. Have you been overspinning your achievements in your essays? Are you really the fast-track star you portrayed yourself as? Recommendation letters provide the reality check. But such corroboration is more than merely factual. Schools are looking to see if your recommenders also confirm your themes, the self-marketing handle you've been pitching in your essays. A recommendation letter that confirms all the factual claims you make about your position and achievements but contradicts the spin you've put on them will hurt you. For example, to evade the "techie" pigeonhole, suppose you downplay your technical expertise in your essays and highlight your informal project leadership and mentorship roles. In his letter, your recommender confirms that you are an unusually skilled software developer who has played key roles in developing six of the company's flagship applications—just as you claimed. However, he completely fails to back up your leadership claims, instead enthusing rhapsodically about your brilliant software development and testing skills. Admissions officers, wondering if you really have senior management potential, slide your file into the wait-list box. Dissonance between recommender and applicant can be fatal.

On a more subtle level, schools can also use letters of recommendation to gauge whether you (1) know how to read people well enough to discern enthusiastic recommenders from the lukewarm and (2) have the negotiation skills to convince busy recommenders to do you a big favor.

Ask a roomful of admissions officials what they value most in a recommendation letter, and you'll invariably hear two words: candor and content. They want to know that the recommender is being honest with them, and they want the honest assessment to be backed up by concrete anecdotes. In other words, they want credibility. Does this really mean that schools will favor an applicant whose recommendations discuss "areas of improvement" over one whose recommendations deny any weakness? It does. No one is perfect, and a recommendation that offers no negative comment loses believability. As you and your recommenders follow the advice contained in this chapter, remember that elite business schools don't admit applicants because they have no blemishes. They admit them because their positives are so consistently striking and substantial as to outweigh their faults.

LENGTH

Unless you're applying to schools like Harvard and Tuck, which impose tight word limits (250 and 300 words per section, respectively), a one-page recommendation letter should be avoided. Short letters, which used to be called "coffee-break recommendations," suggest that the recommender has an enthusiasm deficit or simply lacks enough real examples to document his praise. Two pages (single-spaced) can be sufficient, especially if you are an applicant who—let's be frank—doesn't walk on water. (Two pages are the maximum at schools like Yale and MIT). Three pages—if free of filler and packed with impressive examples—can be very effective. Anything more than three pages is usually too much information.

Though long letters can certainly backfire if they lack examples, are written poorly, or are *too* long, they do tend to show that the recommender thought highly enough of you to take the time out of her busy day to write an extensive endorsement. Fortunately, Harvard and Tuck notwithstanding, most business schools do not place length restrictions on recommendation letters. They want recommenders to feel encouraged to say as much as they want to (perhaps because finding a recommender who *wants* to say a lot is borderline miraculous). And even Harvard will cut a good recommender some slack. In admissions director Dee Leopold's words: "We have suggested word limits for recommenders that amount to roughly a page of text; we do this to give those not familiar with writing recommendations a sense of the response we're looking for. If your recommenders have more to say, that's fine—their file upload doesn't get cut off after a single page or after a certain number of words." Harvard understands that for many applicants, limiting their recommenders' enthusiasm would be criminal.

SELECTING RECOMMENDERS

Deciding who your recommendations should come from can get complicated, but the following screening steps may help:

- Start by listing your direct supervisors from your current and previous jobs, going back no more than, say, five years (include supervisors in your community involvements). "Direct" means you reported to this person and interacted with him or her regularly, such as several times a week (though hopefully more).

- Next, ask yourself which of these people knows you best, through intensive or continual interaction over a sustained period (ideally, six months or more).

- Then ask yourself who is likely to provide a truly enthusiastic endorsement. Who knows about or would not be appalled by your business school plans and basically thinks a lot of you?

- Next, ask yourself who the best writers are.

- Now ask yourself who understands the recommendation letter process best, as in, has experience writing letters, preferably successful ones.

These "screens" should give you a manageably short list of potential recommenders. If your list is still too long (you should be so lucky), you could add additional screens like, who has an MBA? Who has an MBA from your target schools? Who has the most august job title?

Keep in mind that one of your goals in choosing your recommenders is to arrive at a set of letters that presents the broadest range of your skills, experiences, and themes. This breadth will not only portray you as the kind of well-rounded applicant schools covet; it will also enable you to minimize the overlap between the stories each recommender tells. Although it's fine if two recommenders refer to one or two of the same achievements, they should provide a different perspective on each.

One way to achieve breadth is by choosing recommenders from different periods of your recent career: for example, current supervisor and previous supervisor. Another approach is to choose recommenders from your current or recent employment who have each seen different sides of you: your current direct manager, a current manager in another department whom you worked for regularly in a different capacity, an external client or customer who glimpsed another side of you over an extended period. (For schools that ask for letters from two of your supervisors, a client or customer will only work as a third letter, if the school permits one, unless you are an entrepreneur or work for a family business).

A third approach to ensure breadth is to choose a mix of recommenders from your professional and nonprofessional activities (though always lean toward the professional). A manager from work will obviously have seen you in a very different context from your supervisor at the Make-A-Wish Foundation. Choose this third path only if your current direct supervisor has managed you for several years, your previous direct supervisor managed you a long time ago, and/or you have a very strong profile of extracurricular leadership and impact.

By continually keeping the criteria of enthusiasm, direct knowledge of you, and breadth in mind, you will maximize your chances of identifying the most effective mix of recommenders. If you're shrewd in your choice of recommenders—and they come through for you—you'll have taken a crucial step toward convincing the admissions committee that you deserve a spot.

FIRST LETTER: DIRECT SUPERVISOR

Ideally, your first letter will be from your current boss. Yes, schools say they understand why you may not be able to ask your current manager, but you should try to give schools what they prefer, not just what they'll live with. Because schools recognize how risky it can be to ask your immediate manager for a letter, they look favorably on applicants who do. Don't conclude too quickly that approaching your boss is impossible or "dangerous."

The one exception to the direct supervisor rule is if you are applying to business school within three months or so of starting a new job. In that case, your new boss may not know you well enough to write an effective letter. Your schools may actually prefer a letter from your previous manager. If you absolutely cannot get a letter from your current manager, then you must get a letter from another manager at your current employer who knows you well or from your immediate manager at your most recent previous employer.

What the Schools Say

Recommendations are an important part of your application. We would like one of your recommendations to come from your current supervisor. Your current supervisor is in the best place to provide insight to you as a business professional leader. … We are looking for people who can provide true insight into your character and potential. It is always a good idea to choose your recommenders carefully. Also, you should brief and prep them to help you tell your story. Provide them with your résumé, essay one, talk with them about your goals and educate them on the school.

—ISSER GALLOGLY, NEW YORK UNIVERSITY (STERN)

It should go without saying that procuring a recommendation from a CEO type, celebrity leader, or higher—the so-called "God letter"—will hurt your application if the deity in question doesn't really know you. It should go without saying, but hundreds of business school applicants do exactly that every year. Don't be one of them. You may think that a VIP recommender's willingness is an exploitable ace in the hole, but such letters are a bad idea for two excellent reasons. First, the VIP recommender is unlikely to know you well enough to say anything that will interest the committee, and, second, your ace-in-the-hole strategy is actually surprisingly common. Schools are inundated by brief, unhelpful letters of reference from VIPs. Rather than be impressed, they wonder at your judgment.

SUBSEQUENT LETTERS

Admissions committees love letters from supervisors. These professionals have the seniority and leadership experience to judge employees, and evaluating people is frequently a key part of their managerial role. Their opinion comes with a built-in credibility. Assuming that your immediate supervisor wrote your first letter, your second letter should come from your immediate supervisor in your last job or perhaps another manager at your current job who knows you well. Particularly if you're self-employed or work for a family-owned business (letters from dad are out), clients, suppliers, or your accountant, lawyer, or venture capitalist can also make good business-related recommenders.

Although professional-related letters are always preferred, your second recommendation can also come from an extracurricular source. This could be your supervisor at a community organization, provided that your performance for that organization was unusually strong, you believe your community profile needs more bolstering than your professional side, or you're applying to a school that views "social impact" applicants favorably. Except for schools like Stanford that require them, letters from peers should be avoided unless you really have no stronger supervisory alternative. This is because peers have not usually been in a formal evaluative role over you.

Since schools insist that recommendation letters be recent and come (primarily) from business associates, do not dust off the academic recommendations you filed with your college's career placement an eon ago. With rare exceptions, schools discourage academic letters not only because, for most applicants, college was a long time ago, but also because schools glean all the academic-related information they need from your undergraduate transcript. Too often, academic letters sound half-hearted and distant, referring only to classroom grades rather than to extracurricular leadership or other activities that schools might actually be interested in learning about.

What the Schools Say

Answering our specific questions certainly helps. We understand when a busy person prefers to write one letter to a few schools, but the applicant should still ask the recommender to be aware of what we are asking and try to cover that, even if it's not in the format of our questions.

—Gwyneth Slocum Bailey, University of Michigan (Ross)

THE DELICATE ART OF APPROACHING RECOMMENDERS

Now that you know whom to ask to recommend you, don't just fire off a few e-mails and wait for the effusive praise to pour in. A careful, proactive strategy toward approaching and coaching your recommenders can make all the difference between a disastrous "recommendation" and the real McCoy.

The first step is gauging whether your prospective recommenders are willing. In fact, you want them to be more than willing; you want them to be glad to help. The best method is to forthrightly ask them if they think they can write a strongly supportive letter. If you encounter anything short of unhesitating consent, you may want to consider someone else. Recommenders sometimes agree to write positive letters but then, suddenly overcome by a scruple of "objectivity," submit tepid or vague letters that harm more than they help. A recommender who is writing a letter only out of courtesy or duty will probably accept an opportunity to back out if you offer one. So phrase your request in language that invites the unenthusiastic recommender to withdraw.

The Drill

Let's face it. Devoting the multiple hours required to write a detailed letter of recommendation is a big favor. Give your recommenders enough time (two to three months is ideal), and make your initial request in a face-to-face meeting (or two). Bring with you all the supporting documentation you think they need (or will read). Definitely give them:

- Your résumé.

- Your schools' instructions for filling out the online recommendation letter form (or the actual form and a stamped envelope if you're going the hard-copy route).

- A cover memo or general statement explaining why you need an MBA, what your post-MBA goals are, what you think is unique and compelling about your candidacy (traits, not just skills), which stories (accomplishments) and themes you want this recommender to discuss, and which schools you're applying to, with a list of the qualities they seek in applicants.

Consider giving your recommenders:

- Your essays, if you've written them (you did start early, didn't you?). (Note a risk here: the recommender may simply import material from your essay with no new insights or information).

- Talking points for answering *each* of the schools' recommendation questions.

- Highlights and/or quotations from the recommenders' performance reviews of you.

- A sample letter of recommendation (this chapter contains two).

Be sure to tell your recommenders when you need the letter and how much time you realistically expect the process to take. Because all this material may be curbing their enthusiasm, also tell them that you do not expect them to write a separate letter for each of your schools. Rather, tell them this: when they receive the e-mail from your schools containing the log-in information for the schools' online recommendation forms, you would be happy to use that log-in information to go online and collect the recommendation questions for each of your schools. You will then assemble all the schools' questions into a single, composite list (in which the many questions that schools share will be eliminated). Only then will you ask the recommender to begin work.

Provided you don't overdo it, all this information can ensure that your recommendation letters complement your essays while minimizing the chances of a backfiring endorsement. Draw the conversation to a close by telling them that recommendation writing has only one eternal, inviolably sacred rule: each response to an individual recommendation question must contain at least one specific, concrete, and detailed example ("Mary is a true leader. *For example, ...*").

Far from scripting the recommender's response, your supporting documentation may actually jog his or her memory about accomplishments and skills that you overlooked. In any event, your impressive organization and thoroughness will hopefully put recommenders in a more relaxed frame of mind, one conducive to praise.

Educating Your Recommender

You will be the best judge of whether your recommender really understands the recommendation process. Managers in management consulting and finance, the two traditional MBA feeder industries, are likely to be veterans (or beneficiaries) of the MBA recommendation letter game and so may require little guidance. If you work for a small company or a firm in an industry where MBAs are less common, you may have to do some hand-holding.

Your recommenders may be used to the brief reference letters sometimes used as letters of introduction in the business world and dash off your letter accordingly. Similarly, they may think they should approach your letter in the same spirit as your performance review, where a tone of rigorously neutral objectivity rules. In either case, they may believe that an impersonal corporate tone confers weight and authority. Edify them: recommendation letters should start not from a position of neutrality but of energetic advocacy.

WRITING YOUR OWN?

More and more recommenders, weighed down by work and other responsibilities, are asking applicants to draft their letters of recommendation for them. Even if your recommender only intends to use this draft as a starting point, you should resist this request for one good reason: business schools don't like it. The whole point of asking a third party—your boss—to provide some outside perspective on your potential and qualifications is defeated if that outside perspective comes from you.

Given that typical admissions officers read thousands of recommendation letters over their careers, you can rest assured that they have a sixth sense about nongenuine letters. The personal idiosyncrasies of your writing and thinking style are difficult to hide, and after plowing through your essays, the admissions officers are now likely to be acutely sensitive to them. Even if you try to adopt your recommender's voice, the similarity between your essays and your letters of recommendation is likely to be all too clear.

But the likelihood of getting caught is not the only argument against writing your own letters. Another is that it will probably produce a mediocre letter. Admissions officers will immediately sense that your ventriloquized recommendation letter isn't offering any insights or experiences not already found in your essays. Your recommender can probably highlight stories or personal traits that you cannot, and he or she probably understands the larger context in which your contribution has unfolded far better than you do. Finally, even the most egotistical applicants will be hard pressed to describe themselves with the same delighted, spontaneous enthusiasm that a truly supportive recommender can communicate.

What the Schools Say

Do not incorporate anything drafted by the candidate in your recommendation or have the candidate submit the recommendation on your behalf.

—Yale School of Management Instructions to Recommenders

In writing your own letter, in other words, you'll be trading an opportunity to provide a fresh, deeper perspective on your candidacy for warmed-over versions of your essays. So do your best to convince your recommender to write the letter himself or herself. If you can't, try to find another recommender who will.

If you really feel you have no choice but to write the letter for the recommender's signature, consider an alternative that will keep you out of the process. As a consultant with over a decade's experience evaluating recommendation letters, I can interview your recommenders for you and transcribe their comments into a formal recommendation letter for their revision and signature. This removes you from the process, as the schools want, and saves your recommender from the hassle of slaving over nouns, predicates, and indirect objects. He or she may not have two hours to write your letter, but is likely to have 45 minutes to convey comments over the phone.

Using the School's Questions—or Not

Most schools insist that recommenders respond to each specific question on the school's recommendation form rather than submit a generic letter to every school. How do you satisfy this requirement without scaring off your recommender? As I noted earlier, one approach is to craft a single composite letter that encompasses *all* the questions asked on each of your schools' recommendation forms. Since business schools want you to remain outside the letter-writing process, you can then have your recommender send the composite letter to me, and I can take care of matching the relevant content to each schools' specific questions.

If you're lucky, you may have the kind of godsend recommenders who are willing to craft separate letters for all your schools. If you do, simple humanity compels you to limit the number of letters you ask them for to some reasonable level. Alternatively, you could line up a different set of recommenders for your "safety" or less desirable schools. Their letters may not be as strong as your A Team recommenders, but then again you may not need them to be. Your main recommenders will appreciate the lighter burden.

What the Schools Say

We would like the recommenders to fill out our form but realize these are very busy people. We do not look negatively on letters of recommendation that are in letter form but address our questions. We do not like to receive generic letters of recommendation attached to our form—there are reasons why we ask the questions we ask on our form and hope that the recommender will address them in some format.

—SALLY JAEGER, DARTMOUTH (TUCK)

RECOMMENDATION LETTER QUESTIONS: EXAMPLES AND SPECIFIC QUESTIONS

Most schools' recommendation forms ask for similar content. Every school asks the recommender to describe the length and context of his or her interaction with you, and virtually everyone asks about weaknesses (sorry, "areas of development"). The vast majority require recommenders to comment on your strengths and weaknesses, and most ask the recommender to compare you to your peers, characterize your interpersonal skills, discuss your leadership ability or managerial potential, or document your impact.

Fighting Admissions Committee Assumptions

As we've seen, an effective recommendation letter is not only detailed and enthusiastic but strategic. Besides guiding your recommender toward discussing the accomplishments that reinforce your essays' themes, you can also ensure that she helps you combat the assumptions that admissions officers may bring to your application: the quantitatively challenged sales rep, the interpersonally unpolished techie, the individualistic entrepreneur who never saw a team he didn't try to run, the investment banker without a social conscience, and so on.

First, list the generalizations about skills or personality that are traditionally associated with your industry or profession (if you aren't sure, ask me). Pull out your résumé and essays, and, perhaps with a friend's help, check if any part of your application is unintentionally telegraphing these stereotypes to the admissions committee. Is your résumé stuffed with too much technical jargon? Does your list of community involvements start looking patchy after the second activity? If you do find anything that subtly hints at your profession's stereotyped weakness, ask your recommender to help you offset it with stories that work against type, perhaps by giving him outlines of examples that refute them. For example, an applicant who has never worked overseas could encourage her recommender to discuss the details of her success on a multinational project team. The solo entrepreneur could ask his recommender to describe the team-building exercises he implemented at his start-up.

There are also topics that are distinctive to individual schools, such as INSEAD's interest in you "as a person," Columbia's "ethical behavior" query, Duke's request for information on your international experience, and Michigan's curiosity about your "ability to help create knowledge in the workplace (i.e., ask questions, learn, contribute, and transfer knowledge to staff, team members, and supervisors)."

Before discussing specific strategies for approaching the most common recommendation letter questions, let's consider a feature that should be common to all of them: examples. In recent years, business schools have reworded their recommendation questions to make it harder for recommenders to answer in general, unrevealing ways. So-called behavioral questions push the recommender to provide situational examples that prove you have the skills claimed for you by showing those skills in action. An example of a behavioral question is Stanford's, "Describe the most constructive feedback you have given the candidate. Please also detail the circumstances that caused you to give the feedback." It's impossible to answer this question effectively with vague language not tied to a specific event. Bottom line: the days when schools trusted recommenders' flat assertions about applicants' skills are gone. They want credible evidence, or in Yale's words: "Please be as specific as possible and use concrete examples whenever possible."

As we've seen, the most credible evidence is the example or anecdote, which even in a recommendation letter can usually be structured as follows:

1. What was the problem or challenge that the applicant or your organization faced?

2. How did the applicant use his particular skill to resolve the problem or challenge? That is, what steps did he follow in applying this skill and overcoming the specific obstacles he faced?

3. What was the positive outcome (expressed quantitatively, if possible)?

As in essays and résumés, numbers give schools hard data they can hang their hats on, magically transforming the nebulous into the tangible. If your recommenders back up all their claims and examples about you with concrete numbers, your letters will have the weight and credibility that give applications momentum. Another type of evidence that builds credibility is quotations, as from clients, other managers, or the recommender's own performance reviews on you. ("The deal simply would not have gone down without Jason. The client later told me, 'It was a pleasure working with such an efficient, resourceful, and polished young analyst.'")

Finally, it's not enough to provide stellar examples if you don't also provide the context for understanding them. In other words, your recommender shouldn't just state that you presented your market analysis to the CEO; she should explain that only one other associate has ever done that in the history of the firm.

Now let's look at the most common recommendation letter questions.

How Long and in What Context?

"How long and in what context?" is the de rigueur first question of every recommendation letter. Because it asks a straightforward factual question, there's very little "positioning" your recommender can do for you here: she either knows you well or she doesn't. If she does, she can make that knowledge crystal clear by very specifically noting the range and depth of interaction she's had with you. This is where many applicants falter by assuming that this is a no-brainer that can be answered in a single sentence: "I've known Caldwell since October 2002, when he began reporting to me as business development manager." Recommenders need to go deeper than this.

He or she must detail your professional relationship: How did your recommender first get to know you? Did he hire you? What qualities did he first notice in you? What were your job responsibilities when you first began working with the recommender? What, early on, was your hierarchical relationship with the recommender? Did you report directly to him? How often would you meet or talk with him? Continually (offices or cubicles side by side) or intermittently—twice a day, once a week? If only once a week, did you meet formally in meetings, for example? If so, were these group or one-on-one meetings? How have your professional responsibilities and hierarchical reporting relationship changed over time? How frequently do you interact with the recommender now and under what sorts of circumstances—ongoing daily interaction, meetings, travel situations? If you no longer work together, when did you last work with your recommender and how often do you keep in touch?

If all these questions seem like overkill, remember that if your recommender can establish early on that she has extensive and sustained knowledge of you, she will have created a climate of credibility that will make all her upcoming assertions about you more believable. Conversely, if your relationship with the recommender is not close or longstanding, you may want to keep this paragraph short and sweet—or consider another recommender.

This section is also a good place for the recommender to provide a few sentences of background information on himself—where he earned his degree(s) and which organizations he has worked for and in what capacity, up to his present title. Such information enhances the recommender's credibility as someone whose opinion merits respect. Recommenders who have MBAs should obviously note this fact, especially if they are alumni of the school in question.

Having established this detailed context as succinctly as possible, the recommender can conclude this section by explicitly asserting her authority to recommend you: "For these reasons, I believe I'm in a particularly strong position to comment authoritatively on Caldwell's skills and potential."

Strengths

In many ways, strengths are the most important part of the recommendation letter—the recommender's opportunity to describe what really makes you special and to back it up with examples. Which strengths should you emphasize? Again, avoid "hardworking" or "diligent." These worker-bee qualities are assumed and will hardly distinguish you from others as a potential senior manager. You want the strengths that your recommender discusses here to complement the three to five themes illustrated in your essays. The themes need not match identically, of course.

Some variance between essays and the recommendations is good because one of the functions of a recommendation letter is to provide new information. So if your recommender details three strengths, two could be the same strengths you cited in your essays. The same rough ratio might also govern the overlap between the stories described in your essays and those in your recommendations. That is, two could be unique to this recommendation, and one could be a story you discussed in your essays.

The recommender should describe your strengths straightforwardly in a theme sentence or two: "One of Rajesh's special talents is decisive decision making." The body of the paragraph (several sentences in length) should consist of evidence sentences that cite specific examples of your strength. These examples are the payload of the recommendation letter—the proof that your recommender isn't just blowing laudatory smoke rings. Without them, your letter is sunk.

If you are, for example, a finance professional or IT consultant, it goes without saying that you have strong technical or analytical skills. Encourage your recommender to focus on strengths that might not be assumed in your profession, such as leadership, creativity, interpersonal skills, or strategic vision.

Weaknesses

No section of the recommendation letter is more dreaded, important, or misunderstood than the "weaknesses" question (sometimes euphemized as "areas of improvement" or "constructive feedback . . . given the applicant"). It's a question every school poses (sometimes twice). Some schools also want to know how you handle criticism, apparently believing that it's not enough that you be deserving of criticism; you must also be able to take it like a grown-up.

Most letters whistle past the graveyard when it comes to addressing weaknesses. They either ignore them ("If Ralph has any weaknesses, I am not aware of them") or dress up virtues as vices ("perfectionist," "works too hard"). Both approaches fail because (1) they're frankly hard to believe, and (2) too many applicants use them. They fundamentally misunderstand the purpose of the question.

In reality, schools expect your recommenders to be quite supportive, so they do not include the weakness question expecting to learn of horrific faults like "abusive" or "unscrupulous." (A small fraction of recommenders do, of course, report such deal-breaking weaknesses.) Rather than flushing out the bad apples, the main purpose of the weakness question is simply to learn where otherwise outstanding applicants need further development. Many applicants' paranoia about this question's dark intent leads them to immediately think in terms of *personal* weaknesses, and, unsure which kind are acceptable, they offer weaknesses that are really strengths, like "impatient with lower standards." Some schools, like Dartmouth, make it harder to wriggle out of the weakness question by asking the recommender for *three* areas of improvement.

But unless the school's question insists on a personal weakness, a much safer approach is for the recommender to identify *professional* weaknesses. For example, your recommender may commend you on your superb corporate finance skills but advise you to gain formal training in derivatives, risk management, and fixed-income securities. These are hardly weaknesses schools will hold against you—indeed, they strengthen your case for needing an MBA! In other words, steer your recommender toward discussing weaknesses that (1) complement the reasons for needing an MBA given in your goals essay and that (2) no one would expect you to have overcome at this point in your career. The recommender must, however, be specific about these functional or professional weaknesses or the schools may suspect another attempt at evasion.

By asking your recommender both for a professional weakness and, elsewhere on its form, for the one thing they would change about you, Columbia forces a description of a personal weakness. What personal weaknesses are acceptable? It's often a question of degree. A weakness—poor communication skills—that can expedite your file to the ding bin becomes tolerable if it's a mild and correctable form of the flaw: "needs to polish her oral presentation skills." Such repairable weaknesses can include everything from a "tendency toward linear thinking," "too quick to compromise," and "still too risk-averse" to "immature about corporate politics" or "too deferential toward senior management," and the like. If your personal weakness is not an egregious vice, doesn't routinely impede your effectiveness, is a maturity issue typical of younger applicants, and/or can be rectified, then admitting it will not damage your chances of being admitted.

Usually, citing one weakness is sufficient (unless the school asks for more), but a two-sentence response won't cut it. The recommender should provide a brief example in which you demonstrate the flaw. He should then indicate what you have been doing to rectify it (if you have). (Since weakness questions ask for current flaws, the recommender should not imply that you've completely eliminated the weakness.)

Don't fear the weakness question. Even one frank, detailed admission that you aren't the first perfect human being will go a long way toward overcoming the skepticism that schools bring to each new glowing recommendation letter. By providing contrast, weaknesses can actually accentuate your positives.

Interpersonal and Teamwork Skills

So much of your time in business school will be spent in groups that for most applicants the recommender's response to this question is more important than his comments on your analytical or quantitative skills (which in any case the admissions committee can assess through your GMAT score, transcript, and résumé). Moreover, because people skills are a broad and amorphous talent, they must be demonstrated in your recommendation letter through examples, examples, examples.

One way of grasping how important people skills are to business schools is to consider the sheer variety of interpersonal terms that show up on schools' recommendation rating grids:

Handling conflict

Building consensus

Motivating teams

Negotiating successfully

Mentoring subordinates

Multicultural skills

Interacting with peers

Interacting with subordinates

Making presentations

Influencing others

Oral communication

Sense of community

Inspiring trust and confidence

Respecting others

Integrity

Personal accountability for one's behavior

The interpersonal ideal may well be the applicant with a friendly, even fun-loving demeanor who treats everyone with respect while inspiring others to do their best. But there are as many "right" ways to show interpersonal and teamwork skills as there are terms for it. Be sure to provide your recommender with the details of your finest interpersonal moments (she may not have witnessed them). They need not be formal work examples. Sometimes the most effective examples are informal stories like going beyond the call of duty to help a colleague with a personal problem or lifting your group's morale through some personal gesture.

A recommendation that hints at the wrong kinds of interpersonal adjectives—arrogant, harassing, prejudiced, antisocial, introverted, socially inept—can have a decisively negative impact on your chances of being admitted.

Peer Comparisons and Managerial Potential

The rating grid ("outstanding, top 5%") common to many recommendation forms is not the only way business schools ask recommenders to explicitly compare you to your peers. Several schools also ask the recommender to elaborate on your abilities relative to others (MIT: "How does the applicant stand out from others in a similar capacity?"). This is where the hard evidence of true fast-track status—ahead-of-pace promotions, atypical raises and bonuses, unusual job responsibilities or visibility—must go. Here again, concreteness gains the most traction. "Alice is among my top two account representatives (out of twelve)" is far more persuasive than "Alice is one of the most talented representatives I have." This section can close with an explicit description of the ranking the recommender gives you ("top 5%") among a specific pool of peers, for example, "all the marketing managers I've worked with in my career," "the 25 peers in Wue's consultant training cohort," "the fifty MBAs I've interacted with professionally," or "the 30 analysts under me in the Equities Research division."

Your long-term potential is, of course, another way of getting at how exceptional you are relative to peers, and many schools ask the recommender to assess your likelihood of future success. Since the recommender obviously can't know how things will turn out for you, it's tempting to fire off a short, general-sounding paragraph along the lines of, "Tony will succeed at whatever he sets his mind to." This won't score many points with the admissions committee (which probably sees this exact phrase in every other letter), so it's best to approach this question in the following three concrete ways:

1. *Past record of atypical success:* The recommender can quickly cite the evidence that you have succeeded at an atypical pace thus far in your career: early promotions, special management training programs, "high-potential" status, unusual raises and bonuses—anything that shows you outperforming your peers. The recommender can then make the logical deduction for

the admissions committee: your past history of atypical success strongly suggests that your unusual success will continue.

2. *Business school and goals:* First, the recommender can explain why she believes you want and need an MBA. The recommender with an MBA can draw from her own experience of the degree's effect on her career. The recommender without an MBA can simply mention the hard or soft skills that she believes you will gain in business school. Second, the recommender can provide the committee with as much detail as she has about your post-MBA goals. The greater the detail, the more thoughtful and forward-looking you will appear. This will increase the likelihood that the committee will believe that you will actually realize your potential. In discussing goals, the recommender should always make clear why she thinks these goals are reasonable and achievable for you.

3. *Five or ten years ahead:* The recommender can sketch out a likely scenario (synchronized with your goals essay, of course) for you five or ten years down the road—including job title, industry and type of employer, or general responsibilities. This can graphically indicate how much potential he really thinks you have. That is, a recommender who states that you will be roughly on a par with your peer MBAs 10 years from now may not impress the committee. Conversely, a snapshot of you outperforming your peers would confirm the recommender's strong sense of your potential.

LETTERS OF RECOMMENDATION: WHAT *NOT* TO DO

1. Omit examples. This is recommendation sin number one. Letters that lack anecdotes or stories to flesh out the recommender's claims are almost worthless in the committee's eyes.

2. Choose your recommenders poorly. Avoid VIP recommenders who know your first cousin's second wife and met you only once for 30 seconds. This mistake also includes family members and friends or former professors who gave you an A five years ago but never talked to you.

3. Write it for the recommender. Why? Because schools don't like it. Find a recommender who thinks enough of you to write it himself or herself. If all else fails, I can interview the recommender for you, saving him or her time while keeping you out of the process.

4. Use vague, generic language. "Bill is a top performer with a really sharp mind and a winning personality." This is an empty, uncompelling claim. Schools want substantiated facts and anecdotes that reveal personality and distinctiveness.

5. Adopt an impersonal, dry "corporate" tone thinking this lends gravitas and credibility. Recommenders who continually refer to you as "the applicant" will sound like they regard you as a mere cog in the corporate wheel or, worse, can't recall your name. Similarly, an entire letter of sentences like, "Project deliverables were aligned with Ricardo's scope analysis, impacting our strategic benchmarks across all metrics" can ruin an otherwise enthusiastic letter.

6. Wander from the question. Too many recommendation letters suffer from attention deficit disorder. Eager to be enthusiastic but even more eager to avoid specifics, the recommender begins praising one of the applicant's strengths but then quickly moves on to four more without ever illustrating the first.

7. Pretend you have no weaknesses. Many applicants are so psyched out by their competition that they believe a letter that admits even the slightest weakness will scuttle their chances. The opposite is actually true: a letter that omits a weakness loses credibility and may invite suspicions that some sinister personal failing is being covered up.

8. Attempt to evade the weaknesses question by using stale, overused, generic weaknesses like "perfectionist," "works too hard," or "too hard on himself." Better to mention the functional deficiencies that you're going to business school to fix.

9. Contradict your application's themes. Don't be a quant-savvy marketer in your essays, résumé, and interview but a quant-challenged marketer in your recommendation letters. Stay on message.

10. Focus only on factual achievements rather than portraying yourself as someone with a unique set of strengths. A letter that's chock full of impressively detailed accomplishments is light-years stronger than a vague letter devoid of examples. But the ideal letter will place such accomplishments in a broader context to show why your performance was atypical and will connect them to the themes ("innovative leadership," "international profile," etc.) that unite your whole application.

SAMPLE LETTERS OF RECOMMENDATION

The following two actual recommendation letters earned their beneficiaries admission to Stanford and Columbia. Though some business schools frown on long letters, a long, meaty letter will always be more effective than a short one that's generic or vague.

Sample Letter 1: Lian X. (Admitted to Stanford GSB)

Dear Admissions Committee:

Lian X. is a highly intelligent, energetic, and dedicated leader with a bright future in executive management. In comparing her with the MBAs, executives, and Ph.D.s I've managed or worked with in my career, I would rank her in the top 5 percent. I'm sure she will contribute to Stanford's MBA program as substantially as she has contributed to Toyota America.

[Brief section on the recommender's background enhances the letter's credibility, especially since the recommender has had an impressive career.→]
I earned my bachelor's in economics at Harvard University and later earned my Ph.D. in engineering and my MBA at the Massachusetts Institute of Technology. I have been fortunate in my career to have co-developed several major automotive industry initiatives, from the gas-electric hybrid product line and economy SUV products to multiple-platform automotive engineering and the Indian compact car series. Having been present at the creation of many innovative automotive projects I have developed a firsthand understanding of the dynamics of new technology leadership. In 2002 I accepted the challenge of becoming Toyota America's youngest senior vice president for the same reason I believe Lian agreed to come aboard as our youngest director—because we want to play a part in defining the leading edge of automotive design.

1. *Define your relationship to the applicant and describe the circumstances under which you have known him or her.*
   I first met Lian X. early this year when she called me regarding possible openings at Toyota America. By this time, I had already begun the search process for a director of next-generation automotive projects, but after Lian's call I added her name to the hat and invited her in for an interview. She had already impressed us with her reputation in the industry, and she was equally impressive in her interview. I had her talk with several Toyota America managers, and she impressed them with her hard knowledge. To test her, I asked her bluntly what she thought Toyota Motor Corporation should be doing over the next year and what she thought of what we had done so far. She pulled no punches in pinpointing where she thought we had failed; I frankly admired her candor. We offered her the director's position, which actually surprised her, as she later told me she had been expecting to be offered a division manager position. She is our youngest director by four years. Since she joined in June, we have interacted on a daily basis. *[←Though the recommender and the applicant have worked together for under a year, their daily interaction reassures the reader that the recommender knows the applicant reasonably well]*

2. *Please describe the candidate's capacity for hard work, i.e., the ability and desire to sustain a steady and focused effort over a long period of time and over a broad range of tasks and responsibilities.*

Lian's duties at Toyota America are varied and substantial. The research and design initiatives she authorizes potentially affect Toyota Motor's millions of customers, 254,000 employees, and our $11 billion in sales. Lian has played a critical role in establishing our newly created Hydrogen Engine Division and building its credibility as a future power train across Toyota Motor. In specific terms, she is responsible for creating Toyota Motor's future hydrogen fuel cell product line; establishing a framework for and executing all design and research projects and partnerships related to this promising new "green" technology; and proselytizing and pre-marketing hydrogen fuel and future alternative automotive technologies across the industry. *[←Detailing Lian's impressive range and visibility of responsibilities helps her stand out.]* This requires an extraordinary level of energy and a willingness to put in very long hours (she typically works over 70 hours a week). Lian is passionate about what she is doing. I sometimes call her the "pit-bull" because of her unusual energy and commitment. I know I can unleash her on a task and she will deliver.

Despite her wide range of changing priorities, she has the tenacity to stay with a project until it is concluded. For example, when she first arrived I assigned her a many-month mission: get the major power train vendors in several selected regions to participate in a Toyota-sponsored industry conference to promote a hybrid fuel platform. Lian's effort has not faltered over the months and she has been able to draw the support of many major names in the Tier 1 automotive vendor world, which would be critical for the future technical success and marketplace adoption of this new engine technology.

3. *Please provide examples of the candidate's analytical abilities and intellectual curiosity.*

Lian's analytical abilities were well known to us before she even began working for us. I was already familiar with the projects she led on SUV fuel efficiency improvement, diesel conversion, and composite-based body design she had done at Hyundai. She also jumpstarted Hyundai's robotic sedan manufacturing facility in Shanghai in 2007. These were outstandingly impressive and unusual achievements. Several other executive VPs had also admired her rise, and we were even using her career as an external role model case study for our young managers before she arrived.

Lian absorbs new knowledge with astonishing speed and has unusually strong intellectual gifts. For example, in her role as Toyota America's "prime mover" for next-generation fuel cell technologies, Lian established our first thorough process for researching, evaluating, prototyping, comparing, and greenlighting the potential technologies we incubate in our Sapporo "skunk works." Her new evaluation tool balances financial, technological, management, manufacturing efficiency, regulatory, and customer variables to screen out unpromising technologies. This process and the recommendations Lian derives from it are now our main tool for analyzing which technologies to integrate into our latest models and when. It has already helped us greenlight three multimillion-dollar alternative power train technologies planned for our 2010 and 2012 model revisions. *[←Recommender's specificity deepens the letter's credibility.]*

Lian's analytical and intellectual skills were amply displayed in only her second week when her expertise in hydrogen engine technology was put to the test. Still adjusting to a new environment, Lian crafted a report that provided a highly detailed analysis of the next-generation alternative fuels landscape, assessed the potential value of each for Toyota, identified the strategic timeframe in which Toyota should roll out products, identified the leading players in each market segment, and proposed a detailed strategic positioning approach for Toyota. Her work was so solid that it has been presented by Toyota Motors to all of Toyota's regions as the common basis by which Toyota and its subsidiaries should make decisions in the future alternative fuel technology market. I also know that when Lian consulted with Toyota's Tokyo research brain trust to validate her work on this report, they praised her work and set up a meeting to extract insights from it while including part of Lian's analysis in their next report! *[←Extended four-sentence example constitutes compelling "mini-accomplishment."]*

Lian came to Toyota America in part because she felt the promise of hydrogen fuel cells has been unfairly ignored, and she wanted to play a role in bringing them into the mainstream. Like me, she believes in identifying and proselytizing for "paradigm shifting" automotive technologies. Hence, her curiosity about Toyota America's hybrid fuels niche is quite robust. She couples that curiosity with excellent vision and knowledge of the industry. I trust her judgment in evaluating and understanding the new technologies, and extracting the essence for us: i.e., how can we use these technologies and integrate them into our consumer products.

4. *Describe a situation in which the applicant has demonstrated initiative and the ability to understand his or her own strengths and weaknesses. What are some of the candidate's weaknesses?*
Lian brings a remorseless can-do initiative to whatever she does. One example in particular can illustrate this. We are involved with another group at Toyota in attempting to do a major multimillion-dollar deal with a leading American competitor to establish a new hydrogen fuel cell industry standard in Asia and North and Latin America. This group had trouble understanding the market implications of the deal as well as Toyota's four

ongoing hydrogen development projects. I sent Lian in as a facilitator to help bridge the gap in understanding, using both her technological and interpersonal skills. She successfully suggested a common industry standard for the regions that overcame the initial misunderstandings and kept the possibility of the standard alive. Lian also spearheaded an extension of the standard into Europe, which had not originally been included. Specifically, she proposed including in the standard a brand new Toyota technology that even our competitor immediately recognized the value of. This suggestion could open a multimillion market to us.

I can think of no better proof that Lian views her strengths and weaknesses objectively than that she is applying to business school. She is at a pivotal point in her career—indeed, its culmination—and she has already devoted significant time to her education. Nevertheless, she understands that she lacks grounding in the basic principles of the American general management system. As I myself did, she is willing to step away from her career to gain them and later have the same kind of involvement I had in the launching of ground-breaking automotive technologies. I applaud Lian for her commitment to improving her skills and ability to contribute in the long-term. Aside from these functional developmental needs I don't regard Lian as having any significant weaknesses. [←*Recommender dodges weakness question by referring to applicant's need for general management education; a more direct response would have been preferable.*]

5. *Please describe the candidate's attitude and behavior when working with: (a) managers/supervisors, (b) peers, and (c) subordinates.*
Lian has been extremely deft at negotiating the dynamics of our professional relationship. She understands my role and time demands well and complements them with her own skills. She communicates issues that merit my attention succinctly and with a full range of viable, well-considered options. When she comes to me with problems she also brings solutions. She does exhaustive due diligence on potential technologies percolating up to us, creates an evaluative shortlist I can depend on, and always makes an actionable recommendation.

Lian interacts with peers and subordinates with essentially the same guiding attitude—providing the support necessary to drive the process forward. Toyota America's Technology office is a relatively flat organization of 150 people. She is an inclusive, "enabling" manager and colleague. She goes out of her way to tap all sources of information at Toyota Motor, introduces our groups to all relevant parties, and involves many groups on each deal and project.

As a specific example of her interpersonal skills, recently one of Lian's colleagues took an extended leave for serious medical reasons. Not only did Lian assume part of this individual's responsibilities while he was away, but, more important, when the colleague returned Lian spent a great deal of time helping him catch up and updating him on the latest developments and decisions. I have found her a pleasure to work with.

6. *How would you rate the candidate's leadership potential?*
As I mentioned, Lian and I share a dedication to contributing to the inception and evolution of innovative automotive technologies. Being a leader of any enterprise is a challenge; leading the new technology arm of the world's largest carmaker is something else again. I have found it to be a true test of all my resources, and Lian is among a select group of people whom I feel is also capable of providing this kind of strategic, exhaustive leadership. I know she plans to found an automotive technology venture of her own in her native China one day. She has all the personal tools to succeed.

In the few months that we have worked together, Lian has already been intimately involved in several large alternative power train projects, executed two new partnerships with Tier II vendors, and personally green-lighted a technology that may one day change automotive engineering as we know it. She has also stopped two technologies from development that could have cost Toyota America millions of dollars. I see no major limits to her potential. [←*The level of impact the recommender conveys in this short paragraph greatly advances the applicant's cause.*]

7. *Please discuss the candidate's citizenship (as defined by mature, respectful behavior) within your organization and in the community.*
Lian has a buoyant personality and ready sense of humor, but her commitment to the organization and others is quite mature and responsible. She is highly reliable, someone you count on when there is no margin for error. For example, on several occasions, our top management has urgently needed board-level presentations on emerging technologies to counter competitors' threats in the fuel efficiency marketplace. On each and every occasion, Lian completed the presentation and supporting analysis ahead of deadline. That level of reliability and dedication is the definition of corporate citizenship. Outside of Toyota America, I know that Lian is involved in the China-America Century Foundation, which she is promoting at Toyota America through internal and external fundraising events, and that her entrepreneurial plans for China include a significant community-giving component.

Lian deserves a place in Stanford GSB because she has demonstrated repeatedly and impressively that she has the skills that turn promising ideas into revolutionary technologies. I wish her well.

Cordially,

Sample Letter 2: Subodh J. (Admitted to Columbia Business School)

Dear Admissions Committee:

I am very happy to have the opportunity to recommend Subodh J. for admission to the MBA program of Columbia Business School. Subodh has outstanding analytical skills and exceptional individual and interpersonal attributes that will make him a truly exceptional contributor at Columbia and a brilliant leader. [←*Brief introduction establishes tone of enthusiastic endorsement.*]

What is your relationship to, and how long have you known the applicant? Is this person still employed by your organization? If "No," when did he/she depart?

I first met Subodh at the beginning of 2006 when he joined Satyan Partners, the strategy division of Satyan Consulting, as an intern. At that time I was a manager entering my sixth year with Satyan. Over the course of the following two years I had the privilege of supervising Subodh during several strategy engagements, representing fifteen full-time months, with leading Asian personal computer manufacturers. [←*Specific information on nature of recommender's relationship with Subodh builds credibility.*] In January 2008, following an engagement during which we developed the integrated desktop PC strategy for IndiaPC, Subodh decided to join Dell where he took on the operational responsibility of launching their new corporate laptop offerings in Japan. At the time, Dell Japan was the last PC maker to enter the market. Today, with more than 10% market share, Dell Japan is poised to become the fifth largest personal computer maker, just behind NEC.

Following Dell's successful launch in Japan, I heard Subodh was thinking of seeking out a new challenge. I immediately met with him to convince him to return to Satyan Partners, which, happily, he did in autumn 2009. Very soon after his return we had the opportunity to work together on a company-wide operational review for China Computer's entering president. It was our last engagement together. Subodh notably demonstrated his ability to deal with senior members of the Executive Committee, especially with Mr. Xie L., the current head of the Consumer Desktop Division. Subodh also showed his ability to put his technical expertise into practice.

Subodh is still working with Satyan Consulting and enjoying continued success. He recently sold his first engagement, which he is currently managing. As for me, in 2010 I left Satyan to return to my home city of Chennai where I work as a freelance consultant to senior executives at Wipro and Tata Group.

Provide a short list of adjectives, which describe the applicant's strengths.

To name only a few of the most relevant adjectives, Subodh is extremely bright, curious, versatile, efficient, autonomous, team-oriented, ethical, and very mature. The following questions/answers will help to better substantiate why I think these characteristics accurately represent Subodh. *[←Rather than just list adjectives, the recommender refers the reader ahead to the rest of the letter where these adjectives are illustrated with examples.]*

How does the applicant's performance compare with that of his or her peers?

When working with Satyan, I considered myself privileged to work with a group of twenty-five highly talented and motivated individuals. As a Senior Manager I have had the opportunity to manage several consultants who "keep me on my toes." By that I mean that they do not hesitate to challenge my ideas and force me to better myself.

I can truly say that Subodh is the most talented person I've worked with in what is a very strong peer group of twenty-five people. *[←Bold statement of extreme praise makes this letter stand out from less enthusiastically endorsed applicants. Will he back it up?]* I'm not the only one to think this. Our staffing meetings would oftentimes dissolve into heated discussions over who would have the privilege of adding Subodh to their team. He is what we refer to amongst ourselves as a "Fast-Tracker." Subodh received the "far exceeds requirements" notation on his last five evaluations. This is the highest possible ranking and is only awarded to the top 3% in an office. *[←Provides substantial detail to support "most talented" claim.]*

What makes him so effective?

Subodh learns extremely quickly, is very curious, and has the versatility to succeed in any context. After only four and half years of work experience, he has proven his ability to adapt and succeed both in consulting and in industry. Moreover, his software background provides him with much stronger analytical and quantitative skills than most of his peers. During the IndiaPC assignment in 2007, Subodh built a marketing plan with multiple variables that enabled us to model customer acceptance scenarios and compare them. This greatly helped the client make his $175 million investment decision. Few senior consultants could have done this job. *[←Though brief, this example effectively demonstrates Subodh's analytical skills.]* Combined with his experience in corporate strategy and marketing, this analytical/ quantitative skill makes Subodh an "all-terrain" consultant, able to go through complex Excel models and contribute to more qualitative and business-driven projects.

What further sets Subodh's performances apart from those of his peer group are his autonomy and initiative. Subodh will not wait for his project manager to tell him what to do; he will systematically suggest a course of action and propose an implementation plan. Once a plan is agreed upon, he will take full responsibility for delivery and will typically far exceed expectations. This was the case during the last engagement we worked on together for China Computer. The project identified several initiatives for driving efficiency and liberating upwards of $1.5 billion in free cash flow. Subodh contributed significantly to this project by assuming the full responsibility for a whole segment of the project—the consumer laptop division—representing one fourth of the total synergies. Normally, this type of project is awarded to a manager, but we felt Subodh had the required skills and maturity. As usual he proved us right. On the strength of this project in particular he won his ticket to be promoted to Manager in June 2010. [←*Second set of key strengths is also backed up by a concrete example.*]

Another important characteristic of Subodh's is that he has excellent relational skills with clients and does not require the same level of guidance as most of his peers. He is not just a consultant but also a true counselor to his clients, which is demonstrated by the repeat business he generates. Once clients have worked with him they ask for him specifically. Recently, for example, IndiaPC, who remembered his contribution in 2007, directly contacted Subodh. Subodh went on to sell this client an $800,000 project; a feat rarely achieved by first-year managers. [←*Third set of strengths backed up by a concrete example.*]

How has the applicant grown during his/her employment with you? Please comment on the applicant's maturity.

Subodh has progressed at an exceptionally rapid pace in all dimensions expected of a consultant: analytical capability, aptitude to "storyboard," client impact, ability to take on growing responsibility within projects and manage cross-functional teams.

Furthermore and as previously discussed, Subodh has also been able to develop his marketing skills and recently sold an engagement to IndiaPC in difficult market conditions. I believe that this latest achievement is in good part related to his experience in industry. I can remember that our discussions were often punctuated by Subodh's concern for putting his consulting experience to the test of business reality. And indeed, I witnessed a positive difference in his abilities after his eighteen-month Dell experience. On top of his former assets, Subodh had developed a better knowledge of operational constraints and had more empathy for the client.

As far as maturity is concerned, one clear sign of it is that despite his growing reputation and influence Subodh has remained true to himself: easygoing, always helpful and extremely professional. In short, Subodh takes his work and clients very seriously but does not take himself too seriously which, in my mind, is a very strong sign of maturity.

Comment on the applicant's ability to work with others, including superiors, peers, and subordinates. If the tables were reversed, would you enjoy working for the applicant?

Subodh is very easy to work with. All stakeholders in a project always appreciate him because he naturally creates good personal connections thanks to his smiling personality.

As previously stated, senior managers, partners and clients will specifically request Subodh for almost any type of project because of his autonomy, versatility, and efficiency. Subodh clearly understands the roles, responsibilities as well as the strengths and weaknesses of these stakeholders. He knows when to involve the right players to maximize his work's potential for success. This was confirmed to me when I observed the way he worked with managers on several assignments. He was able to quickly understand each environment and efficiently adjust to different styles of management.

Subodh's peers respect his judgment and will oftentimes turn to him as they would to a project manager for expert advice. More importantly he contributes to the success of all projects because he is a "true team player." I have personally and frequently seen Subodh help a colleague complete an assignment after he himself had already put in a sixteen-hour day. During a strategic project that we worked on for six months I saw another example of his commitment to the team. Because of some last-minute adjustments we had spent all night working on a business plan. Our presentation was at 8:00 am and by 6:00 am we had hardly finished. Subodh took it upon himself to finalize the deck and get everything ready so that I could take a shower and gather my thoughts prior to making the presentation to a twenty-person project committee. Trust me, had he not offered to do this, what turned out to be a successful presentation could have been a disaster. [←*Revealingly specific anecdote shows Subodh's human side.*]

Subodh's subordinates value the fact that he sets out a clear direction, takes the time to work closely with them, and "teaches" them the skills required to be a good consultant. First, in terms of knowledge transmission, Subodh has the ability to adapt to his audience and make tricky concepts sound simple. This greatly helped us integrate consultants into assignments that required strong technical backgrounds. Secondly, Subodh has an excellent capacity to translate technical insights into something meaningful for the client's business.

Finally, I would enjoy being managed by Subodh because he gains respect; he does not impose it. I know that he would provide me with strong direction as well as the room I need to develop my own views and opinions. Moreover, he would provide the input and support I would need to improve my deliverables and myself.

In what ways could the applicant improve professionally? How does he/she accept constructive criticism?

Subodh's attitude towards seeking out professional feedback is exemplary. In each of the five evaluations I conducted on him, he explicitly asked for weaknesses and made sure to work on them for the next evaluation. He is one of the rare consultants who is more interested in the feedback session than the discussion about pay and bonus, although this also mattered to him, of course.

As I said previously, Subodh is superbly talented, and as one of our very best consultants, he does not have many weaknesses. However, as his background is in engineering he would definitely benefit from the formal management training provided by the Columbia Business School MBA program. He will acquire new skills and knowledge such as financial analysis, entrepreneurial management, and organizational behavior that will complement his own technology expertise. Interacting with Columbia Business School's diverse student body will allow him to broaden his perspectives and overall boost his ability to anticipate and manage change. Subodh is a very talented person and clearly a future leader, so the MBA will round out his skills. [←*Recommender takes advantage of Columbia's request for a professional weakness by naming functional areas Subodh can address in business school.*]

How well has the applicant made use of available opportunities? Consider his or her initiative, curiosity and motivation.

Subodh is inherently curious. When most consultants are presented with a new project they will typically ask if it is a strategy engagement and if it is in their industry of choice. In contrast, Subodh seems to first ask himself what he can learn from working on the project. In terms of his initiative, as previously discussed, this is an area where he definitely sets himself apart from his peer group. For example, on a project in which his team lacked information about new technologies such as home-based networked computing, Subodh decided to organize a four-week benchmark in London, U.K. He first got a few agreements in principle to meet with some U.K. start-ups and then successfully sold the idea to our Managing Partner and the client. The benchmark proved very helpful to the client and became a reference used by Satyan practitioners throughout the European practice, involving five offices and representing more than five hundred consultants.

Another example of Subodh's motivation to make full use of opportunities is the work we did on integrated desktop PCs in 2007. [←*The recommender's repeated ability to cite supportive examples makes his enthusiasm for Subodh seem eminently logical.]* Early that year Subodh was asked to work on an initial assessment of the integrated desktop PC business plan for a competitive manufacturer. While he knew almost nothing about this technology he rapidly became a reference with the client at both the engineering and marketing levels, and delivered much more than was initially asked of him. As a result, he was instrumental in turning this small engagement into a fifteen-person project that lasted for nearly a year and a half. Three years later, when the client wants to further develop integrated desktop computing, he asks for Subodh.

Comment on your observations of the applicant's ethical behavior.

Subodh is a straight shooter. He calls it as he sees it and does not shy away from stating his opinions. On one occasion, a client had asked us to "stretch" the numbers for a business plan. We were considering following the client's request, because we were getting a lot of pressure from the client and internally. But Subodh vigorously reminded us that doing so might well serve our interests in the short term but it could ultimately come back to haunt us.

Given the amount of pressure on us, it really took a lot of backbone for Subodh to speak his mind and defend his opinions. I honestly cannot think of any other consultant in Subodh's peer group who would have held their ground in the face of direct resistance from the Managing Partner. *[←Impressive claim.]* Furthermore, and more importantly, he was simply right.

What do you think motivates the candidate's application to the MBA program at Columbia Business School? Do you feel the applicant is realistic in his/her professional ambitions?

Subodh is a realistic person. Unlike many consultants I have encountered, he has always adopted a pragmatic and hands-on attitude in the way he sets his goals and makes decisions. In the years 2006–2007, like many technology consultants, Subodh had many opportunities to join start-ups working on very promising technologies such as wireless home computing or PC-based home theater technology. Notwithstanding those attractive possibilities, Subodh decided to work on the launch of integrated desktop PCs, a technology that is encountering important success in India today. In retrospect, this choice happened to be the right one at the time. While this could be viewed as chance, I know for a fact that Subodh considered all options available to him and chose the one he felt was the most realistic, had the best chance of success, and would best enable him to develop professionally. Because of the maturity of integrated desktop PCs as a technology and the conclusions Subodh had drawn from his four-week benchmark in the U.K., Subodh finally chose integrated desktop PCs versus wireless home computing and PC-based home theater, which were not yet mature technologies for the Indian market.

This exemplifies why I am convinced that Subodh has realistic professional ambitions and that his decision to apply to Columbia is well thought through. Personally, I think that Subodh's solid experience in industry and consulting is the key to understanding his wish to attend an MBA program now. This is truly the perfect time for him to complement his skills and experience with the richness, rigor, and diversity of a Columbia MBA. I am convinced that Subodh has the required talent to achieve his goals and make the most of his past experience in developing new PC technology on a large scale.

As regards Subodh's choice of Columbia, I like to think I had a slight impact on his preference. I can remember how attentive he was when I would tell him about my personal experience working in New York as a consultant during my graduate studies in electrical engineering. I frequently used the services of Columbia's library and learned to appreciate the quality of your facilities. Subodh and I had these discussions quite early in our relationship but I recall that Subodh was already very interested in the prospect of studying at Columbia. *[←Personalizing Subodh's application to Columbia by mentioning recommender's own esteem for Columbia is a nice touch.]*

Obviously, Subodh's choice of your MBA program has much to do with its outstanding reputation. However, I would venture to say that the renowned diversity and hands-on approach of your program are likely the key drivers of his choice.

Arc there any other matters, which you feel we should know about the applicant?

I sincerely believe that Subodh would prove a valuable addition to your esteemed MBA program. I believe that his experience, strong technical expertise and well-rounded personality will make him an asset to your program and his classmates. Moreover, he is simply a great person to be around. He possesses a contagiously positive outlook on things, is the personification of the term "team player," has a strong sense of ethics and is consistently driven to better himself and his environment.

There is absolutely no doubt in my mind that Subodh possesses the skills to successfully graduate from your program and hold up the Columbia tradition of excellence in the international business community.

Sincerely,

Parting Thoughts

If you've invested your valuable time and money in this book, it's probably because you know as well as anyone what an MBA can do for your career and your life. You realize it can do more than give you world-beating management skills and an intense learning experience you'll never forget. It can also open doors, launch lifelong relationships, and maybe even change the way you understand yourself and the world.

Like anything offering that much value, there are no magic shortcuts into the promised land. After helping hundreds of applicants win admission to the world's best business programs since 1997, I can assure you that the essays that will get you in are not those with the best-executed "value proposition," the shiniest brand, the cleverest angle, or the most polished prose. No, the essays that succeed do it through self-knowledge, vivid detail, hard work, and a little bit of creativity. The odds of application success are directly proportional to the amount of candid personal insight and time you put into your essays.

Admissions officers recognize sincerity, individuality, and hard work and reward them with admission more often than you might think. So be real, and give each essay the time it needs to really capture you. If you want experienced guidance to help you through the rough patches, contact me directly at paulbodine@yahoo.com for a free, no-obligation consult.

1

In the Flesh: Admissions Interviews

Some business schools try to interview all their applicants; some interview only those who've survived an initial screening review; and other schools' interview policies fall somewhere in between. Whatever the policy of the schools you're applying to, the business school interview will be an important stage in your MBA admissions hunt. Whether you interview with admissions staff, alumni, students, or even faculty, a lousy interview performance can sink your chances, and a brilliant one can advance them.

We've seen that most B-school essay questions can be categorized into a handful of basic topic categories. The range of possible interview questions is much wider. After all, where most business schools limit themselves to three to six essays, even a 30-minute interview can cover 10 or more questions, ranging from why you majored in physical education to which kind of vegetable you would be (if you were one) and why, to what you think of the Chicago Bears.

The impossibility of predicting the interview questions is partly why business schools continue to conduct them: they test you in ways essays do not. Nevertheless, there are several interview questions that you can be fairly confident will be asked in some form. I provide sample responses for these core questions in this appendix. These core topics are followed by sample responses for three broad categories of questions that you should also practice for: behavioral questions (in which the interviewer asks hypothetical or situational questions to see how you would act in certain circumstances), tough questions ("Tell me about yourself"), and questions you should be ready to ask the interviewer when your interrogation is over.

If you need to practice your interviewing skills (and who doesn't), schedule a Skype video interview with me at paulbodine@yahoo.com. Using actual questions asked by your target school, I'll walk you through a realistic admissions interview, critique your responses afterward, and then send you a recording of your interview embedded with my "postgame analysis."

THE CORE QUESTIONS

"What are your career goals?"

- My short-term career plan after Stanford is to work for a couple of years at a venture capital firm like Kleiner Perkins Caufield & Byers or General Catalyst. Evaluating alternative energy firms for possible funding, I'll have a great opportunity to recognize emerging technologies, develop my venture analysis and mentoring skills, refine my own business plan, and establish contacts in the energy and VC industry. My long-term career goal is to launch an alternative energy firm that will focus on sustainable but also scalable alternative energy solutions such as wind-powered desalination plants or non-silicon-based solar power farms. With a Stanford MBA I'll be ideally positioned to ensure that my firm attracts enough seed money, recruits top scientific talent, and aligns itself with a major energy company that can help us leverage our technological breakthroughs. I'm really excited about the opportunities that are emerging.

- My short-term post-MBA goal is to work as an investment research analyst covering emerging markets either for an investment bank with a strong presence in Southeast Asia, such as HSBC, or at a mutual fund specializing in the region, such as Matthews International's Pacific Tiger Fund. Combined with the special insights I have gained through my knowledge of China and Vietnam—both their cultures and their economies—this career phase will give me a rich and nuanced foundation in the market and its companies. In the long term, I plan to exploit my investment research experience through a position as a fund manager. Based in the United States, Singapore, or Shanghai, I will run a Southeast Asia emerging markets fund that enables me to travel frequently to the region to visit companies and speak to company managers. Eventually— say, 10 to 15 years out—I hope to start my own fund focused on Southeast Asia or maybe even entirely on Vietnam, which I expect to grow as quickly as China did during its initial breakout period.

"Why do you want an MBA?"

- Well, it's really only been in the past one or two years that I've known for sure that private equity is the path I want to devote my career to. Carlyle Group's acquisition of my firm forced me to learn in a hurry what private equity firms do and what kinds of impacts they have. When I began to see the positive effects they were having on Remington's operations and strategy, I sought out some of Carlyle's contact people for our firm and learned a lot more. That led to informational interviews with managers at TPG Capital and Permira. I just became really passionate about PE at that point, and I knew it was what I should be doing. Needless to say, with my background in engineering there's no way to break into private equity unless I "retool" with an MBA. And at 27, it doesn't make sense to wait.

- The skills I've gained in project management at General Mills have given me a great foundation for my post-MBA marketing career. But technology management to marketing is a big career switch, and I need the MBA to help me fill in my specific knowledge gaps, for example, the principles of advertising, how to interpret statistical data from market research, how to price products, strategic marketing planning—even the use of branding partnerships with other companies. The MBA is the best way to quickly but also thoroughly ramp up my knowledge of these areas. Of course, an MBA program will also enhance my "soft" leadership skills, sharpen my quantitative and analytical skills, enable me to network with sharp, talented people from different backgrounds, and experience a summer internship that will open a door for me to transition into marketing.

"Why our school?"

- I first learned of MIT Sloan before I was even seriously considering an MBA. Mary Goffin, a Sloan MBA at my firm, was and is very active as an alumna, and she was always singing the praises of MIT's MBA program. When I became serious about the MBA, I remembered what she had said about Sloan's superlative technology resources, including the Center for Information Systems Research, Productivity from Information Technology, and Center for e-Business. I began exploring the program on my own, including a campus visit last spring, and was impressed by the students I spoke with, including Tim Zhang, Beatrice Ellfeldt, and Vijay Singh. I loved the idea of the "First-year Challenge," the emphasis on experiential learning through the leadership courses, and the unique Sloan Innovation Period. Since entrepreneurship is my goal, the $1K Warm-Up Business Idea Competition and the MIT $50K Entrepreneurship Competition will be fantastic opportunities for me. I'd be happy to go into more detail about the Sloan classes, professors, and student clubs that I'm excited about.

RÉSUMÉ-KEYED CORE QUESTIONS

"Walk me through your résumé."

▪ I majored in biochemistry in college because I planned on becoming a doctor. A summer job as an equipment tester at my father's pharmaceuticals firm and a macroeconomics course sparked my interest in business. So after eye-opening internships at E*Trade and Mercer Consulting, I accepted an offer to become an associate consultant in the Chicago office of McKinsey & Company. McKinsey's hypothesis-driven approach to problem-solving fit my science background perfectly. I also wanted a general introduction to finance, marketing strategy, or operations in a variety of industries, which consulting for McKinsey could give me. A McKinsey project gave me my first taste of entrepreneurship. My colleague and I created from the ground up the business plan for a client's technology start-up, working directly with their CEO and dozens of client staff. Our plan was accepted and implemented, and it ultimately led to a business that today generates $100 million in revenue. This project sparked my interest in entrepreneurship, so after three years at McKinsey I moved to Warburg Pincus to get insight into new ventures from the operational and investment side. My year at Warburg has really broadened the way I think about companies. I have developed an in-depth knowledge of finance and have been able to work with companies' balance sheets much more than I would have at McKinsey. After three years in consulting and one in private equity, I'm ready to get the skills to become a successful entrepreneur.

"Why did you leave Stragetel after only six months?"

▪ That was a difficult experience for me, but one I take full responsibility for. I had been working there as an IT contractor for about six months in the sales and marketing department. Because I was looking for ways to break into technical sales, I loved the environment and the department. My client manager knew of my interest and went out of his way to expose me to some of the sales functions. When a full-time opening came up for a technical liaison with the development department, the sales and marketing client manager suggested that I take it and promised me it was really a stepping-stone position into a direct technical sales position. That would have been just what I wanted, but it didn't turn out to be the case. In fact, the full-time position took me even further from Stragetel's sales and marketing functions, and turned out to be a straight technical role. I should have done more due diligence rather than rely on the client manager's assurances. Anyway, when Intel offered me a true technical sales position—exactly what I had been looking for—I decided to jump at the chance. I learned a lot about doing my "homework" and taking responsibility for my actions from that experience.

"Could you explain this gap of six months on your résumé in 2008?"

- Sure. As you know, the subprime crisis led to Bear Stearns's purchase for pennies by Morgan Stanley, and in April, my entire department was downsized—15 people in all, regardless of experience, seniority, education. As the credit markets were still reeling, most of the companies I would have looked to for work were not hiring. I interviewed at over 20 firms in the space of six months, networked at at least 10 industry events and conferences, and used my personal network to do informational interviews outside the industry. But the job market was crowded with people with my skill sets by then. Fortunately, I also used my time between jobs to deepen my involvement at The Hope Place, mentoring two kids, who are now my good buddies. I also completed my CFA III exam, studied for the GMAT, and began visiting business schools, including Anderson. It was a challenging period for me, but I never gave up, and finally this May, Banco Popular offered me an interesting position in its merchant services group. Since this aligned with my post-MBA international goals, I decided to take it and apply for your Fully Employed MBA program.

BEHAVIORAL QUESTIONS

"If you were working on a project with a team of peers late at night and they had an opinion entirely different from yours, how would you manage the situation so that the team completed the assignment the next day?"

- In these kinds of situations, I first ask a lot of questions so I can clearly understand each person's point of view. If the explanations they give me persuade me that my position is flawed, I back off my position as appropriate and offer a new solution that integrates their position and the elements of mine I'm still confident in. We can then proceed forward. If their answers to my questions fail to convince me that my approach needs revising, I need to consider how important it is to me that our project's success take priority over my team's unity. I mean, I might be willing to accept a less-than-optimal solution for this project because I don't feel I have time to convince my teammates, or I believe there will be long-term negative impact on the team's cohesiveness if I try to push my position on this project too hard. It would depend very much on the context.

But if I believe so strongly in my position—for example, if I believe my teammates' solution could have extremely negative consequences—I will use all my persuasive and analytical powers to make the best possible case for my solution, specifically identifying the reasons why I believe their positions are flawed. Wherever possible, I will offer compromises so they won't feel "defeated" or resent my resistance. For example, I might offer to support their position on some other project if they buy into mine on this one. Or I might try to incorporate aspects of their position that won't be harmful to the net outcome if they agree to follow my position on the really mission-critical aspects of the project. If I am certain my position is the best solution for the project, I have enough confidence in my negotiation and interpersonal skills to believe that I could eventually persuade them. I have encountered some examples of this kind of situation from my professional life if you'd like me to share them.

"What kind of manager are you? How do you motivate people? What is your managerial style?"

■ I consider myself to be an inclusive, collaborative manager with high standards but a nonconfrontational style. I developed this leadership philosophy as class president at McMaster University and refined it at as a corporate manager for Sand River Systems in the United States and Lenovo in China. It's based on three basic principles: taking initiative and motivating team members through encouragement, synergizing skills, trust, and shared vision; welcoming criticism as feedback toward improving the process; and solving problems through rigorous analysis and hard data. When I first joined Sand River in 2002, for example, the company had just been dealt a major blow when the virtualization industry standards group omitted its core technology from the industry standard. When Sand River's stock nosedived, management called a meeting, but because we had just enjoyed a successful round of venture funding, no one really sensed the urgency. Though I was only a junior manager I stood up and made what I meant to be an inspiring speech on behalf of focusing less on our promising but still-incubating products and putting greater energy into reducing the time-to-market for our more fully developed products. I was surprised by how much flak I received for that, but I didn't let it rattle me. I asked for time to put together a detailed proposal and timeline for repurposing our product development efforts. I also explicitly asked my critics to review my proposal and offer their feedback. This won over management and some of my critics, and two weeks later I presented a proposal, which had definitely been rigorously worked over and improved by my critics. Because that proposal was thoroughly backed up by data from our product development staff, competitor intelligence, and a couple of germane case studies, it won the day, and today I'm working directly with the CTO and the entire product development staff in implementing my new time-to-market plan. I'll bring this same leadership style to my Tuck study group.

TOUGH QUESTIONS

"Tell me about yourself."

■ Sure. Though I was born and raised in Peoria, Illinois, I think I can say I've led a pretty unusual life. When I was 10, my father took a sabbatical from his teaching job and bought a sailboat, which he and my mother, sister, and I sailed around the Caribbean for two years. The exposure to the cultural variety of this region was an incredible revelation for me, and ever since then I have been a travel and language nut. So far I've lived or worked in four countries, including Norway, Panama, and the U.K., and I speak three languages fluently: English, Norwegian, and German. I think I can offer a lot in terms of cross-cultural insights to my Yale classmates. When I was 16, my family moved to Oslo, Norway, which was a bit difficult for me at first because of the cold winters and language barrier. I worked hard at learning the language though, and eventually made friends who showed me Scandinavia's hot spots and backpacked with me through Europe and Russia.

My technology knowledge grew directly from my desire to be an "international person." I joined Germany's SAP right after graduating from Humboldt Universität. SAP was an exciting place. I worked on SAP's business process outsourcing efforts, and in my spare time I started a successful travel-rating Web site similar to TripAdvisor but Europe-focused. This entrepreneurial experience gave me an interest in product marketing, which I pursued by joining the start-up Crescat Group, a global technology consultancy. Within a year, I was promoted to director of development, in charge of all of our business development activities for the firm's Western Europe region. Leading teams as large as 15, I played a key role in growing Crescat's top-line revenue by 350 percent.

My success gave me the resources to start SeaGuide, a travel-based youth leadership program similar to Outward Bound but more nautically based. That's grown by leaps and bounds. We now have chapters in nine countries. To get social entrepreneurship skills to professionalize and expand SeaGuide is the reason I'm seeking the MBA. I'm confident my cross-cultural, technology management, and social entrepreneurship skills will enable me to add a lot to my INSEAD class.

"Why should we accept you? What would you add to the program?"

■ Well, I think I can bring a pretty diverse perspective to my classmates that will really enhance their experience. Professionally, I have unusual leadership exposure to both the public and private sectors. As the commander of gunnery crews on two Singaporean navy frigates, for example, I was exposed to the military's unusual technical and organizational demands at sea. But I was also later assigned to develop a system for motivating and tracking the performance of naval recruits and to command a naval facility on the Malaysian border. As a technical manager at Flextronics I have learned how to quickly build teams to manage the complexity, competition, and change of the outsourced electronics manufacturing industry.

Personally, I can offer the insights of someone who led effectively in Singapore's armed forces, a melting pot of Malays, Chinese, Indians, and Eurasians. As both a Singaporean and ethnic German, by any definition I would be considered a "diversity" applicant. But as an avid scuba diver I also bring my unique vision of the global community. Scuba diving opens up an entire "global community" of life that most people never experience. I have found that diving with people from every walk of life always creates bridges across cultural and language difference as we appreciate and explore the diversity of the underwater world that binds everyone on earth. My family's story and my involvement in the Pacific Rim Environment Fund add to the diverse contribution I can bring to London Business School, and I'd be glad to talk about them.

"What is the primary weakness in your application?"

■ Probably the fact that early on my career basically centered on research, so I didn't gain any leadership opportunities for three or more years. However, I began to address this two years ago when I pursued and won a lab manager position at Fusion BioEnergy and then helped start GreenFuel. I think I proved my managerial potential by leading the efficiency changes in this group during the integration of Fusion and BP. Moreover, in the process of launching GreenFuel, I was able to set a vision for the company, begin to implement that vision, and achieve tangible results. When you look at my management successes of the past few years—all achieved with only my technical degree and my own leadership instincts—I think I have demonstrated strong leadership potential.

QUESTIONS FOR THE INTERVIEWER

You must be prepared for the moment near the interview's end when the interviewer turns the tables on you and asks you to fire away. Saying you have no questions will be interpreted as either laziness or lack of interest. Similarly, asking questions that anyone could find on the school's Web site or that show more interest in getting admitted than in the school itself will send equally unflattering signals. What you ask will depend to some extent on who's doing the asking.

For the Admissions Committee

If an admissions committee member is interviewing you, you should ask questions that show you have a fair amount of knowledge about the school already but have specific questions related to your academic or extracurricular interests. You can assume the admissions committee member has the depth of program knowledge to answer such fine-grained questions. Avoid any questions that suggest anything negative about the school or display your anxiety about the admissions process.

- "Is the new dean planning any major changes that will affect next year's entering class?"

- "Second-year Brett Delmar said a new trek to South Africa was being planned. Is that true?"

- "At University of Oklahoma, I was very active in convincing alumni to meet informally with students for professional networking opportunities. Will there be opportunities for me to help out the Career Services Office in any similar way?"

- "I read that Dean Chen wants to expand your offerings in the human resources specialization. What changes are likely within the next year or so?"

For Student Interviewers

If you are being interviewed by a current student, you can ask much more specific questions about the curriculum, professors, and the student experience. Never forget that students, more approachable though they may seem, are evaluating you as potential peers: stay positive and professional.

- "Have you taken any courses with Professor Jenarczak or Thirumalai? What are they like as teachers?"

- "Which student clubs are most popular in your class?"

- "Can you recommend any off-campus neighborhoods for first-years?"

- "What has surprised you most about Chicago since becoming a student?"

For Alumni Interviewers

Alumni interviewers are the most unpredictable. You may be lobbed softballs for an hour with an avuncular alum eager to smooth your way, grilled rigorously by someone with a mysterious chip on his shoulder, or be frozen out entirely by an alumnus who seems more interested in his own story than in yours. Don't ask questions that assume they have current knowledge of the program, and remember that most people are flattered by questions about their own experiences.

- "How has an INSEAD MBA helped you in your own career?"

- "What aspects of your MBA experience have been most useful to you in your post-MBA career?"

- "How helpful has the school's network been to you since you graduated?"

- "What are the opportunities for alumni to stay connected or involved with the school? Is the chapter here in San Jose pretty active?"

Still Alive: Wait-List Letters That Work

Congratulations! Sort of. You weren't rejected; unfortunately, you weren't accepted either. You're in that peculiar purgatory known as the wait list. How long your stay there and what steps, if any, you can take to shorten it will depend not only on the school that wait-listed you but on the unpredictable characteristics of the applicant pool you're competing against. Truth be told, a great deal will simply be beyond your control.

But that doesn't you mean you must simply passively wait and hope. You must adopt a positive and proactive attitude—there's really no alternative. First realize that the wait-list letter means that you qualified for admission. You passed. You may have been wait-listed because the school has already admitted applicants with your profile or they found your qualifications impressive, but found someone else's even more so. The point is that they believe you can handle their program; they just ran out of room. Finally, remember that most schools do not rank their wait-listees, so who gets pulled off may well come down to subjective factors such as demonstrated enthusiasm.

What can you do to enhance your chances of being plucked off the list when a space opens up? For the resourceful and strategic, even purgatory represents an opportunity. Do you have what it takes to convince the school that you really belong there more than anywhere else? All else being equal, it is the motivated applicants—the ones who create and execute a sustained and enthusiastic wait-list campaign (for schools that permit such campaigns)—who get in more often than any other. Viewed in these terms, the wait list is the school's way of testing that enthusiasm. So pass the test.

WAIT-LIST PROCEDURES

The wait list is simply an administrative yield management tool that enables schools to achieve their targeted class size by offsetting the applicants who've turned down their offers of admission by letting in wait-listees. Naturally, business schools with high yields (say, 85 percent) will need to rely on the wait list less than will schools who matriculate only half (or less) of the applicants they admit.

Typical Business School Wait-List Notification

Your application to the University of Chicago Booth School of Business has received the careful consideration of our Admissions Committee. While we are impressed with your application, we are unable to provide you with a final decision at this time and will place you on our **wait-list** for future consideration. I want to assure you that being placed on the wait list signals our sincere interest in your candidacy.

This year, our admissions process was highly competitive. While Chicago Booth is grateful to have so many talented students seeking to join us in Fall 2010, we are simply not able to admit all of our most qualified candidates at this time.

During the coming months, the Committee will review wait list candidates for admission as a part of our Round 3 evaluation process. Decisions will be released as part of our Round 3 process on May 12th. While we hope to enroll as many wait-list candidates as we can at that point, the possibility does exist that some students will continue to be on the wait list into the summer months.

You are more than welcome to visit Chicago Booth at any time, though this is not necessary and will not directly impact your admission decision. In the meantime, we ask that you stay in touch should you choose to make other plans and no longer wish to be considered for a spot in the Class of 2012.

As we continue with the Admissions process for Fall 2010, please contact our office directly via e-mail regarding any questions you may have (admissions@chicagobooth.edu). We appreciate your patience during this process and wish you the best.

Sincerely,

Some schools assign each wait-listee to a specific admissions staffer who becomes his or her point of contact throughout the process (in these cases, it obviously behooves you to treat this person courteously). Other schools assign no specific name at all, requiring applicants to submit updates to an anonymous e-mail address.

Some schools may review their wait lists frequently; others will wait until the end of a round or some other natural breaking point. Some schools periodically remove wait-listed candidates who they no longer believe have a chance of eventually gaining admission. Final wait-list decisions can be made by the admissions director or by the admissions staff as a whole. They typically occur in the late spring or summer (though sometimes as late as the first day of class) when schools finally know who will be accepting and who won't.

WAIT-LIST LETTERS: WHAT TO DO

Seize the initiative and launch a wait-list campaign. Unless the school completely discourages further contact, take a proactive approach. Plan a strategy of regular, but not annoying, contacts designed to demonstrate your enthusiasm for and your fit with the school's program and culture. The exact particulars of your campaign will vary depending on the school and exactly when you are put on the wait list, but it can include letters, an additional visit to the school, an offer to interview, letters of recommendation or support from others, and occasional substantive phone calls.

The following general steps can help maximize your chances of eventually gaining admission, but you should always follow to the letter the instructions provided by your school.

Step One: Say Yes

Follow closely the instructions provided in the letter advising you of your wait-list status. Promptly accept the offer of wait-list limbo, in whatever manner is required. Indicate that you will be following up with a full-scale wait-list letter in a few days. If the school's notification letter says, "Jump!" and you want to go to that school, you should think and respond, "How high?"

If you have not visited the school, do so. Ask for a tour, attend a class (or two), and meet with students. The greater your distance from the wait-listing school, the more impressive your gesture of a visit (or revisit) will be (but don't put undue financial strain on yourself). If you have visited, consider doing so again. Develop a practical plan for visiting the school, and carefully and courteously inquire whether you can also set up an appointment with a member of the admissions committee. It may be possible to meet one of them unannounced during a campus visit, but having a prearranged appointment is far more preferable.

If you didn't interview and an opportunity to interview still exists, seize it. If you interviewed already but only with an alumnus, try to schedule a face-to-face on-campus tête-à-tête with an admissions official. This official may not offer you a formal interview, but find a way to get to campus anyway and speak with a professor (or two) or meet students. If they won't set something up for you, then reach out informally to students on campus. Learn what you can. Then after the visit send a thank-you to whomever you spoke with. In the note, reiterate your interest in their school and show how the visit was valuable in confirming that interest.

Step Two: The Letter

Within a few days of your initial acceptance of the school's wait-list offer, send out a one-page but certainly no longer than two-page letter. You have already shown that you are qualified to attend the school. Now give the adcom additional reasons to admit you. Address the letter to the wait-list contact person designated by the school. If you are not given a name, address the letter to the person who notified you of your wait-list status or, failing that, to the admissions director. You may also want to send a copy to your interviewer to keep him or her in the loop (you never know who can help).

The wait-list letter may have five parts, discussed in the following sections.

The Introduction

Explain that you are writing to formally accept wait-list status. Thank the adcom effusively for continuing to keep your life and future suspended in uncertainty. Ruthlessly expunge any notes of disappointment or ambivalence. This introduction should establish a positive, optimistic, grateful tone. It should also directly and succinctly state the topics to be addressed in the letter, namely, your reaffirmation of your fit with the school, your updates on developments in your career and life since you applied, and your efforts to compensate for weaknesses in your application (if you feel sure enough about what those are to address them). Your introductory paragraph might also let the committee know that you've included an additional letter of recommendation from a new recommender who will add a fresh perspective on your candidacy.

The Body: Reaffirm School Fit

Reinforce your commitment to and interest in this school's program but do it in an original way. For example, feel free to mention how the school's culture matches your educational preferences and goals but don't just cut and paste from your essays. Reword your original material, or better yet, cite new examples of resources that illustrate this philosophy or approach. For example, demonstrate how your recent visit confirmed and deepened your interest in the program. Perhaps you sat in on a class (Which one? Who taught it? What were your impressions?) or chatted up three second-year students in the cafeteria (What were their names? What did they say? What impressed you about them or what they told you?). Or perhaps your work or research interests have recently led you to explore a faculty member's work or touched on the mission of one of the school's institutes. If so, deliberately and specifically flesh out the bridge between your work or research interest and that faculty member or institute. Admissions committee members want to know if there are real affinities between you and their program.

The Body: Recent Developments

Inform the school of new achievements, initiatives, and developments in your life. Show the adcoms that you're an even stronger applicant than you were five months ago. This could include promotions, new leadership roles at or outside work, or technical skills acquired on the job. Have you led a project or organization? Volunteered? Have you taken your department, business, or club in a new direction? Have you earned a patent? Launched a business? Received a promotion or assumed additional responsibility?

In short, mention any recent accomplishments that you did not discuss in your application and ideally tie them back to some of the themes or experiences you presented in your essays. If you don't have promotions or even particularly notable achievements, don't fret. Basically, anything *new* that has occurred in your professional or community life since you applied can—if you analyze it—be presented as a development that has strengthened your candidacy (though never try to exaggerate a nonaccomplishment into an accomplishment).

Demonstrate that you are "new and improved" since you initially applied, and you'll increase your chances of successfully surviving the wait list.

The Body: Addressing Concerns

Read the school's wait-list notification letter for any hints of deficiency in your profile. Some schools will tell wait-listees of their concerns or issues in the wait-list notification, for example, recommending explicitly that they retake the GMAT. Some schools will simply invite you to contact them, and your contact person will supply sometimes quite specific and helpful advice. Of course, other schools will leave you entirely in the dark. But even in these cases it's usually possible to arrive at some idea of what's holding you back, particularly if you're working with an experienced consultant like myself. For example, it's easy enough to find out if your GMAT score is below the school's average—if so, consider retaking it. The vast majority of application deficiencies involve poor numbers (GMAT and/or GPA), vague career goals or weak work experience, insufficient community or extracurricular involvement, poorly demonstrated interest in the school, or inadequate emphasis on what makes the applicant's profile or potential contribution unique. Evaluate your application closely to see whether any of these deficiencies pertain.

If your nonquantitative courses in college brought down your GPA, then consider taking a class in writing for business or business communications. If your grades in calculus, statistics, accounting, or economics were mediocre, enroll this minute in an evening course in these topics or at mbamath.com— and let the school know about it. Especially if you're from a liberal arts background, take calculus and statistics. If you're still on the wait list when you earn an A in one of these classes, get that transcript in their hands as soon as possible. If you are not admitted, those classes will help you when you reapply in the fall. If you are admitted, they will help you in your classes.

In other words, whatever your perceived shortcomings are, address them— without highlighting them. For example, if you enrolled in Toastmasters to improve your English, inform the school that you joined Toastmasters two months ago, that you won the extemporaneous and most-improved awards, and that the whole thing's been an enjoyable experience because of the friends you've made and the confidence you've gained. But *don't* say that you also did all this because you were concerned about your low TOEFL or substandard verbal score. The school will get the drift.

Note: You don't need to reaffirm school fit, discuss recent developments, and address concerns in that order. A wait-listed applicant who believes that the school is mostly concerned about her level of interest in its program might want to position her "reaffirm fit" section first. An applicant who's made good progress offsetting glaring weaknesses might want to lead with that section. Also, it's very likely that you can combine parts of your "recent developments" section with your "addressing concerns" section. For example, if you had a weak history of community involvement but were recently named to the board of your local charity, this constitutes both an accomplishment and successful damage control on your application's weakness.

Whichever particular organization your letter takes, keep it short and sweet—two pages max. Don't succumb to the temptation to rewrite or even summarize your life history or essay(s). Stay focused on what you have accomplished since applying, the school fit issue, and your perceived weaknesses.

The Conclusion

Your conclusion should repeat the gratitude and enthusiasm themes of the introduction without using the same language. You could also, space permitting, briefly recap the three or five contributions or uniqueness factors you believe you can bring to the school. If you are certain that you would attend this school, make it clear that it is your first choice and that you will immediately and enthusiastically accept an offer of admission. If you are not enclosing an additional letter of recommendation but one is on its way, let the school know who will be sending it and perhaps even what aspects of your application he or she will shed light on. Perhaps assure the school that if there is anything you can do to improve your candidacy, you will be happy to do it. You may want to express your willingness to provide any additional information the committee needs. Definitely thank the committee for its time.

Step Three: More Than a Letter

As important as it is, the wait-list letter is just the beginning. As soon as you learn you're on the wait list (and it's the wait list of a school that's open to new information from you), dust off any unused letters of recommendation (only those that shed new light, however) and consider which ones to enclose in the wait-list letter. If you have none, you should begin identifying people who can add new insights on your professional, community, or even personal life and can do so with enthusiasm.

You need, in other words, to enlist your fan club. You could seek additional letters of recommendations from former or current supervisors on and off the job, assuming they didn't write one of the letters of recommendation included in your application. Since your wait-list status is evidence that your application may have a flaw, these additional letters of recommendation offer you a perfect opportunity to have a third party do damage control on this weakness by emphasizing offsetting facts or skills. Remember, these wait-list recommendation letters do not have to be as lengthy as your original letters of recommendation, nor do they have to written by someone who knows you as well as your original recommenders.

You could also consider soliciting the help of contacts among current students and alumni of the school that wait-listed you. If your relationship with them is strong enough, ask them to call the admissions office on your behalf and/or write brief letters of support (as distinct from full-fledged letters of recommendation). Bear in mind that this highly proactive and somewhat unorthodox tactic is explicitly frowned upon by some schools and can backfire at other schools that may see such organized, last-minute endorsement campaigns as manipulative. Other schools may actually applaud your initiative in "organizing a support campaign." If you are wait-listed by schools such as Harvard Business School, which explicitly instruct you *not* to send in new information once you've been wait-listed and also explicitly frown on letters of support, *follow their instructions.*

At schools that do not discourage such fan letters, these notes can talk about your recent professional or community developments for you, and they can and should emphasize your fit with the wait-listing school. They are best if they come from students and recent alumni. A bigwig can help but he or she must know you and have something substantive to say about you.

Whether you enlist the help of traditional recommenders or last-minute inside supporters (or both), try to synchronize their efforts so that their letters arrive at the school, say, two weeks apart. A batch of enthusiastic letters arriving all at once is a waste of goodwill. Save your ammo. And, again, observe the school's wait-list instructions as well as online forums where admissions officials clarify them. Some schools draw the line at submitting *two* additional letters of recommendation—you should know this!

How soon after your initial wait-list letter should you begin sending supplemental letters of support? Generally speaking, three to four weeks later is appropriate. If you are still on the wait list, consider also sending a new update or wait-list letter. Even if you have very little new to relate, do your best to emphasize the new and create a sense of momentum. Follow up this second letter with a phone call (if the school permits this) and offer to interview, either in person or over the phone. How many wait-list letters will it take? Stanford GSB has been known pull wait-listees from purgatory after as many as seven update letters.

The point is to never give up until you absolutely have to. The wait list is the ultimate test of your passion for attending a particular school. The upside of that test is that schools may respond if that passion is sustained and genuine—and you've got a bit of good luck.

WAIT-LIST LETTERS: WHAT *NOT* TO DO

1. Fail to follow directions. Again, read the school's wait-list letter or instructions very carefully. If they say, "Don't call," then—guess what—*don't* call.

2. Whine or moan. Regardless of how you may actually feel, your wait-list letter should avoid any trace of desperation, complaint, special pleading, or anger at the sheer injustice of it all. Be professional and positive.

3. Repeat information they already have. Never use anything verbatim from your original application. Don't send a new letter of recommendation if the recommender simply rehashes experiences and virtues that a previous recommender has extolled. Keep it fresh and new. If a point bears repeating, rephrase it thoroughly.

4. Include a promotion or development as an "update" in your wait-list letter when it actually occurred *before* you submitted your application.

5. Tell the school that because it is your first-choice school you will immediately and enthusiastically accept its offer of admission if, in fact, you would choose another school over it. There are other ways to express strong interest in a school's program short of claiming it is "number one" when it isn't.

TWO CASE STUDIES

The following case studies are actual former clients of mine who were wait-listed at the University of Michigan and Chicago, respectively, before gaining admission. Only the proper names, industries, and dates have been changed to protect their privacy.

Case Study 1: Sanjay B.

Sanjay B. was an outstanding applicant. He had a good GPA (3.4) at a Big Ten university; work experience that included three blue-chip firms, General Motors, Dell, and GE Capital; significant international experience including assignments in Paris and Singapore; unusually strong leadership exposure for someone so early in his career; and well-articulated goals. His was the profile of a fast-rising, tireless, make-it-happen future manager. But Sanjay also had huge weaknesses: a GMAT score of 580, roughly 100 points below Michigan's (then) average, and only one and a half year's of full-time work experience at the time of his application. What's more, he had no deep extracurricular involvements or unusual personal or cultural profile to offset his glaring negatives. The fact that Michigan wait-listed him bordered on the miraculous (and said something about the strength of his essays). But how could such a "marginal" candidate realistically hope to survive the end-of-season wait-list weeding?

Sanjay did it by launching a sustained guerilla wait-list campaign that included regular update letters detailing substantial professional advances and enthusiastically discussing specific features of Michigan's program. Here is Sanjay's first draft of his Michigan wait-list letter (with my annotations indicating its many weaknesses).

Sanjay B.'s Wait-List Letter: First Draft

Dear Admissions Committee,

I am writing to thank you for consideration into your MBA program. *[←Not grammatical English.]* Unfortunately, as it stands now, I am on the wait list. *[←Striking negative note is unhelpful.]*

I would like to update you on some events that I have experienced since I first prepared my application packet several months ago. I am proud that my reputation as a peak performer has convinced GE Capital to continually choose me for its most challenging assignments. *[←Vague, flabby statements. Should cut straight to the "meat."→]* Most recently, I was selected to a four-month assignment in Brazil. I will be managing and training a group of new Investment Analysts that will serve our GE Capital Sao Paulo office. This will be my forth *[sic]* international assignment and will further expose me to just how business benefits from diversity. I look forward to sharing these experiences with the diverse student body at the University of Michigan.

In November 2007, one of our clients was underperforming. *[←Transition into new example is too abrupt. Context needed.]* I was chosen to lead a team of seven Investment Analysts spanning three U.S. cities in a modified scope analysis of the client. *[←Good use of specific numbers for concreteness.]* The work we were performing was not typical—GE picked me to lead the team because of my past performances in high-pressure environments. Our team was brought in to perform a liquidation analysis to determine how much we could collect in a worst case scenario. While performing our work I discovered that our client had not been paying its vendors. The company's financial situation was much worse than GE had anticipated. Our team needed to act fast. I contacted the appropriate people at GE to privy *[sic]* them to our findings. This came as a shock to them. GE Capital's position in the deal was that of an agent. Therefore we were the lead financier amongst a group of banks. Management at GE informed me that this new information would have to be brought to light in a bank meeting. Our team needed to supply a report of our findings, so that the bank committee would be properly informed. I was proud because this feat had not only put myself *[sic]* in the spotlight, but also our Investment Analyst group as a whole. *[Good story, but Sanjay takes too long telling it.]*

In December 2007 the fruits of my labor with respect to recruiting came forth. *[Transitions too abruptly to new example; wording is awkward.]* I was the lead recruiter for the Investment Analyst position at GE Capital. As the lead recruiter, I was accountable for the budgeting and conducting information sessions at the undergraduate universities we recruit at. Additionally I was responsible for coordinating and conducting on-campus interviews of undergraduate candidates. This task was a challenging one. Students who are interested in our Investment Analyst program are also interested in similar programs at Investment Banks. Although GE Capital has a strong brand name and reputation, it was still difficult to compete with the salaries that the investment banks were offering. It was my job to convince these students that the experiences they will endure [*sic*] at GE Capital would far outweigh that of any investment bank. The results of my recruiting work—1) 11 out of 14 offers accepted, the highest acceptance rate in the history of our group and 2) the lowest cost per acceptance in the history of our group. I was able to work smarter and (more importantly to GE) cheaper than my predecessors. [*Excellent, concrete results, but example is wordy.*]

I will not be shy to point out that the University of Michigan is my first choice. The University of Michigan is a perfect fit for me for several reasons. Through my research of MBA programs I found that many top tier schools have a disproportionate percentage of graduates working in investment banking and consulting. Michigan, on the other hand, does not "pigeonhole" its graduates into banking or consulting careers. I want to join a manufacturing firms [*sic*] financial management development program for MBA graduates. All the firms that appeal to me (General Electric, Ford Motor Company, Microsoft, Intel, IBM, and Dell) have such programs for Michigan MBA graduates.

The fact that Michigan's program is flexible by design will allow me to customize my MBA to meet my future career goals. As noted in my essays, my long-term goal is to become the Controller or CFO of a large company. I know to reach this goal I will need to obtain my CPA certificate. As a Michigan MBA student I will be able to customize my second year courses to take advantage of accounting courses that will help prepare me for the challenges I will have ahead on my path to the CFO's office. Additionally, I would take advantage of two examples of Michigan's innovative curriculum—"Electronic Commerce on the Internet" and "Network Infrastructure in e-Business." [*Convincing, detailed reasons for claiming Michigan as his first choice.*]

If I am given the chance I know I can make a strong contribution to the excellence and richness of Michigan's program through the quality of my leadership in the classroom, in the workplace, and in the community. I ask you for that chance. [*Nice, from-the-heart touch.*]

Thank you for your consideration,
Sanjay B.

Sanjay's first draft was solid, but its abrupt transitions, sloppy writing, occasionally overly general statements, and overall wordiness needed work. Sanjay's final draft addressed all these concerns.

Sanjay B.'s Michigan Wait-List Letter: Final Draft

Dear Admissions Committee,

I am writing to thank you for considering my application to the University of Michigan's MBA program. I am honored to still be in the running for a place in this fall's class. In this letter I would like to update you on some substantial recent developments in my career that may impact the Committee's perception of my candidacy.

Since I prepared my application packet several months ago, GE Capital has decided to award me my fourth international auditing assignment, this time for a four-month engagement managing and training three new Investment Analysts for GE Capital's Sao Paulo office. I am proud that my reputation as a peak performer has convinced GE Capital to continually choose me for its most challenging assignments. I know this experience will give me further first-hand exposure in just how much business benefits from diversity, and I look forward to sharing my experiences with my diverse Michigan classmates.

Shortly after submitting my application in November 2007, GE gave me another unusual vote of confidence when I was chosen to lead a team of seven Investment Analysts in analyzing how much GE Capital could collect from a critical, under-performing client in a worst-case scenario. Chosen to lead the team because of my past performance in high-pressure environments, I soon discovered that our client's financial situation was much worse than GE knew. Quickly contacting the appropriate managers, I was told to prepare a report on our findings, and GE's bank committee soon had all the information it needed to control the crisis. I was proud of this high-visibility assignment because it not only put me in the spotlight, but brought much-deserved attention to our Investment Analyst group as a whole.

In December 2007 GE also decided to make me the lead recruiter for its Investment Analyst position, which meant I was responsible for the information sessions we hold at colleges as well as coordinating, budgeting, and conducting the on-campus interviews for undergraduate candidates. GE Capital has a strong reputation, but we were competing with the higher salaries offered by the investment banks. My challenge was to convince these students that GE Capital could offer them more meaningful work experiences than any investment bank. My work resulted in the highest acceptance rate (11 out of 14 offers) and the lowest cost-per-acceptance in the history of our group.

I will not be shy in stating that the University of Michigan is my first choice. Although the graduates of many top-tier schools often choose careers in investment banking and consulting, Michigan's flexible, broad-based MBA program will make me a strong candidate to join the financial management development program of one of the manufacturing firms that appeal to me most (GE, Ford, Microsoft, Intel, IBM, and Dell). I will need my CPA certificate to realize my ultimate goal of becoming the controller or CFO of a large manufacturing firm. Michigan's program will enable me to take accounting courses in my second year, while I take full advantage of such innovative courses as "Electronic Commerce on the Internet" and "Network Infrastructure in e-Business."

If given the chance, I know I can make a strong contribution to the excellence and richness of Michigan's program with the quality of my leadership in the classroom, in the workplace, and in the community. I respectfully ask you for that chance. Thank you again for your consideration.

Sanjay B.

Unfortunately, even this strong letter was not enough. Two months later, as June wore into July, Sanjay was still on Michigan's wait list. From his São Paulo assignment, Sanjay watched as time and his hopes ran out. Fortunately, he had outstanding news—he was receiving a major promotion, incontrovertible new evidence of the fast-track profile he had hammered away at in his Michigan essays eight months before. Heartened, Sanjay crafted the following letter, and then drove its message home by arranging two enthusiastic, genuine, and knowledgeable reference letters from new senior managers at GE Capital.

Faced with a candidate who had deepened his impressive professional profile with a promotion and new overseas assignment, was clearly and consistently articulating his passionate commitment to their program, and was backing up his self-advocacy with two new glowing recommendations, Michigan decided to overlook Sanjay's youth and undeniably weak GMAT score. A month later he was finalizing his move to Ann Arbor.

Sanjay B.'s Follow-up Michigan Wait-List Letter

Dear [First Name],

When I last updated the Admissions Committee, I was embarking on my fourth international managerial assignment for GE Capital, this time in Brazil. In the past two months, I have enjoyed managerial growth and challenges that few second-year analysts ever have the opportunity to experience. But I have never lost sight of my real goal—gaining admission to Michigan's MBA program and refocusing my career in corporate finance.

My unprecedented promotion to Manager of Underwriting and Business Analysis in June has presented me with the exciting challenge of being completely accountable for my team's performance while I learn to adapt to the cultural and technical differences of doing business in a foreign country. Thankfully, the fantastic, diverse group of talented individuals who work for me have made that transition an easy one. I am the only American; one of my team members is from Australia, and the remaining five are from Chile, Brazil, and Bolivia. Many applicants say they embrace diversity, but in the past two months I have been given an opportunity to actually practice it by learning how to thrive as the minority member of a multicultural team. I was sent on this assignment to pass on my knowledge of our business, but I am the one who has truly been learning.

While here, I have been able to reflect further on my goals. No matter how I examine it, this fall remains the best time for me to earn an MBA from Michigan. My work in the States and my four international assignments have given me the equivalent of several years of intensive, high-level business experience, which I believe can benefit my Michigan classmates. Moreover, waiting another year to gain experience that won't help me move into corporate finance would be counterproductive. I am fortunate to be on the fast track here at GE, but I know that I could make an even greater contribution if I were to align my career with my passion. Because of the accomplishments I mentioned in my April letter and my recent promotion to manager, I believe my experiences since my original application have strengthened my application significantly. Today, more than ever I know I can benefit from and contribute to the quality of the University of Michigan's MBA program.

Because of the nature of GE Capital's assignments, it is still uncertain how long I will be here in Brazil, though I believe I will be returning to the States in early August. If my hopes for the University of Michigan do not materialize I will need to begin positioning myself for my next assignment at GE Capital right away. Again, gaining admission to the University of Michigan is my number one priority—please do not hesitate to contact me if you have any questions. I have attached an updated version of my résumé for your files.

Best regards,

Sanjay B.

Case Study 2: John D.

John D. applied to the University of Chicago with a master's degree in economics, a decent GMAT (690), an impressive title (director of import purchasing) in an unusual industry (hospital supply), and job responsibilities that included managing four people, overseeing a $35 million budget, and frequent travel around the world. Moreover, as a Ukrainian immigrant, he had a distinctive cultural profile and very clear and specific reasons for making Chicago GSB his number-one choice.

Alas, John had made the mistake of applying in the third round, and that fact, combined with a weak track record in extracurricular/community activities, landed him on Chicago's wait list. He was determined and motivated, however. He immediately asked his admissions contact at Chicago for feedback. She advised him to submit a letter "reiterating your interest in the Chicago GSB, how you plan to contribute outside of the academic arena, and talk about anything that has happened since you applied." He also showed his essays to Chicago GSB students who were willing to help. One student's advice helped focus him on making the impassioned, concrete case that Chicago needed from him: "Write from your heart. Tell us why you want to sell your house and move family to this cold city for two years. Why is it so important that you do that?" Another sounded a gloomier note: "Not having any meaningful community service in the past few years is going to hurt you. … The GSB wants future CEOs, not just people who can analyze data. … Trouble is, if all you talk about are things you did years ago in college, it will look really bad."

John came to me anxious, even frantic: "I have been talking to at least three current students about my wait list and one GSB alumni. I do have lots of information and ideas, but meanwhile, I am lost, losing focus. That is the reason I ask for help from you to clear my thoughts. … If there is only one spot open, I need to take it! This is my goal!" John's high motivation was a very good sign. The outline we crafted helped him "clear his thoughts" and write a strong wait-list letter that addressed exactly what Chicago recommended: further reasons why Chicago was his best match, details on his plans for community leadership to compensate for weakness in that area, and his latest professional accomplishments.

John D.'s Chicago Wait-List Letter: Outline

I. Lead:
   A. Thank you very much for your letter of [date] notifying me of my wait-list status for the Graduate School of Business Fall MBA class.
      1. Appreciate competitiveness of Chicago's admission process
         a. Honored, thrilled to be on wait list.
      2. Writing to reaffirm deepening interest, how plan to contribute to Chicago GSB, update on significant recent developments.
      3. Also submitting additional letter of recommendation, from colleague/former manager, to provide committee with fuller picture.
II. In essays, stated I believe Chicago offers resources aligned with career goal—international private equity finance—and unavailable from other programs:
   A. Ability to concentrate in entrepreneurial, investment management.
   B. Outstanding faculty like Kaplan, Schrager.
   C. Variety of electives.
   D. Past three months: explored Chicago's program more closely—more convinced than ever of relevance, uniqueness:
      1. Chicago's research culture:
         a. Leading-edge business knowledge taught, created here
      2. Chicago tradition of analytical rigor, intellectual curiosity:
         a. Ideal for transitioning into analytical profession like private equity
         b. B school is way to make career change—also grow intellectually

      c. At GSB: take real courses from demanding departments in every discipline

    3. Expectation of maturity, self-knowledge, focus:

      a. Flexible curriculum means those who know what they want benefit most

      b. 6-plus year career: sharply defined my goals

      c. Specialize in investment finance in first semester at Chicago to prep for private equity-oriented summer internship

  E. Chicago best program for me

    1. If admitted will accept.

III. At GSB: can use expertise to make contribution to community:

  A. GSB's location—Chicago, Hyde Park: many worthy community organizations to help.

  B. GSB's Giving Something Back group offers many opportunities:

    1. Tutoring at Ray School.

    2. Ronald McDonald House.

  C. Expertise in hospital supply industry helps me have bigger impact on Habitat for Humanity

    1. Volunteer at building sites.

    2. Also use knowledge of logistics and hospital supply industry to supervise at sites, negotiate favorable contracts with suppliers.

  D. Use bilingual skills to tutor Chinese immigrants in English.

  E. Continue promoting intellectual, cultural exchange between U.S., Ukraine through Chicago office of Ukrainian Association of Professionals in Science and Technology.

    1. Help create new international trade opportunities for Chicago business.

IV. Since applying continuing to develop professionally, impact my organization

  A. Efforts as Director of Import Purchasing led to EuroHealth Supply Association award.

  B. Deepened international business skills: trips to Spain, Mexico.

  C. Proud now recognized as industry authority.

    1. One of few experts asked to provide trend surveys for hospital supply industries of Spain, Italy, Mexico.

    2. Led to nomination to board of directors of new hospital supply company in Arkansas.

  D. Second time in 3.5 years helped startup get off ground.

V. Close: Ms. [Last Name], I want to contribute unique knowledge of my industry, unusually deep international experiences, multicultural skills to GSB class.

A. Wait list: GSB confident I can thrive at Chicago, make contribution to
organization, community.

B. Let me demonstrate that confidence is well placed

John D.'s Chicago Wait-List Letter: Final Version

Dear [Director of Admissions]:

Thank you very much for your letter of May 18 notifying me of my wait-list
status for admission to the Fall 2008 entering class of the Graduate School of
Business. I appreciate the competitiveness of Chicago's admission process, so
I am honored and thrilled to be among the talented applicants still under
consideration. This letter is to reaffirm my deepening interest in the Chicago
GSB, to elaborate on my plan for contributing to the Chicago community,
and to update you on significant personal developments since I applied.
*[Straightforward introductory paragraph that officially accepts wait-list sta-
tus while avoiding negative overtones, subtly compliments both the school and
the applicant on their selectiveness, and informs Chicago that he will discuss
the key points they want addressed.]*

Chicago has always held a special attraction for me because of its extremely
impressive faculty and superb academic reputation. No other business school
has produced so many Nobel Prize winners. The knowledge and ideas of
Chicago's thought leaders has shaped business practices around the world.
*[This paragraph's somewhat generic-sounding lead sentences are greatly off-
set by the concrete and impressive sentences that follow.]* I was first exposed
to the excellence of Chicago's faculty as a whole during college when I studied
Professor Milton Friedman's classic economics text *A Theoretical Framework
for Monetary Analysis*. Later, during graduate study at Florida State University,
I came to know the works of Professor George Stigler and other members of
the "Chicago School" of economics. Even now, my experience as a board advisor for GyroTech International benefits from the eHubs concepts of GSB
Professor Steven Kaplan, whom *BusinessWeek* has named as one of the best
entrepreneurship teachers in graduate management education.

Since applying in February I have explored GSB's program more closely by
speaking with Chicago students as well as GSB alumni. *[←Ideally, he would
have named them.]* I am more convinced than ever that Chicago is the most
appropriate school given my specific goals.

The GSB offers me a combination of resources that are not only closely
aligned with my career plan but are also unavailable at other programs. First,
Chicago's tradition of analytical rigor is ideal for someone making a transition,
as I am, into an analytical profession like private equity finance. In contrast to
the "fluffy" approach of some schools, GSB's disciplined-based program will

help me focus on developing my critical, problem-solving, and decision-making abilities—the intellectual tools that will help me cope effectively with a constantly changing global business environment.

Second, I believe Chicago's amazingly flexible curriculum most benefits students who know what they want. My six-plus-year professional career has enabled me to sharply define a career goal in international private equity finance. Moreover, because I already have degrees in business and economics, Chicago will enable me to build on my previous education while avoiding wasteful repetition. Specifically, I plan to begin specializing in finance during my first year at Chicago through courses like "Entrepreneurial Finance and Private Equity" and "Private Equity/Venture Capital Labs" to prepare myself for a private equity – oriented summer internship.

Third, the quality and size of GSB's alumni network is impressive. Every alumnus or alumna I have interacted with has shared the same strong enthusiasm and loyalty for their alma mater. To me, this is the ultimate validation of the quality of the program.

Finally, the GSB will enable me to use my expertise to have a greater impact on my community than I could in other programs. GSB's location on Chicago's south side will afford me many opportunities to help Hyde Park and surrounding communities complete their exciting urban renaissance. I am very interested in joining the GSB's "Giving Something Back" club and look forward to tutoring at the Ray School or volunteering at the Ronald McDonald House. However, I believe my expertise in the hospital supply industry will enable me to have an even bigger impact at Habitat for Humanity. In addition to volunteering my time at building sites, I also hope to use my knowledge of logistics and supply management in the hospital and health-care industry to play a supervisory role and negotiate favorable contracts with Habitat's suppliers. *[←Not only gets specific about the Chicago community activities he'll get involved in, but makes it believable by showing how he'll contribute his particular skills.]* Furthermore, as a member of the Chicago office of the Ukrainian Association of Professionals in Science and Technology, I will continue to promote intellectual and cultural exchange between the Ukraine and the United States and help Chicago-area businesses find new opportunities for international trade.

Because the unique combination of all of these resources makes Chicago's MBA program the best choice for me, if admitted I will definitely accept. *[←Signals Chicago that he is one answer to their concerns about yield.]*

Since applying I have continued to develop professionally and believe I am an even stronger candidate than I was three months ago. My efforts as Director of Import Purchasing for GyroTech led directly to the company's receiving in May the Importer of the Year award from EuroHealth Supply Association. I have also continued to deepen my international business skills through trips to Spain

(March), China (April), and Mexico (May). I am proud to be one of only a handful of international industry experts who are asked to provide trend surveys for the hospital and health-care supply industries of Italy, Spain, and Mexico. This industry prominence was rewarded in March when a business associate named me board advisor for Advance Treatments, Inc., a new hospital supply company in Little Rock, Arkansas. *[Concrete, impressive new developments.]*

Ms. [Last Name], I recognize that the knowledge and experience each of GSB's students brings to the class are critical to the success of the program. I believe my unique knowledge of the hospital supply industry, my unusually deep international experience, and my multicultural skills will enrich the learning experience of the GSB Class of 2010. Once again, thank you for offering me this opportunity to further explain my reasons for accepting wait-list status at the University of Chicago GSB. I hope you will give me the opportunity to demonstrate that the confidence the admissions committee has shown in my application thus far is indeed well placed. Thank you for your time and consideration. *[Maintains tone of gratitude and sincerity with a few personal touches thrown in.]*

Sincerely,
John D.

Six weeks later, John's eagerness to do everything he could to survive wait-list purgatory paid off when Chicago offered him admission.

ABOUT THE AUTHOR

One of America's most experienced admissions consultants (serving clients since 1997), Paul (paulbodine@yahoo.com) has helped hundreds of clients earn admission to the world's top business, law, medical, and graduate schools as well as elite colleges for Accepted.com and his own firm, paulsbodine.com—the only admissions consultancy that offers both a low-price *and* a success guarantee. Year in and year out, Paul's MBA clients have consistently earned admission to the most selective business schools, from Harvard, Stanford, Wharton, MIT Sloan, and Kellogg to Chicago, Columbia, Dartmouth Tuck, Berkeley Haas, Michigan, London Business School, INSEAD, and NYU Stern, among many others.

Paul is the author of *Great Application Essays for Business School,* first edition (named "Best MBA Book" by The GMAT Club in 2010), *Perfect Phrases for Business School Acceptance, Great Personal Statements for Law School, Perfect Phrases for Law School Acceptance, Perfect Phrases for Medical School Acceptance,* and *Perfect Phrases for Letters of Recommendation* (McGraw-Hill). He has been interviewed by *Business Week, Christian Science Monitor,* MBAPodcaster, Law School Podcaster, and Law School Interactive. He lives in Southern California.